WRITTEN IN THE RUINS

Cape Breton Island's Second Pre-Columbian Chinese Settlement

PAUL CHIASSON

DUNDURN
TORONTO

Editor: Michael Melgaard
Design: Laura Boyle
Cover Design: Courtney Horner
Printer: Webcom
Front cover image: Andrews Map of the Maritime Provinces, 1853.

Library and Archives Canada Cataloguing in Publication

Chiasson, Paul, author
Written in the ruins : Cape Breton Island's second Pre-Columbian Chinese settlement / Paul Chiasson.

Includes bibliographical references and index.
Issued in print and electronic formats.
ISBN 978-1-4597-3312-1 (paperback).--ISBN 978-1-4597-3313-8 (pdf).--
ISBN 978-1-4597-3314-5 (epub)

1. Cape Breton Island (N.S.)--Discovery and exploration--Chinese. 2. Chinese--Nova Scotia--St. Peter's--Antiquities. 3. Excavations (Archaeology)--Nova Scotia--St. Peter's. 4. St. Peter's (N.S.)--Antiquities. 5. Cape Breton Island (N.S.)--Antiquities. I. Title.

E109.C5C483 2016 971.6'9801 C2015-906678-6
C2015-906679-4

1 2 3 4 5 20 19 18 17 16

We acknowledge the support of the **Canada Council for the Arts** and the **Ontario Arts Council** for our publishing program. We also acknowledge the financial support of the **Government of Canada** through the **Canada Book Fund** and **Livres Canada Books**, and the **Government of Ontario** through the **Ontario Book Publishing Tax Credit** and the **Ontario Media Development Corporation**.

Care has been taken to trace the ownership of copyright material used in this book. The author and the publisher welcome any information enabling them to rectify any references or credits in subsequent editions.

— *J. Kirk Howard, President*

The publisher is not responsible for websites or their content unless they are owned by the publisher.

VISIT US AT

Dundurn.com | @dundurnpress | Facebook.com/dundurnpress | Pinterest.com/dundurnpress

Dundurn
3 Church Street, Suite 500
Toronto, Ontario, Canada
M5E 1M2

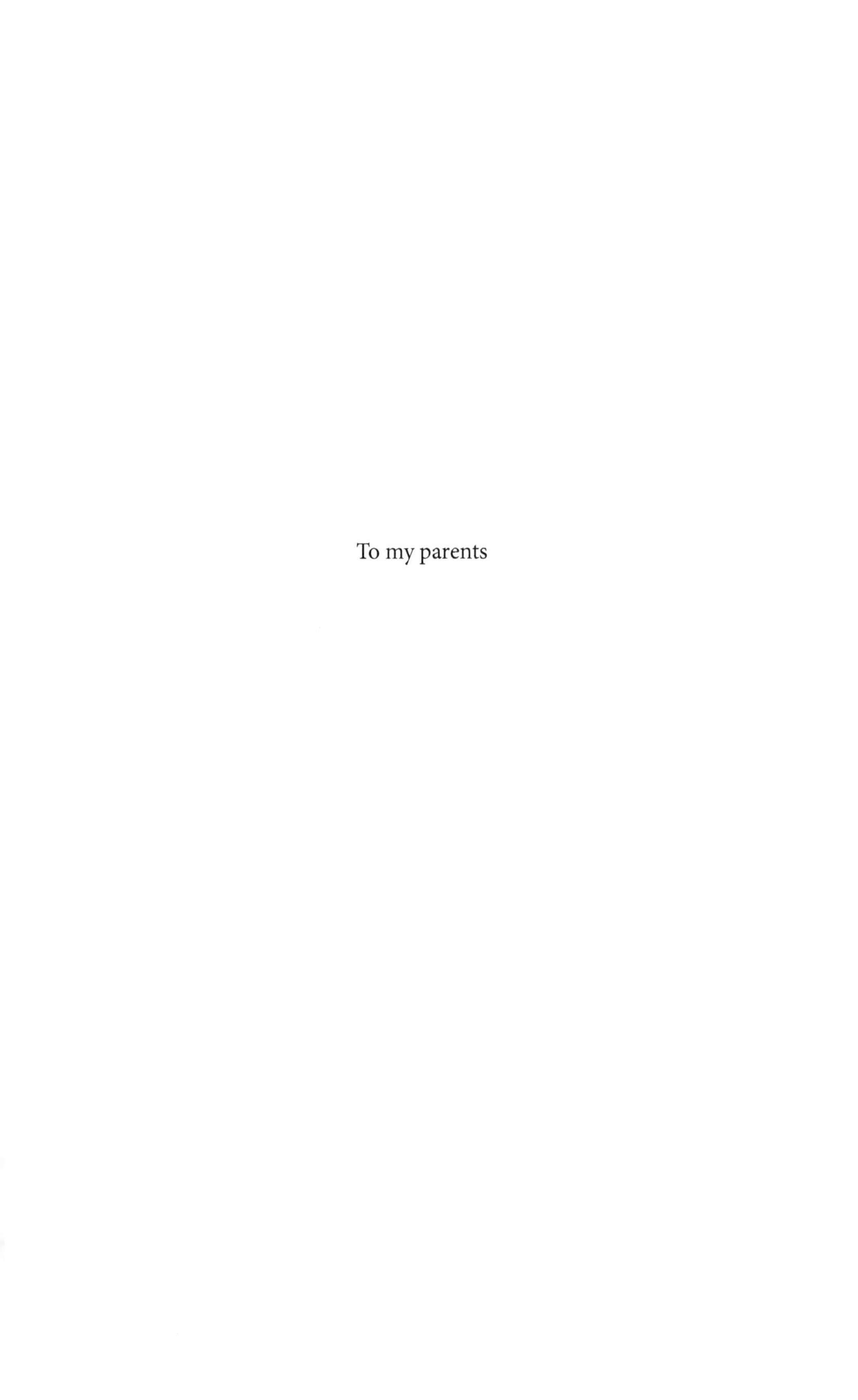

To my parents

Contents

Prologue: A Shipwreck's Tale 9

Introduction: The Path to the Second City 13

Part One: The Second City

1 The Ruins on the Shore 27

2 Rovers of the Sea 38

3 The Ruins on Mount Grenville 47

4 The Mark of an Ancient Canal 61

5 A Cannon from the Past 76

Part Two: Rovers of the Sea

6 The Adventures of David Ingram 87

7 The Treasure Fleets 94

8 A Culture Forgotten 101

9 History Through a New Lens 109

Part Three: History Derailed

10 History Takes a Turn 117
11 Nicolo Zeno of Venice 132
12 Evolution of a Myth 138
13 The *Zeno Stories* Come of Age 151
14 The Battle for History 159
15 Myth Becomes History 169

Epilogue: Attend to the Original Facts 188

Acknowledgements 193
Notes 194
Selected Bibliography 205
Index 212

Prologue:
A SHIPWRECK'S TALE

With its rocky coast surrounded by the often-stormy Atlantic Ocean, Cape Breton Island's stories of shipwrecks and the men and women who survived them are many. One of the best known and most complete of these narratives was written in the late eighteenth century by a young British seaman, Samuel Walter Prenties. His narrative contains just a passing mention of a small settlement on Cape Breton Island called Saint Peters, but the claim he makes is remarkable enough to highlight the ancient mystery that the town now seems to keep watch over.

Ensign Prenties, the eldest son of a Quebec innkeeper, entered the British navy in July 1778 in the midst of the American Revolution. A prolonged period of bad health kept him from his duties until the late fall of 1780, when he was entrusted with a packet of military orders that were to be delivered from Quebec City to Sir Henry Clinton, the British commander then in control of the city of New York. On November 17, Ensign Prenties sailed out from his station in Quebec aboard the ship *St. Lawrence* and headed for the port of New York. He was twenty-five years old.

It was a cold northern November, and as Prenties's ship sailed out the St. Lawrence River into the open water of the Gulf of St. Lawrence the weather turned dangerously cold. Heavy packs of ice surrounded the vessel and the nineteen people on board — thirteen "indifferent" seamen, according to Prenties's account, and six passengers — were kept busy cutting the frozen sea from the sides of the ship while simultaneously working the pumps in the hold to keep her afloat. Prenties later noted that during this early and exhausting period of their voyage the ship's captain "remained continually in a state of intoxication in his cabin."[1] To add to the crew's fears, after they entered the Gulf of St. Lawrence the ship that was accompanying them went down with all on board, lost to the foul weather and the icy waters.

The weather worsened, and as the *St. Lawrence* continued through the Gulf past Prince Edward Island, the ice thickened. The pumps keeping the ship free of water finally froze. The hold flooded, and on the fifth of December the *St. Lawrence* was grounded off the west coast of Cape Breton Island, about forty metres from the shallow rocky shore at the mouth of the Margaree River, which cuts through one of the most beautiful valleys on the island.

Using the small lifeboat, the crew were able to ferry themselves and the passengers to land. In all of this, only two people were lost. Both were passengers: a young boy who fell into the water while trying to board the lifeboat and an older man who had fallen asleep and frozen to death while still on board the *St. Lawrence*. Within days of their shipwreck, three more men died, all from the cold, all having first lost their lower extremities, and all after suffering a period of delirium. This left fourteen to live over the winter on a diet of salt beef and onions that had been salvaged from the wreck. By the first of January, after staying on the shore for close to a month, six of the fourteen decided to head north along the coast in the lifeboat that had originally ferried them from the wreck.

Over the next two months, the coldest of winter, this small group of six was able to round the northern tip of Cape Breton and sail south down along the eastern coast of the island. By mid-February the group had run out of provisions. Hungry, cold, and exhausted, they made the decision that one of the men should be sacrificed to cannibalism. They would eat him so the other five could live.

On February 28, having arrived in St. Anns Bay, approximately midway along the eastern coast of the island, the men settled down to their final meagre meal before the gruesome task of killing one of their own. Then their life changed again. They were startled by the voices of two Mi'kmaq men who must have been just as amazed to see the six bedraggled sailors crouching over the last embers of their fire. These sailors, having travelled almost 250 kilometres along the icy coastline in their tiny lifeboat in the middle of winter, were rescued just as their hope was fading. The six were taken to the nearby Mi'kmaq encampment where they were fed and cared for. From the description Prenties gave to the Mi'kmaq of where his ship had come aground, they were able to find their way back to the original camp and the men who had been left behind to fend for themselves. Only three remained alive. From nineteen, they were now only nine.

The remainder of Prenties's narrative tells of how this group of nine survivors travelled to the small French settlement of Saint Peters, and then across the narrow stretch of water, the Strait of Canso, to the mainland of Nova Scotia and the village of Canso, the shipping centre of the region. Eventually they made it to Halifax, the primary military centre along the coast. In his old age, Prenties would become a farmer in Quebec.

Aside from the story of courage and endurance, the record Prenties wrote is important because of his mention of Saint Peters. During his short stay there, Prenties observed the remains of what could only have been a canal. This was 1781, over a generation after the French military had abandoned the small fort they had built earlier in the century near the narrow isthmus that joins the two sides of Cape Breton together. We know from the records of the period that the French fort had been a small, minor affair. However, according to Prenties's observations, he had seen a large canal that he believed only the French military could have built. He wrote that the French "had formed a design of cutting through this narrow neck of land and opening a communication on that side between the ocean and the lake, in order to bring their large ships of war to lie during the winter in the lake of St. Peter's [the Bras d'Or]."[2] Given that eighteenth-century French warships were large multi-masted vessels, this must have been a sizable canal that Prenties was describing. Someone had cut a deep channel through this rocky isthmus. However, the contemporary records are clear — the French had done no such thing.

Who built a canal at Saint Peters that allowed "large ships of war" to sail through to the Bras d'Or Lakes that run up the centre of the island? Who was building canals before Europeans began arriving in the New World? The Prenties narrative makes only a simple, short mention of a manmade "cut" here, but this eye-witness account by an experienced seaman and his reference to the size of the ships this canal could handle narrowed my attention to the small town of Saint Peters. My previous investigations into pre-Columbian visitors of Cape Breton Island had led me to believe that is was the Island of Seven Cities, settled by the Chinese Treasure fleets in the fifteenth century. I had already found evidence of one settlement on Cape Breton Island; could this passing mention in an all-but-forgotten shipwreck's tale be a clue to a second city?

Introduction:

THE PATH TO THE SECOND CITY

In a small town on Canada's East Coast there is a mysterious historical puzzle that needs to be solved. The town, Saint Peters (sometimes written with an apostrophe, often written without) is located on the southeastern coast of Cape Breton Island in the province of Nova Scotia. There are two old ruined structures in Saint Peters, the suggestion of a man-made canal on the earliest maps, and a nineteenth-century report of an ancient cannon that was found buried in one of the ruins. Framing all these elements is an old Mi'kmaq legend claiming that the two ruins in Saint Peters were left by foreign visitors who had come to Cape Breton before the earliest French settlements on the island — before Europeans began arriving. The ruins, the canal, and the ancient cannon have never been fully explained. Their story may change history.

From the very beginnings of the European Age of Discovery, Cape Breton Island was considered unusual. In 1497, at least a century before any attempt at European settlement in the region, the explorer John Cabot had referred to Cape Breton as the Island of Seven Cities. The history of the area includes early references to the island having once been the land of the Chinese. Even more surprisingly, the Mi'kmaq were the only Aboriginal people of North America who had a written language when Europeans first arrived. Early missionaries described how the Mi'kmaq, even the children, were reading and writing in a character-based script. This writing, their clothing, and their customs suggest an early Chinese presence.

That there were pre-Columbian Chinese visitors to North America is a very real possibility. Before Europeans started their voyages of discovery in the late fifteenth century, the Chinese had already been masters of the oceans for hundreds of years, with ships and crews that dwarfed those of Europe. In the early fifteenth century, during the Ming dynasty (1368–1644), already with a long history of sailing and navigation, China launched massive fleets of ships they called the Treasure Fleets. These fleets consisted of hundreds of ships, some the largest wooden vessels ever built, manned by tens of thousands of highly trained crew. The Treasure Fleets are known to have sailed throughout the Indian Ocean as far as the east coast of Africa, but they could have sailed much farther. Their extensive visits to foreign ports over a period of almost thirty years are believed to have been aimed less at trade and discovery, and more as acts of diplomacy to proclaim China's greatness among nations, but we know very little of the specifics of these great journeys. As China began to turn inward by the middle of the fifteenth century, the Treasure Fleets were stopped and the records of their voyages destroyed. Much of China's long maritime history — where their ships sailed, whom they visited, and what they accomplished — remains one of the great mysteries of world history. However, given what we do know of China and its early sailing history, it is possible that early Chinese settlers had come to dig for Nova Scotia's rich minerals, settled and lived among the Mi'kmaq, and then left before Europeans began arriving later in the century. It is the one theory that may answer all the questions posed by the island's curious, unresolved past.

Several years ago, my interest in the mysteries of Cape Breton Island led me to a place called Cape Dauphin, the long arm of Kellys Mountain, a low stone coastal mountain that reaches out into the Atlantic Ocean precisely where the eastern shore of Cape Breton turns abruptly northward. There were ruins there that I believe to be the remains of stone foundations that had been left behind by early Chinese settlers before

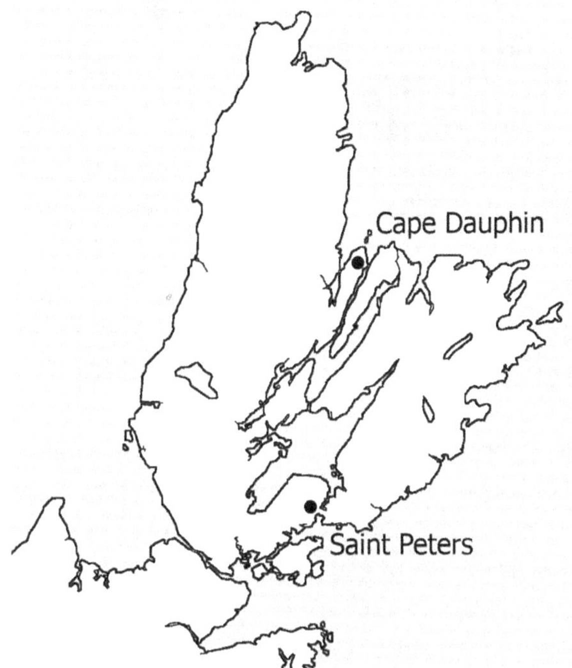

Cape Breton Island, showing the sites of the ruins at Cape Dauphin and Saint Peters.

the European Age of Discovery. These ruins appear to be flat stone platforms built into a large, clear, open, rectangular area cut out of the thick spruce forest near the summit. There are also the remains of a wide and once well-made road leading up the steep side of the cape to the site. In many places the road is still lined with the ruins of low stone walls, the sections at the top of the mountain clearly made by human hands. Early aerial photographs suggest there may have been town walls built in certain sections of the site. In 2006 I wrote a book, *The Island of Seven Cities*, about my discoveries.

A recap of my evidence that the Cape Dauphin site is Chinese can be seen in three short videos available online,[1] but beyond the research and the theory, it is important to briefly explain how such a revolutionary idea has been viewed by traditional historians. Soon after the Cape Dauphin book was published I began to sense that this discovery business is a difficult and dangerous thing. When a new discovery comes along, the sort of discovery that forces a change in fundamental ideas, it appears that the same general pattern plays out. It was expressed clearly by one of Charles Darwin's early supporters thirty years after the theory of evolution was first published. In 1888, Thomas Henry Huxley wrote of Darwin's work, "It was badly received by the generation to which it was first addressed, and the outpouring of angry nonsense to which it gave rise is sad to think upon. But the present generation will probably behave just as badly if another Darwin should arise, and inflict upon them what the generality of mankind most hate — the necessity of revising their convictions."[2] This is in no way a personal comparison; but the theory — even the suggestion — of early Chinese settlement in North America, appears to be suffering the same treatment. Anger and frustration are being directed at the very logical idea that Chinese may have reached the Americas at least a century before Columbus.

Several months after my book was published, in the summer of 2006, the Nova Scotia government sent a group of five archaeologists to the Cape Dauphin site. The group was led by David Christianson, the Curator of Archaeology at the Nova Scotia Museum. Christianson spent one afternoon at the site. There was no digging and nothing was disturbed. Afterwards, Christianson, acting as the official voice of the province, gave interviews with the press. It was Christianson's position that his group had found nothing on Cape Dauphin. No ruins, no walls, no ancient road. Nothing. He declared that there was no sign of human habitation on the site.

Another vocal critic of my theory, whose alternative theories were argued loudly and publicly after my book's release, was a hydrogeologist who had been contracted in 1989 by a gravel company to conduct an environmental impact assessment of Cape Dauphin. The hydrogeologist had reviewed the impact of the company's plan to mine, crush, and remove thousands of tons of gravel from the top of Cape Dauphin. Her study found no areas of archaeological importance in the area where the work was to take place. She claimed that the road, three kilometres long up the eastern side of the steep cape, was not ancient at all — even with the remains of low stone walls that continue to line its sides — but had been built as a fire road by a single firefighter in five hours on the morning of July 26, 1952, and then recut and used by the gravel company to access their site many years later. She also claimed that the rectangular site of stone ruins near the summit, which I have referred to as the Town Site, was simply a result of the same forest fire for which the road was built, and that the wide stone remains of the surrounding wall were built as a fire break by the same crew fighting this 1952 blaze. Since publication of the Chinese theory, the study she wrote for the gravel company has become the guiding light of detractors. As a hydrogeologist, she appeared to act as an objective expert, and using the precise language of an expert, she quoted specifics to add strength to her argument.

Her research adds new information that helps explain the condition of the site and how much of it has been destroyed over time. Nonetheless, her basic belief that the entire archaeological site was a result of a 1952 fire seems illogical. She makes no mention of the two parallel town walls, one with what appears to be a circular entrance, the faint outlines of which can be seen on aerial photographs,[3] nor of the ruined stone platforms that can still be seen on the cleared hillside of the Town Site.[4] According to her, the road up the side of Cape Dauphin did not exist before the fire. It did. The road can be seen on a 1931 aerial photograph of the cape.[5] Nonetheless, this theory, as well as several others, have developed into a range of various explanations of the ruins. These have been accepted and become a source of scorn aimed at the Chinese theory.

The official position of the local government was then and continues to be that nothing exists on the Cape Dauphin site. Despite this, growing public interest in my work led to an invitation to meet with the premier of Nova Scotia, Rodney MacDonald, a couple of years after my first book was published. My meeting with the premier was set up in order to open a line of communication with official government channels. I had come up against a wall of disinterest from those in the Heritage Division of the provincial government, the office responsible for archaeological sites in the province, but I felt it was important that the premier's office at the very least understand the project, if not address it directly. I felt that someone in authority had to know that this research was beginning to be taken seriously.

Introducing an idea as unusual as ancient Chinese ruins on the East Coast of Canada might appear to many to be the ravings of a lunatic. My experience has been that some people are fascinated, some are scared, and some are angry that their long-held views are being doubted. Others just walk away. In the case of my meeting with the premier, I had less than fifteen minutes to present the evidence. I didn't have a moment to waste. I took off my jacket, rolled up my sleeves, and began to talk while the premier sat in front of my small computer screen.

My fifteen minutes must have gone well. Premier MacDonald became excited and was quick with his questions. It was obvious he could see the project had some merit. In fifteen minutes it was hard to convey the magnitude of the discovery or the change that it could eventually mean for his province, but he was interested enough to appear supportive. He was very curious about the Mi'kmaq; surprisingly, few Nova Scotians are aware of the descriptions left by early visitors. He was also fascinated by the early dates of European voyages to Cape Breton. He seemed curious about it all.

Despite this meeting with the premier, the indifference of the local government remains. Officially, there continues to be nothing on Cape Dauphin — no ruins on this site, nothing to study, nothing to protect. When something exists that is so new, perhaps difficult to imagine and contrary to traditions, history proves that we find it easiest to ignore, to not look through the lens. As was said of Darwin, changing long-held convictions is one of the most difficult of human journeys.

However, I have not met with such disbelief from everyone. The unfailing curiosity from China has helped propel my theories forward. At first, the Chinese scholars who heard of my theories were skeptical; however, that did not stop them from asking questions and wanting to dig deeper into the research I had done. On closer investigation of the facts, they saw something important in what I had found, not only in the ruins on the site but in the early history of the region and in the culture of the Mi'kmaq. For them, there was something to this theory.

After *The Island of Seven Cities* was published, a number of Chinese news reporters wrote about the project. The interview that stands out most clearly was by a Toronto-based Chinese-Canadian television station. It was set up in my publisher's offices in downtown Toronto. As I sat down at the desk watching the technical crew arrange their equipment, the reporter arrived, a thin Chinese woman in her forties, well-dressed in a dark suit, who, after introducing herself, was quick to tell me that she had very little respect for these foolish theories of early Chinese settlement. She believed I was completely wrong. It appeared to be the beginning of a rough interview.

She had not read my book, so I was sitting across from a viewpoint of cynicism and mistrust not informed of my arguments. Her natural disbelief began to change as the interview progressed and we began to talk about the project. When she saw the early twentieth-century photographs of the Mi'kmaq for the first time, she appeared startled. She looked at me as if I had made a mistake. She asked the date of the photographs and where they had been taken. She was bewildered that these Mi'kmaq were living in Canada. They were dressed in Chinese-like clothing, and the patterns sewn on the borders of their coats and dresses and the ornaments they wore appeared to be Chinese. She showed the photographs to the camera, lighting, and audio technicians. The young Chinese men gathered around her. It was obvious from their expressions that they were surprised, perhaps even a bit excited. The disbelievers were converted. As she was leaving, she promised she would read the book. It was another step. This was the type of attitude I have seen consistently from the Chinese: cynicism and doubt followed by growing interest.

In December of 2006 I gave a lecture at the Chinese Cultural Centre of Greater Toronto. The Cultural Centre had been asked by the Chinese government to mount a travelling display celebrating the fifteenth-century voyages of the naval commander Zheng He, who had commanded the Chinese Treasure Fleets, and I was invited to present my evidence for the Cape Dauphin site. The Cultural Centre showed a short movie on Zheng He and the Treasure Fleets, then I spoke. There were questions, and I saw that there was excitement. The Zheng He film had made the Cape Breton settlement appear possible. We know the Treasure Fleets had hundreds of ships, crews of tens of thousands, and the most advanced navigation system in the world. It would be a surprise if Chinese ships had not made it to the Americas. The audience had reason to believe that I could be correct, and that meant a great deal to me.

A few days after the lecture, I received an email from the Ottawa office of the Honourable Bill Casey, a senior Canadian statesman who was then a Member of Parliament from Nova Scotia. He had been asked by the Chinese ambassador to investigate my findings. In response to the request, I suggested to Mr. Casey's office that I come to Ottawa to present my work. However, after having contacted me to get more information,

Mr. Casey's office and the Chinese ambassador in Ottawa fell silent for several months. I assumed Mr. Casey had discussed the project with the archaeologists from the Heritage Division of the Nova Scotia government who would have told him that my theory of early Chinese settlement was impossible. At the time I felt that there was little I could do. The Heritage Division remained the final arbitrator of things archaeological.

While waiting for a response from Ottawa, I heard about a course being taught at McGill University in Montreal that was specifically focused on my book and the theory of early Chinese settlement on Cape Dauphin. For me that proved to be a very significant development in the project. The course was offered by the McGill Institute for Lifelong Learning, a school at McGill University that makes non-credit university courses available to local retirees. It was listed in their catalogue as "The Discovery of a pre-Columbian Settlement on Cape Breton" and had been organized by a Chinese man named Cheong Pak Chow who, before his retirement, had been the director of civil aviation in Singapore.

The course ran for ten two-hour sessions in the winter of 2007. *The Island of Seven Cities* was used as the text, sixteen students signed up, and small groups were given one or two chapters of the book to research in depth. I remember thinking that this course was exactly what the Cape Dauphin project needed, someone to provide solid, objective, and well-considered criticism of what I had written.

I was invited to McGill to attend the final class in March, and as I began to discuss the project with the students, it became clear that they had brought a passion and seriousness to their investigations that both surprised and excited me. Several students admitted that they had stood fervently against the ideas presented in my book, but having reviewed the research, the maps, the historical documents, and the legends of the area in great detail, and with all the mistakes inherent in a new theory accounted for, they all became convinced that I had found something of importance on this wilderness mountainside in Cape Breton. The students also believed that the facts pointed consistently in a single direction: to ancient China.

After the class, I began to realize that the most unnerving part of my meeting with the McGill students had been my inability to give a specific, clear plan for the future of the Cape Dauphin ruins. When they asked, I had no answers. I was very uncertain what would happen to the site, who would be involved, and how it would be investigated. The course reminded me that all discussions with archaeologists and the Nova Scotia authorities aside, the future of this project depended on cold hard finances.

Later that month, an interview I had done with a Chinese journalist appeared in the *People's Daily*, China's main newspaper. The *People's Daily* is the voice of the Chinese government, so the article on the Cape Dauphin project was important. The book had not yet been published in China, which meant the article was the first fully sanctioned introduction of the theory to Chinese readers. For the future of the project, that was a critical step. I began to realize that the Chinese had started to investigate, to probe, to ask questions, and to slowly and carefully become involved in the project.

Several weeks after the interview with *People's Daily*, I finally presented the project to the Chinese ambassador in Ottawa. From what I came to understand, the ambassador's curiosity had grown after several of his friends and colleagues read the book and suggested it to him. He took an interest in the project and had spoken with Bill Casey about it because they sat on a committee on international relations together. The Ambassador asked Mr. Casey to establish contact with me. They had been out of touch with me for five months because Mr. Casey's office and the Office of the Ambassador had been trying to organize their schedules to allow them both an afternoon together to meet.

I was nervous about the meeting, but had little reason to be. For all the elaborate ceremony of the Canadian Parliament Buildings, our meeting was informal and efficient. For a senior politician, Mr. Casey was very easygoing. As has often been the case with this project, there appeared a series of coincidences which made our mutual trust almost immediate.

Mr. Casey was the elected federal representative of the area of Nova Scotia that had once been home to many of the first Acadians, including some of my ancestors. In that region, along the northern coast of the Bay of Fundy, the Acadian port town of Beaubassin had grown up during the seventeenth century. The Acadians, including several members of the Chiasson family, were part of the earliest history of the town, an important trading centre up until 1755 when the English deported the Acadians, destroyed

Beaubassin, and successfully erased the memory of the Acadian presence in the area. Until recently, few people other than historians and those with Acadian blood knew that the area was widely and successfully settled by the French well before the English arrived and destroyed the French settlements. Ruins of the early French town had been discovered, and because of Mr. Casey's interest and intervention in the project, an archaeological team had been organized to begin surveying the site. From his involvement in the Beaubassin project, Mr. Casey understood fully the official road blocks I had been facing. Even before the Chinese Ambassador arrived and I presented my work to both of them, it was clear that I had, at the very least, the sympathy and understanding of at least one senior Canadian politician.

My meeting with the Ambassador was held in the Privy Council Chamber, on the upper floor of the Centre Block of the Parliament Buildings. With only four people at the meeting — the Ambassador, Mr. Casey, Mr. Casey's assistant, and me — we were able to forgo the formalities of a prepared presentation on a large screen. The four of us simply sat around my computer as I went through the photographs of the site and its history. They had questions. The issue of pre-Columbian Christian iconography among the Mi'kmaq had raised Mr. Casey's eyebrows for a moment, but an explanation of the very early Christian communities among the Chinese helped explain how that iconography might have arrived. The ambassador seemed most curious about the Mi'kmaq history. Over the space of two hours, I sensed that both men seemed to realize that one of the greatest strengths of the theory of Chinese settlement was simply that it answered many more questions than it raised.

On my way back to the airport, it was impossible for me to tell if the meeting had been a success. I had seen other plans for the project unravel, so I had few expectations about where the meeting would lead. However, I sensed that the meeting had gone as well as it could have. Over the following days, the responses I received from both Mr. Casey and the ambassador were encouraging. They remained reluctant to believe without proof, but both men suggested that they would support any steps necessary to have the site studied and protected. I could not have expected more. I had gone to Ottawa searching for some glimmer of interest from the Canadian and Chinese governments, and it appeared that I had had it from both.

In 2008, one of China's most respected publishing houses, SDX Joint Publishing Company, decided to translate and publish *The Island of Seven Cities* in China. Since the translation and the various articles in Chinese newspapers and journals, I have spoken several times to Chinese groups. There is always a certain degree of skepticism, but the images of the site and of the Mi'kmaq clothing and written language consistently seem to win over even the most cynical members of the audience.

I have watched as the Chinese audiences began asking questions; I have listened while journalists dug through the research to uncover the story; I have seen the interest on the faces of the audience at lectures and informal presentations of my work; and I have witnessed the excitement of the Chinese ambassador. Little by little the Chinese have investigated the entire project. Their involvement has been slow and well-paced, and it has increased with time and understanding. Cautiously, a foundation of information, insight, and then trust has been built. I have been watching patience in action.

Since I first began sharing my theories in 2005, before the discovery was published a year later, I received inquiries from documentary makers wanting to tell the Cape Dauphin story. Getting a team of filmmakers involved was a critical step in the project because it meant the possibility of raising the funds necessary for both Western and Chinese archaeologists to look at the site together, which was the next logical step in the project. There were a number of false starts in the making of the documentary. I managed to find an interested company, Ellis Entertainment, but the first archaeologist hired by the documentary team refused to have me involved in the project. She also refused to have a Chinese archaeologist on the team. Ultimately she proved to be too inexperienced, and her application to dig on the site was rejected by the Nova Scotia authorities. With the growing realization that with limited financing and a host of bureaucratic hurdles a full-scale archaeological dig would not be possible, Ellis, in conjunction with History Television, eventually produced a one-hour documentary of the site, *Mysterious Ruins: Cape Breton*. The documentary reviewed the research and gave both the Western and Chinese reactions to the project, but there was no dig.

The Ellis team brought a local archaeologist up to Cape Dauphin for a couple of hours to review the ruins. To this local archaeologist, there was nothing of interest to see. As he claimed, "I wouldn't give a dime for this site." However, aerial video footage and photographs of the ruins were also shown to historians in China who had worked on similar, fifteenth-century ruins. Contrary to the local Nova Scotia archaeologist, the Chinese scholars believed there was something here. In the eyes of the Chinese, there were definite signs of early occupation on the site. It was an archaeological site that needed further investigation, and so I continued to find myself caught between the Western attitude on one side and the Chinese on the other.

Throughout this slow and consistent development of the Cape Dauphin project, I began to collect additional pieces of research that suggested there were other sites of ancient ruins on Cape Breton Island. One possible site was Cheticamp, the village of my Acadian ancestors on the west side of the island. Given Cheticamp's location outside the regular shipping channels, the early French interest in and settlement of this specific area was unusual and unexpected, and so I started to investigate the first records of the region. The other site I started to look at was Ingonish, a small village on the northeast coast of the island. Here, too, there was mention in the early records of unusual elements that I thought might be interesting.

I had not initially looked at Saint Peters as one of the possible Seven Cities referred to in early European legends of Cape Breton, even though there were two old ruins that existed on the outskirts of the town. I knew of the ruins from my childhood — they are well-known in the area — but they appeared to have been explained by the traditional history of early French and English settlement in the region. There did not seem to be anything unusual about the place. However, Saint Peters kept insinuating itself into my research, and soon I began to realize that there was something there that was asking to be investigated. There were questions there that had never been answered.

Part One:

THE SECOND CITY

1
THE RUINS ON THE SHORE

There are ruins in Saint Peters: a small fortress on the shore that is now believed to have been left behind by a seventeenth-century French settlement, and another slightly larger fortress on the hillside overlooking Saint Peters Bay that historians now claim was built by a small English garrison in the late eighteenth century. During my research into the history of Cape Breton Island, I had originally accepted the explanations for these early ruins and so had very little interest in documents relating to the history of the Saint Peters area. I felt that the ruins could have nothing to do with pre-Colombian settlement of Cape Breton.

My interest in Saint Peters grew when I began looking at the history of Cheticamp, the Acadian village on the west coast of the island. Early on in my research I found a shipwreck narrative from 1823 about a small group of sailors, led by a man named Samuel Burrows, that described in great detail how these sailors were rescued and cared for by the local villagers. Some of my ancestors were mentioned. Any story of great bravery in the face of seemingly insurmountable odds is captivating, and these various accounts of young sailors fighting for their lives, having their frozen feet and hands cut off with primitive tools, and then being nursed back to health in Acadian homes, were so fascinating that I looked for other shipwreck narratives from this region. That is when I found the Prenties account from 1780. Initially it was how the lost sailors were rescued by the Mi'kmaq that made the story so appealing, but Prenties's mention of large French warships sailing across the isthmus of Saint Peters had a certain shock value. His casual observation that the French "had formed a design of cutting through this narrow neck of land, and opening a communication between the ocean and the lake" stayed with me. My curiosity regarding Prenties's apparent canal forced me to go digging through the historical documents in search of what we actually know of this canal and of these two old ruined fortresses. First, I looked at the ruins.

The one set of ruins that appears most conspicuously through the centuries is a flat earth platform with wide earth walls, located in a cleared area near the shore of Saint Peters Bay. It is just west of the modern, nineteenth-century canal. This canal cuts across the narrow isthmus from Saint Peters Bay to the Bras d'Or Lakes, just as the earlier canal in Prenties's narrative had. I remembered the ruined fort from when I was a boy growing up in Cape Breton; the ruins were well known on the island. They still are.

These ruins on the shore on the western side of the isthmus were first recorded and mapped by the French surveyors and cartographers who visited the island in 1713. Although these French reports gave the first concrete descriptions of the ruined structure on the shore, the ruins had been mentioned twice before, by two French companies that had tried to establish fishing and trading businesses in Saint Peters during the seventeenth century. The first mention came in 1640, almost seventy-five years before the French military arrived. It is a note in the records of a trading company based in Paris, the *Compagnie de Cap-Breton*. The company was established in 1633 by Pierre Desportes, a Paris merchant, with the hope of building a fur trading post in Saint Peters.[1] In one document left by the company, dated March 1640, mention is made of *Le Fort St. Pierre*, the Fort of Saint Peters, for the first time. The captain of a ship contracted by the *Compagnie de Cap-Breton* was told that when he arrived at Cape Breton he was to follow the orders of the commander stationed at Fort

Saint Peters, to "*suivre les orders de Louis Parguier, commandant pour Desportes au fort Saint-Pierre*" (to follow the orders of Louis Parguier, Desportes's commander at Fort Saint Peter).[2]

In the mid-seventeenth century, among the reports of early settlements in the Americas, the term *fort* sometimes simply meant a settlement, what the French also called a *habitation*. The two terms *fort* and *habitation* were sometimes used interchangeably. This first mention of the Fort Saint Peters could simply have meant the settlement of Saint Peters. Perhaps the building — the fort — had not existed yet. Perhaps this fort was just a collection of houses. However, in the case of the documents of the *Compagnie de Cap-Breton*, the two descriptions also appeared together, the *fort* and the *habitation*, "*le fort et habitation de Saint-Pierre.*"[3] It appears that this company regarded the fort and the habitation as two different things. *Fort Saint-Pierre* appears to reference an actual structure of some sort that existed apart from the *habitation*. The settlement — the location of the living quarters — was considered a separate entity.

With no earlier mention of matters relating to the construction of a fort in Saint Peters, it seems to have appeared in the French records already made. It appeared as if the fort was already part of the landscape when the French first began arriving in the mid-seventeenth century.

It is unlikely that the *Compagnie de Cap-Breton* built the fort. According to the company's records, it was a very small enterprise. In 1641 the company contracted a nail maker and a single carpenter to work in Saint Peters. They had a two-person workforce, too little to have left anything of substance, and they were forced out of Saint Peters by 1647. Would they have built what the French military would later describe and draw on their maps as a solid earth platform, earthen walls, and a trench or moat, all surrounded by an extensive area of cleared land? The *Compagnie de Cap-Breton* may have used what was there, but logic suggests they did not build it.

The next time this structure on the shore was mentioned, seventeen years later in 1657, was in a letter from Nicolas Denys, a French fisherman and fur trader who had lived on and off in Saint Peters since 1650. Writing to one of his business partners back in France, Denys complained about the way the fort had been laid out. He claimed that the fort, having been partially ruined by a competitor of his, needed to be rebuilt. More important, he also complained that it was necessary to have a new entrance to the fort at Saint Peters made because he felt the original entrance was in the wrong place.[4] He gave no other explanation other than the original entrance was "*très mal place*" (very badly placed). The later French surveys show the single entrance centred on the southeast wall. It is not clear from Denys's letter where he wanted it moved. The important thing about this brief note about a misplaced entrance is that it seems inconceivable Denys would have built something this significant, complete with extensive cleared land, earth walls and a moat, and then wanted it changed. Would Denys have misplaced the door if he had built this fort? His complaint makes it doubtful that Denys was the original builder.

Like the earlier *Compagnie de Cap-Breton*, Denys appears to have used this strange little fort near the shore on the west side of the isthmus for the location of his business — his trading post. He built a few simple wooden buildings within the walls of the fort for storage and offices that were eventually abandoned after a fire destroyed his business in the winter of 1668–69.

More important for our understanding of the history of Saint Peters, Denys actually claimed to have built the main fort for his settlement — and in this case he used the term *fort* in his description — in another location.[5] So that there would be no doubt to his claim, Denys also drew a map of Saint Peters Bay and located his flag exactly where he said this main fort was, east of the small fortress on the shore that he had used as a trading post before the fire and east of what is now the modern canal, on a point of land referred to locally as Jerome Point. Denys's written description matches his map, so there is no reason to doubt him.

The location of Denys's settlement — the new fort that Denys claimed he built where his settlers lived — has been substantiated by those who came after him. A 1752 census done of the island, *Tour of Inspection Made by the Sieur de la Roque*, refers to this tip of land to the east of the harbour as the "*Pointe de l'ancienne Intendance*"[6] (Point of the Old Intendant). The term *ancienne Indendance* could only refer to the Denys settlement. In 1653, Denys had been appointed Governor of the region, including Cape Breton Island, after he had purchased it from the Company of New France. He was the Old Intendant. The same term and the same location was used in a series of letters written during the same period by Thomas Pichon, a secretary stationed in Louisbourg who would later become known as "the Spy of Beausejour." Jerome Point was referred to as "the point of the old intendance."[7]

It could be that Denys, while claiming to have built the fort for his settlement to the east of the isthmus, at the base of the mountain, actually built a second fort with its flat platform, earth walls, and surrounding moat on the other side of the bay, near the shore on the west side of the isthmus. Logically however, the fort and the settlement would be built as a single unit, the settlers either living inside the fort or in very close proximity. Where safety was an issue, in the wilderness, it would have seemed highly unlikely, even foolhardy, to separate the fortress on the west side of the isthmus and the settlement to the east of the isthmus on Jerome Point. Moreover, why would he build two forts? It appears that the small fort on the shore west of the modern canal already existed before Denys arrived. It was too small for his settlement, so he used it simply as a trading post.

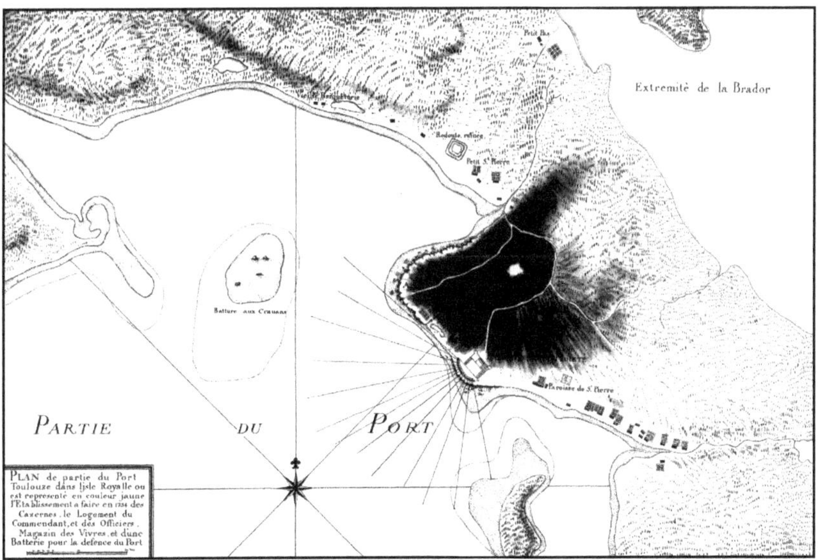

A French map (ca. 1730) of Saint Peters showing the ruins on the shore.

"PLAN de partie du Port Toulouze dans Ijsle Royalle ou est representé en couleur jaune l'Etablissement a faire en 1734 des Cazernes, le Logement du Commendant et des Officiers, Magazin des Vivres, et d'une Batterie pour la defence du Port." Library and Archives Canada, MIKAN No. 4125764, NMC34354.

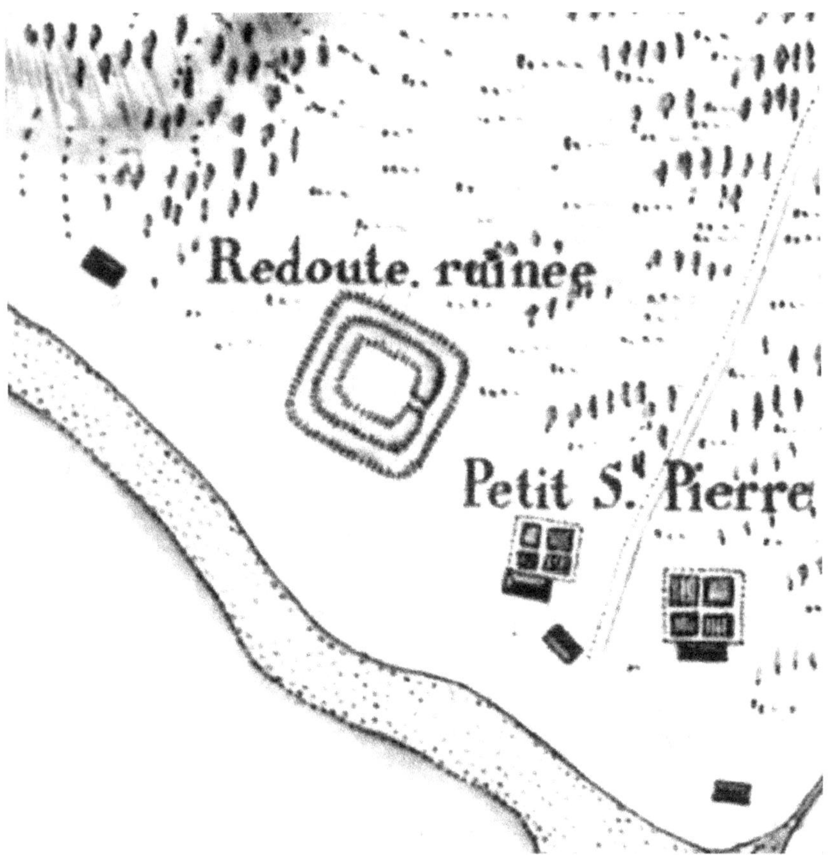

Detail showing the ruined structure on the shore marked as the *Redoubt ruinée.*

"PLAN de partie du Port Toulouze dans Ijsle Royalle ou est representé en couleur jaune l'Etablissement a faire en 1734 des Cazernes, le Logement du Commendant et des Officiers, Magazin des Vivres, et d'une Batterie pour la defence du Port." Library and Archives Canada, MIKAN No. 4125764, NMC34354.

These ruins on the shore to the west of the modern canal were recorded by the French military when they mapped and recorded the geography of Saint Peters beginning in 1713. The structure on the shore on the west side of the isthmus was labelled by the French as a "*Redoubte ruinee,*" a ruined redoubt, or a small ruined fortress.

Surveyors reported that they had found a square structure, twelve *toise* on each side. An early French *toise* equaled just over two metres, so the ruined fortress, when first officially surveyed by the French in the

A photograph of the shore ruins. The nineteenth-century caretaker's house sits inside the low earth walls.

early eighteenth century, was a simple square structure about twenty-five metres per side. According to this survey, it was surrounded by a trench — a moat. The surveyors appear to claim that the walls were made of earth. Much more recent archaeology of the fort claims the walls were built of sod or horizontal layers of soil. The French report mentioned two openings, although the cartographers only showed a single opening in the southeast wall. The actual description reads, "... *un fort quarré Revestu de Gazon avec un faussée qui en fait Lanceinte. chague coste peut avoir douze Toises en face. Le faussé a deux ouvertures et un Glacit d'Environ dix autres qui Tombent sur la Rade....*" (a square fort covered with grass, with a trench surrounding it. Each side may measure twelve toises. The trench has two openings with a buffer area, and about ten others [toise] that open onto the harbour).[8]

The report also claimed that the condition of the structure was still so good that it could be rebuilt at little expense.[9] A French map from around 1730 shows the perfect square geometry of the structure, its earth walls are solid and in good condition, it is surrounded by a wide ditch, and sited inland from the shoreline. It is surrounded by a large area of cleared land that must have once been forest. Faint traces of these ruins still exist.

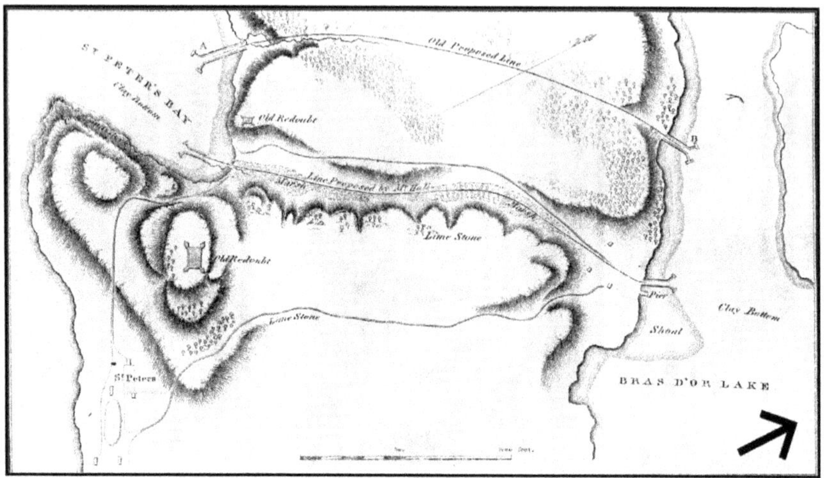

A map of the isthmus of Saint Peters from Thomas Haliburton's 1829 *An Historical and Statistical Account of Nova Scotia* showing the two old redoubts. North is shown by the arrow in the lower right.

Thomas C. Haliburton, Esq., *An Historical and Statistical Account of Nova Scotia, in Two Volumes* (Halifax: Joseph Howe, 1829), 238-239. Toronto Reference Library, Baldwin Collection.

Over a century after the French military reports from the early eighteenth century, the first modern historian to make note of the ruins was Judge Thomas Chandler Haliburton. He was a lawyer from a family of lawyers, a well-known historian and a member of the Nova Scotia government. For twenty years in the early part of the nineteenth century he acted as the district judge in Cape Breton. He knew the island's history and its lore well. In his 1829 history of the region, *An Historical and Statistical Account of Nova-Scotia,*[10] Haliburton included a map of the isthmus of Saint Peters that had been drawn four years earlier, in 1825, and had been used to show the location of the canal project being discussed to link the southern tip of the Bras d'Or with Saint Peters Bay.

The canal would not be started for another thirty years. However, on this map of the area, along with the proposed line of the canal, there were also two tiny but unmistakable icons of typical bastioned fortress-like structures. These are the two sets of ruins in Saint Peters: the one located on the shore on the west side of the isthmus and the other on Mount Grenville (sometimes written as Mount Granville), which I discuss in

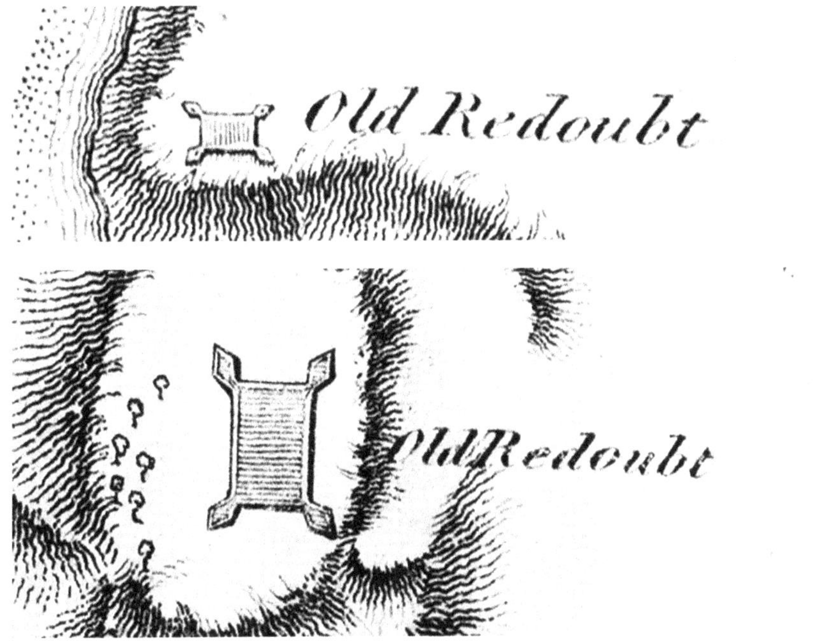

The symbols on Haliburton's map showing two sets of ruins.

Thomas C. Haliburton, Esq., *An Historical and Statistical Account of Nova Scotia, in Two Volumes* (Halifax: Joseph Howe, 1829), 238-239. Toronto Reference Library, Baldwin Collection.

more detail in chapter 3. Both were labelled "old redoubt," as the French military had labelled the lower ruins on the shore a hundred years earlier.

Later in the century, Judge Haliburton's son, R.G. Haliburton, also a historian, claimed that his father had been told by the local Mi'kmaq that the two raised mounds in Saint Peters had been built by "white men before the arrival of the French."[11] The French were the first settlers in the region, so the ruins, according to Mi'kmaq oral history, predate the coming of Europeans. This means the ruins are very significant, and Judge Haliburton knew it. This was the first official history of Nova Scotia. By including the map that showed these two mysterious ruined structures, the highly respected Judge Haliburton called attention to them. He recorded them for modern history.

Haliburton's *History of Nova Scotia* was the first definitive history of the region written by a well-known scholar and politician, and with a map drawn by a professional engineer. It was a combination that must have had an air of great seriousness about it. More than anything, Halliburton realized that the ruins were a precious memory of a long-forgotten history, of very early settlers, of "white men before the French." He did not know what these strange ruins were, but he seemed to know that they were important. He must have had more questions than answers. However, given that he had been told by the Mi'kmaq that they had been built before the French, Haliburton did not let them pass without notice. He left the mystery to us. Judge Haliburton was followed by other historians of the region. In reading those histories, one thing becomes clear. To nineteenth-century thinkers, the history of Saint Peters and its ancient relics needed to be told, however incomplete and unsure it may have seemed. There was something important here that they believed should not be forgotten.

The first thorough history specifically of Cape Breton Island was written forty years after Judge Haliburton's book, in 1869, by another noted historian of the region, Richard Brown. Brown's book, *A History of the Island of Cape Breton*, did not mention either of the mysterious ruins shown on Haliburton's map. However, Brown clearly and precisely substantiated the location of Denys's settlement and fort. It was exactly where Denys had said it was. Brown wrote, "At Saint Peters, in Cape Breton, he [Denys] had a large establishment defended by a fort mounted with cannon, erected upon the rocky point on the right hand of the cove near the narrow isthmus which separates the head waters of the Bras d'Or Lake from the sea."[12] This rocky point of land is Jerome Point, to the east of the current canal, on the right-hand side of the cove.

Later in the century another historian, John George Bourinot, was equally as clear that, "the establishment formed at Saint Peters Bay by Denys was situated as far as can be ascertained, on a rocky neck of land in a little cove to the right of the entrance of the canal; and in this same neighborhood from the days of the French there has been always a small settlement of fishermen and traders."[13] To these historians it must have seemed best to point out what was known and leave it at that. Historians kept affirming the same historical layout of Saint Peters, with the Denys fort located on Jerome Point on the eastern side of the cove. The small ruins on the western shore remained a mystery.

At the end of the nineteenth century, in 1890, the ruins on the shore were finally mentioned. A historian of the region, the Reverend George Patterson, writing about the eighteenth-century French military establishment in Saint Peters, claimed, "The remains of their [the French] work here are still to be seen a little to the east of the entrance to the canal, in a position which commands the whole harbour. But about 100 yards to the westward of the canal are found earthworks, the remains of a similar structure, but undoubtedly much older. The place is still known as 'the old fort,' and formerly had in the neighbourhood the name of the 'pirate fort.'"[14]

Patterson was describing the seventeenth-century fort, seemingly used by both the *Compagnie de Cap-Breton* and Nicolas Denys, the eighteenth-century *redoubt ruinee* of the French surveyors, and the icon on Haliburton's map. Patterson supported this reference to the "old fort" or the "pirate fort" with a footnote that read, "The fact of this name being given to it by the first settlers, shows that they knew it was not built by either the French or the English, but by some persons who had been there before them. Not knowing any nation by whom this could have been done, they naturally regarded it as the work of some rovers of the sea."[15]

There is a certain consistency to the reports on Saint Peters over the centuries. None of them suggests a conventional source for the ruins on the shore. First the mention of an existing fort by the *Compagnie de Cap-Breton;* then Denys wanting the entrance moved; then the French military and their map and description of an earth platform, earth walls, and moat; then Judge Haliburton and the Mi'kmaq and the claim of "mounds" built before Europeans; and the nineteenth-century historian suggesting pirates may have done it. For hundreds of years there was a consistent agreement about where the French settlements had been built — on the point of land to the east of the canal — yet there was also this mysterious structure on the western shore that was impossible to ignore. Critically, both the Mi'kmaq and the local settlers claimed that this structure existed before the coming of the first French pioneers. Nineteenth-century historians were certainly faced with the questions asked by these ruins, but the questions remained unanswered. The ruins could neither be ignored nor explained. Who was responsible? Pirates? Rovers of the sea? Or some other source?

2

ROVERS OF THE SEA

With the information I had found — from Denys's history, from the French military surveyors' reports and maps, from Judge Haliburton quoting Mi'kmaq oral history, and from these early historians — I was forced to ask if these "rovers of the sea" were part of the Chinese Treasure Fleets. One after the other, these voices from history, all with bits and pieces of a strangely consistent story, have described the coming of an earlier people. They were clear in what they reported. They had found something. They simply did not know what these ruins were or who had left them behind.

Remarkably, this "pirate fort" on the shore of Saint Peters is currently believed by historians, scholars, archaeologists, and the Canadian government — by just about everyone — to be something Nicolas Denys built in the early 1650s, his *Fort Saint Pierre*. Now, to our modern history, it is nothing more than a small, seventeenth-century French fort. However, from looking at historical records, it is clear that this current historical certitude is a complete reversal of what, up until the early twentieth century, had been thought of as good, honest historical reporting of a strange unsolved mystery.

The change in perception was the result of a single individual, William Ganong, a well-respected botanist with an interest in history who got rid of those pieces of the Saint Peters puzzle that were problematic and explained away the dilemma. In 1907, in a footnote included in the first English translation of Denys's memoirs, *Description geographique et historique des costes de l'Amerique septentrionale*, Ganong, the manuscript's translator and editor, became the final word on what up until then had been a rather interesting and possibly important story that had been surveyed, reported, and investigated for hundreds of years. Ganong has never been challenged.

Ganong wanted to get rid of the possibly embarrassing, unknown history of Saint Peters — to explain away the ruins that were not easily explained. He employed Nicolas Denys to do it. In order to fit the difficult pieces of the puzzle into standard history, Ganong used his translation of Denys's memoirs not only manipulate Denys's own claims, but also to discredit or dismiss the entire lot of earlier historians who had written about the history of Saint Peters. To Ganong, the ruins on the western shore were just Denys's *Fort Saint Pierre*. He claimed Denys's fort was not located at the foot of Mount Grenville, on Jerome Point on the east side of the bay, at all. According to Ganong, Denys had not really meant what he recorded when he wrote his memoirs and drew his map. The later French reports supporting Denys's location appear to have been ignored as well. Ganong then contradicted every major nineteenth-century historian of the region who had come before him. It was insightful to see how he did it.

Denys, in his memoirs, claimed that his fort had been built "at the foot of a mountain which is almost quite vertical." He placed a flag on the map he drew to indicate a position on what is now called Jerome Point at the base of Mount Grenville. The following is Ganong's footnote in his translation of Denys's claim. It is worth quoting at length because it was Ganong's goal to change the history that preceded him:

> The site of Denys' fort is perfectly well known locally and marked with ample remains. Even without these the detail of our author's description would enable us to locate it. Yet there is much error about it in our principal books. In an article in the Popular Science Monthly for May 1885, R. G. Haliburton

> [the judge's son] cites Indian tradition to the effect that these remains antedated the arrival of the French, and, on the basis of a curious cannon found here, he suggests that they may be Portuguese. This was adopted as probable by Patterson in his work on the Portuguese in North America in Transactions of the Royal Society of Canada, VIII, 1890, ii, 168. Both writers were entirely ignorant of Denys' establishment here, and their theory is wholly groundless. Again, Bourinot, apparently following Brown's usually accurate book, gives in his work on Cape Breton a very unfortunate, if not erroneous, location to the site of Denys' fort, which he seems to have confused with the ruins of Fort Toulouse, erected much later just east of Jerome Point; and he has been followed by MacLeod in his Markland, 494, who has attributed to Denys' fort the extant plans of Fort Toulouse mentioned below.[1]

Ganong's arguments have won a resounding victory. No one speaks of the Mi'kmaq mounds any longer. Stories of the old redoubt or the pirate fort are long forgotten. Now these strange ruins on the shore of Saint Peters are simply considered something Nicolas Denys built in 1650.

The mystery of Saint Peters had been around for hundreds of years. Then came Ganong. He usurped Denys description, "at the foot of a mountain," to mean instead at the foot of the mountain, across the canal, and on the other side of the bay. Ganong was clever, assuring us that the site was "perfectly well known locally and marked with ample remains." The problem was, from all the records that preceded his 1907 translation, Ganong appears to be wrong.

Until Ganong, everyone agreed, including Nicolas Denys himself, that Denys's seventeenth-century *Fort Saint Pierre* had been located over on Jerome Point, along the same stretch of shoreline where the French military would build their wooden palisaded fortress during the eighteenth century. What Ganong claimed was a Denys's construction was, in fact, one of the Mi'kmaq mounds built before the French, the "*redoubt ruinee*" of the French surveyors, the strange pirate fort of local lore. In a bold sweep, Ganong used his scholarly footnote to discredit the long list of respected nineteenth-century historians who had come before him. Ganong claimed that the whole lot were ignorant of the facts, confused in their arguments, and wholly groundless in their theorizing.

Ganong's lone voice of 1907 should have been of very little importance in the face of generations of earlier scholars. However, that was not the case. Ganong was not ignored. Instead, he and his footnotes were embraced by generations of scholars that followed. His was the first, and remains the only, English translation of one of the more important documents of early Canadian history. Denys's memoirs are one of the key records of the seventeenth-century European fishing industry in North America, and they are considered one of the most valuable early accounts of the French in Acadia. Almost immediately, Ganong's translation of Denys's memoirs became one of the bibles of New World history, unquestioned and believed. His lengthy footnotes, often running to pages, were assumed to be historical fact. Moreover, Ganong was speaking with the power of his publisher behind him, the Champlain Society, and that cannot be underestimated.

The Champlain Society was founded in the earliest years of the twentieth century by a small group of Canadian businessmen and historians under the leadership of Sir Edmund Walker, the president of the Canadian Bank of Commerce. The Society's aim was to publish documents that had been written during Canada's early history. These documents were to be translated into English for an English-speaking, Canadian audience, annotated and clarified as necessary. It was one of the Champlain Society's founding principles that, because these were the type of books that would not interest most commercial publishers but were deemed critical to the country's history, it was a necessary and highly beneficial service they would be performing. Their first year of operation was 1907. Ganong's translation of Denys's memoirs, with its dismissal of the mysterious ruins, was published immediately.

William Ganong was an Acadian from New Brunswick with an undergraduate degree from Harvard and a doctorate in biology from the University of Munich. For most of his life, from 1894 until 1932, he was professor of botany at Smith College in Massachusetts. In 1907, the same year his English translation of Denys's memoirs was published, he was appointed president of the Botanical Society of America. He has a science building at the University of New Brunswick named after him. There is a

Mount Ganong in northern New Brunswick. He also wrote history in his spare time. Nicolas Denys was one of his interests. When the Champlain Society commissioned him to translate and edit the Denys book, Ganong had already published a number of articles on the genealogy and nomenclature of early New Brunswick. Given his credentials as a leading botanist and teacher in the United States, along with his Acadian heritage and interest in local history, Ganong must have seemed to the Champlain Society like an obvious choice to deal with such an important document.

Whether Ganong had specifically aimed to explain away the mysterious ruins in Saint Peters is unknown, but the more the evidence is surveyed, the more it looks like that had been his goal. At some point, the old ruins in Saint Peters must have become an embarrassment for historians. No one really knew what they were. Talk of Mi'kmaq mounds and old pirate forts, however honest and forthright the descriptions, must have seemed out of place in the scholarly lecture halls of a new and modern century. For whatever reason, in the face of centuries of previous history, Ganong took it upon himself to make the mystery of the ruins disappear. He aimed to set all the puzzling facts in Saint Peters into some easily understandable and acceptable idea of local history.

Ganong argued that all the earlier historians of Saint Peters had simply been wrong. Even though the location of the Denys fort was long established, Ganong claimed it was on the other side of the bay. He then explained that the ruins of an earth platform and earth walls all surrounded by a deep moat could easily have been the work of Nicolas Denys. He wrote with authority and without any sense of doubt or hesitation in his conclusions. He was convincing.

After dismissing the other written histories, Ganong's footnote went on, "Denys' fort stood on an elevated glacial bank about two hundred and fifty feet west of the present entrance to the canal."[2] He explains that the front face of the fort, the side facing the bay, was missing. However, he then claims that the "steep bank," now exposed, had once been a shoreline cliff face that had been washed away by the sea. However, this was the front edge of the earth platform, part of a deep moat, and according to all previous reports the fort had never been constructed directly on the water's edge. The plot of land it was built on may have been a glacial bank, but according to the early French surveyors, the ruins were an earth platform surrounded by a deep ditch located about twenty metres inland from the shore. Comparing the map that Ganong drew in 1907 with the French survey map from the early eighteenth century and the engineer's map that Judge Haliburton published in 1829 only serves to highlight the problem. This ancient, unexplained platform with its surrounding moat cannot be explained away as having risen naturally as the face of a shoreline cliff. That was not the case when the French surveyed it, nor when Haliburton reported it. Ganong appears to have added a superfluous description to the history of the ruins that only serves to confuse. This small fort was near the shore, but there is no reason to believe that it was built on a cliff on the water's edge. The destruction of the front face of the fort may have occurred during construction of the mid-nineteenth century canal, when much of the surrounding infill was created artificially. Ganong may have been confused by the relatively recent changes in what he saw.

Ganong then described the fort site as, "surrounded on three sides by a low embankment, from one or two up to three feet in height, which formed, no doubt, the stout wall for the pickets which enclosed the fort."[3] According to Ganong, this mystery structure was simply a now-ruined seventeenth-century wooden fort. The reason there appeared to be a raised platform was because its face had once been eaten

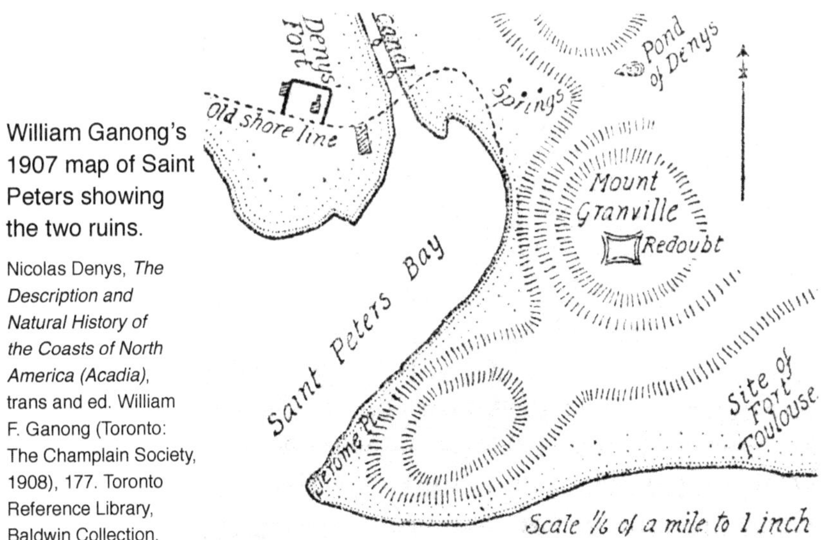

William Ganong's 1907 map of Saint Peters showing the two ruins.

Nicolas Denys, *The Description and Natural History of the Coasts of North America (Acadia)*, trans and ed. William F. Ganong (Toronto: The Champlain Society, 1908), 177. Toronto Reference Library, Baldwin Collection.

away by the tide. The ruined wall now surrounding the fort on three sides had simply been a low base for a palisade. Yet these were the remains of the same wall in which Denys had wanted the entrance moved two hundred and fifty years earlier. It was the same solid earth wall shown by the French surveyors. Their maps show no palisade, and no evidence of either pickets or post holes has ever been found.

It is in that same footnote in which Ganong tried to rearrange the difficult pieces of the Saint Peters puzzle that he was forced to address the person who must have been the greatest threat to this new understanding of these ruins, Judge Haliburton. Ganong had been able to write off Judge Haliburton's son, R.G. Haliburton, as being "totally ignorant of Denys' establishment," and his theory of earlier settlers in Saint Peters, "wholly groundless," but the judge himself could not be dismissed so easily. What Ganong had to deal with in 1907 was the engineer's map that Haliburton had included seventy-five years earlier in his history of Nova Scotia, the map that showed two old unexplained forts in Saint Peters, ruins claimed by the Mi'kmaq to be pre-European. Ganong needed to address these ruins as Haliburton had shown them, both the one on the shore and the one on the hillside. He could not use terms like ignorant and groundless in commenting on Judge Haliburton, who was well respected, well liked, and an important historical figure. Haliburton had been a writer, a historian, and a politician of note both in Nova Scotia and Britain.

The final section of the paragraph in which Ganong attempted to lay to rest the confusing history of the ruins was dedicated to appeasing Judge Haliburton's claims. After describing how Denys's fort had stood on an elevated blank on the dotted line of an imaginary shoreline, Ganong declared that, "The appearance of the place prior to the building of the canal is well shown in the map given by Haliburton where it is designated as 'Old Redoubt.'"[4] Ganong's tone suggested that Haliburton agreed with him, or vice versa. He complimented the Judge on how "well shown" the place was. However, Ganong's claims do not match Haliburton's at all, they contradict him. The sea never washed against the front face of the fort. There was no cliff there. There had been a deep ditch and an earth platform as the French surveyors had shown. Moreover, Judge Haliburton seems to have known perfectly well that this fort had not been built by Nicolas Denys. Haliburton did not know what it was or who had left it behind, other than what the Mi'kmaq had told him, but he knew it was not Denys. It had been built before the French arrived.

Sadly, the claims of the Mi'kmaq were forgotten. With the Champlain Society's imprint and Ganong's footnotes providing the newly minted, undisputed framework for Denys's seventeenth-century memoirs, doubt surrounding the ruined fortress to the west of the canal appeared to dissolve effortlessly into a sense of historical sureness and permanence. Denys did it. Who else could it have been? In 1931, with Ganong's research providing the historical foundation, the Historic Sites and Monuments Board of Canada recognized the ruins of the old fort on the shore as the location of Denys's seventeenth-century trading post. The ruins were now called Denys's *Fort Saint Pierre*.

In 1985, the Historic Sites and Monuments Board hired a small team of archaeologists to substantiate the claim that these ruins had been left by Nicolas Denys. According to the archaeologists' report, their mandate had been, "to verify the location" of Denys's fort and to, "assess the significance of the archaeological remains."[5] After a three-week dig, the archaeologists found the charred remains of the wooden buildings that had belonged to Denys. Denys had built within the fort walls. That seems to be why he wanted the entrance to the fort moved. However, the archaeologists stopped when Denys's buildings were found, digging no deeper. They did what they had been hired to do.

However, the fort itself, that structure described and drawn by the French engineers in the eighteenth century, lies below and around these simple wooden buildings. The report then went on to explain that, "Most likely, this core is the 17th century fort wall.... its original thickness had been about 1.5 m [and] would have survived to a height of about 0.50 m [when the canal was constructed in the mid-nineteenth century]."[6] The archaeologists described the wall as having been constructed of layers of sod, horizontal layers of earth. Most importantly, after admitting that the original height of the walls was unknown, the archaeologists claimed, "One would expect that they had been topped with a palisade."[7]

Before Ganong wrote about the ruins in 1907, no one had suggested that there might have been a typically European wooden palisade surrounding the fortress. The walls were always thought to be of earth. If it had been a palisade built by Denys's carpenters, Denys's carpenters could have easily moved it. It seems that he would not have had to complain to his associates in Paris about it. The French surveyors showed the wall as earth on their maps. The archaeologists hired by the Historical Sites and Monuments Board admitted that even though the team had looked for the remains of post holes that would have proven the use of a wooden palisade, they found none. No palisade, no posts, no pickets. However, the archaeologists' suggestion that "one would expect that they had been topped with a palisade" is perfectly in keeping with Ganong's claims.

The archaeologists hired by the Historic Sites and Monuments Board also claimed that they had found a small section of ruined construction at a level of excavation that predated the Denys fire. Their report states that a section of the construction was not burnt, as the other wooden ruins had been. "As it definitely is situated beneath [underlined in original archaeological report] the burnt floor, it seems possible that it represents a piece from a building predating the Burnt Structure."[8] Perhaps what the archaeologists found under the burnt floor was simply an earlier Denys's structure. It might have been destroyed and built over before the final fire in the winter of 1668–69. Or it might be from the *Compagnie de Cap-Breton*, the trading company that had hired a carpenter and nail maker to come to Saint Peters a decade before Denys. Or perhaps it is something else entirely. It may be part of a much older building. What the archaeologists saw below Denys's burnt wooden structures may be part of the original structure shown by the French surveyors, this earth platform with its thick earth walls surrounded by a deep moat, an ancient, pre-European ruin, a mysterious structure built by rovers of the sea, white men before the French. Rather than strive to understand the reports, the maps, the surveys, the Mi'kmaq oral histories, and the legends of the local settlers, Ganong assured that he had solved the puzzle. Perhaps he hoped all those earlier files would be firmly closed and forgotten, that the rovers of the sea would be lost to time.

3

THE RUINS ON MOUNT GRENVILLE

When William Ganong wrote that the small fortress on the shore of Saint Peters Bay had been built in the mid-seventeenth century, a certain clarity descended on the ruins and on our history. The region's multi-layered and often muddied past and its stories of pirate forts, ancient builders, and strange unknown rovers of the sea was pushed back into the darkness of an ancient time by a modern sense of simplicity and logic. Nicolas Denys did it, and that was the end of the mystery. However, should we not try to better understand these often confused accounts of our past? These early legends point to an unknown source of wonder, memories without written records, an almost forgotten long ago that is hidden behind centuries of change. There appears to be a lost story written in these ruins, a story that continues to haunt the earliest history of the Americas.

The Mi'kmaq voices that spoke of an ancient time, of settlers who came before the French, indicated to the first historian of the province that there were two pre-European ruins in Saint Peters. The Mi'kmaq voices were clear; but who had built these ancient ruins in Saint Peters is a mystery. The first of the ruins, the one on the shore, is now referred to as the seventeenth-century wooden palisaded fort of the French fisherman and fur trader Nicolas Denys. The second ruined structure in Saint Peters referred to by the Mi'kmaq is located on Mount Grenville to the east of the shore ruins, about a fifteen minute walk up the side of the hill. These ruins, too, have been given a European attribution, but, like the shore ruins, this old fortress on the hill is a voice from history that may be saying something very different.

Here on the summit of this low mountain are the ruins of a single raised earth platform that has no obvious, clear explanation. These ruins overlook the isthmus to the west and the full expanse of Saint Peters Bay toward the south. For the most part, the walk up the hill towards the ruins winds through a provincial park that is run as a public campground. It is usually busy with campers and families having picnics during the summer months, but the ruins are located off to one side of the park, near the summit of Mount Grenville, and are usually quiet. In their stark empty simplicity, these ruins too may be the memory of an ancient, unsolved mystery.

This ruined structure near the summit is a rectangular, manmade earth platform. The platform measures roughly twenty-five by thirty metres, larger than the fort on the shore, but it is still relatively small. In places the platform is almost two metres above the surrounding hillside, and in certain places along its perimeter edge there are the remains of what appear to be mounded walls. These walls that once defined the perimeter of the platform are low, less than a metre high, and in their ruined state are a couple of metres wide in places. In certain areas there is what seems to have been a ditch or moat outside these perimeter walls. The platform is overgrown by the forest that surrounds it and, being made of earth, blends easily with the surroundings. The ruins have never been surveyed.

Like the ruins on the shore and the reports of an ancient canal that once crossed this isthmus, the various stories told of these Mount Grenville ruins are confusing. It appears that something of significance existed here at one time, but it is not clear who was responsible for its construction, when it was built, or when it was first deserted.

After the *Compagnie de Cap-Breton* and Nicolas Denys left Saint Peters in the middle of the seventeenth century, the area remained quiet

A partial view of the ruins on Mount Grenville.

until the French military arrived in 1713. When the French surveyed Saint Peters, they made it clear that there was something up on Mount Grenville, a rectangular platform of some sort, with a purpose and origin that were a mystery.

The French cartographers must have been in a professional quandary. Should they record faithfully the reality of what they saw, or should they ignore the ruins. It appears they tried to do both. On the French map from 1733 showing Mount Grenville, the raised earth platform was rendered as an obvious white rectangle against the jet black of its surrounding hillside. The telling white rectangle is clear. It is where the current ruins are located. On another copy of the same map, the ruins are rendered less clearly, but they are still there. They are the ruins of something. There are also roads shown climbing Mount Grenville. Who had built them? The eighteenth-century French knew something was there, but the surveyors appear not to have known what it was or why it had been built. Though the French never actually acknowledged the raised platform by labelling it as a ruin, a "ruined redoubt," as they had on the shore, they found the platform on Mount Grenville impossible to ignore.

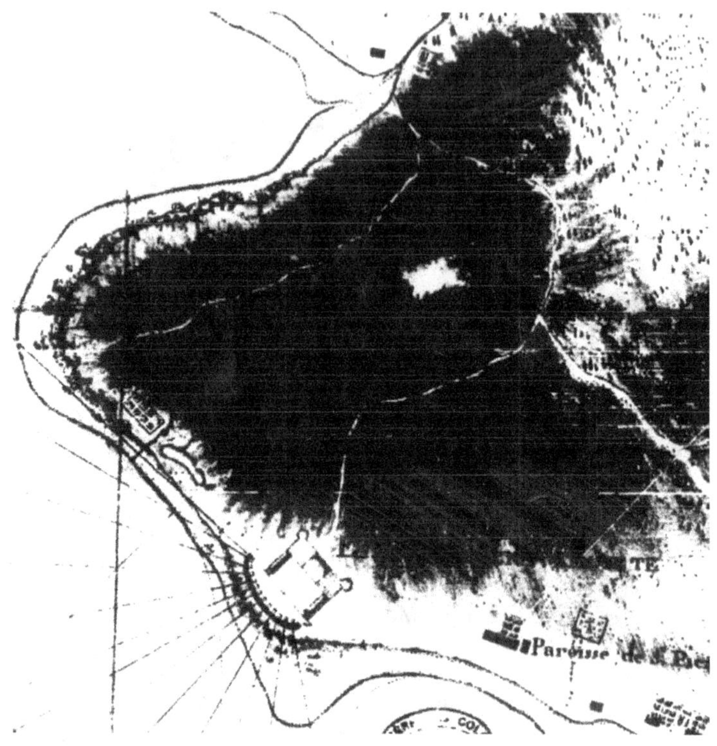

A detail of a French map of Saint Peters (ca. 1730) with a graphic suggestion of the ruined platform on Mount Grenville and the road system connecting it to the shore.

"PLAN de partie du Port Toulouze dans Ijsle Royalle ou est representé en couleur jaune l'Etablissement a faire en 1734 des Cazernes, le Logement du Commendant et des Officiers, Magazin des Vivres, et d'une Batterie pour la defence du Port." Library and Archives Canada, MIKAN No. 4170356, NMC657.

Perhaps the French believed that if they did not label this thing on the mountain, as they had the lower platform, the strange construction up there would not officially exist. It could be ignored and forgotten. It was only a simple raised flat platform of earth, after all. Perhaps they considered it a primitive thing, not worthy of explanation. This was French land now; perhaps they thought the old ruins on the hill would soon be gone.

When the French occupied Saint Peters during the first half of the eighteenth century they renamed the settlement Port Toulouse. They built minimal fortifications. Records and drawings from the period show that those buildings were located on the shoreline at the base of Mount

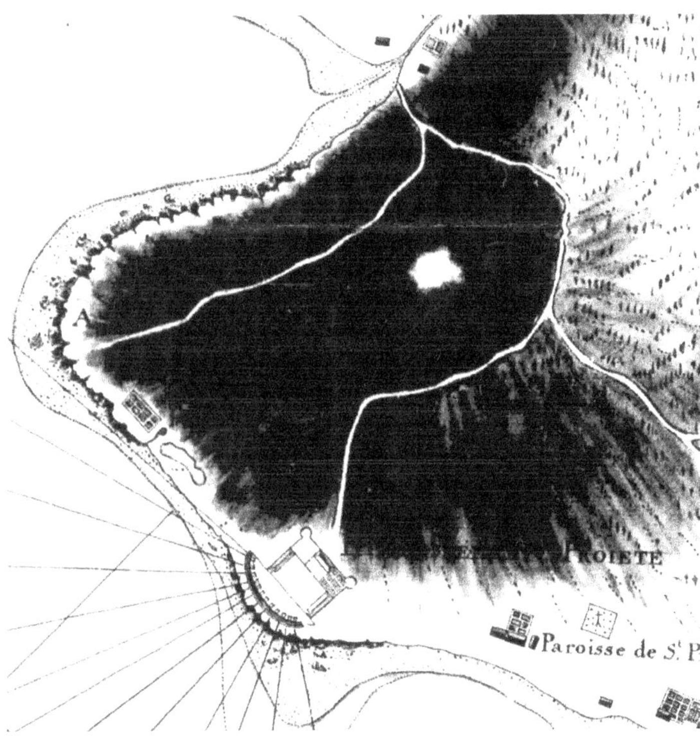

A detail of a second French map of Saint Peters (ca. 1730) with a similar graphic suggestion of the ruined platform on Mount Grenville and the road system connecting it to the shore.

"PLAN de partie du Port Toulouze dans Ijsle Royalle ou est representé en couleur jaune l'Etablissement a faire en 1734 des Cazernes, le Logement du Commendant et des Officiers, Magazin des Vivres, et d'une Batterie pour la defence du Port." Library and Archives Canada, MIKAN No. 4125764, NMC34354.

Grenville, near the place where Nicolas Denys had built his settlement on Jerome Point. By 1717 what the French garrison had built was small, primitive, and wooden. Throughout the fifty years that the French military occupied Cape Breton, statistics suggest that the port remained a small operation. In 1725 there were 60 soldiers in the garrison. The numbers declined from there. In 1734 there were 34, in 1739 there were 25, in 1744 there were 21.[1] In 1745, the French fort at Port Toulouse was destroyed by the British. With changing treaties, the French returned by the end of the decade and built a new fort, but in 1751 the buildings were reported to be both inadequate in number and poorly constructed.[2]

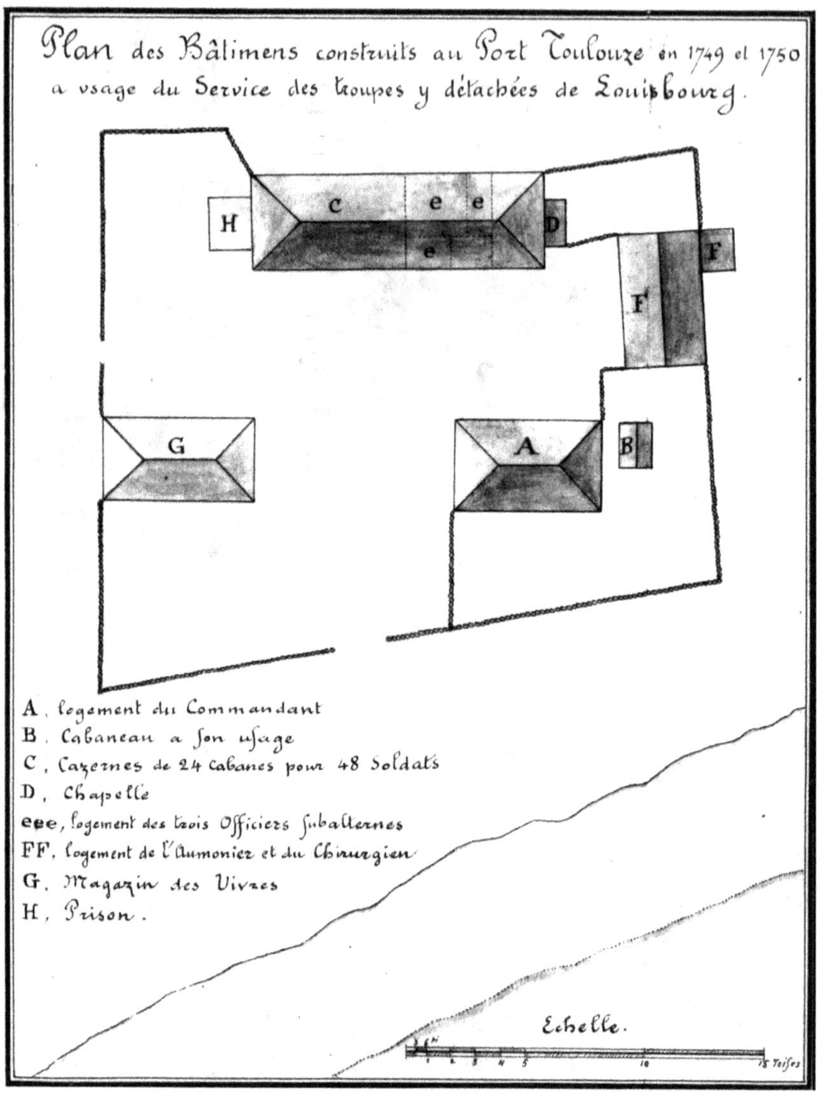

A plan of the eighteenth-century French fortifications built at Port Toulouse (Saint Peters) in 1749 and 1750.

"Plan des batiments construits au Port toulouze en 1749 et 1750 à usage du service des troupes y détachées de Louisbourg." Library and Archives Canada, MIKAN No. 4132931, NMC1005.

After 1751, there was no more French construction in the area except for a road that they built in 1752 to connect St. Peters Bay to their main fortifications at Louisbourg.

It is relatively easy to get a clear image of the simplicity of the French settlement in the mid-eighteenth century. The French military left drawings of what they had built. On a site plan of their fortifications titled "Plans of Buildings Constructed at Port Toulouse in 1749 and 1750," there are only five small wooden structures shown, surrounded by a wooden palisade.

The buildings were rudimentary, all on the shore. Planned and built by a military force at the height of its power in the New World, it is insightful to compare the simple palisade to the mysterious ruins that the French surveyors found further up the hill. The French fort on the shore of Jerome Point was asymmetrically laid out to easily and cheaply provide a sense of a projecting bastion at one corner, and it was constructed of rough logs driven into the ground. Whatever the ruins on the hill had been, its construction would have been a much grander undertaking. Though simple in concept, a flat earth platform near the summit of a hill of uneven terrain is difficult to construct. It would have required moving large amounts of earth in an area that was heavily treed. In contrast, the shore where the French built was already flat and clear by nature. It must have been obvious to the French that they had found something on Mount Grenville that at one time had been important.

It appears that the French made plans to use the ruins on Mount Grenville as a foundation for other buildings. Throughout their occupation of Saint Peters, military architects made proposals to build on the hillside, seemingly on top of and around the mysterious platform that their surveyors had drawn. From the beginning of their occupation in 1713, the French proposed the site for the location of their main fort, and throughout the next forty-five years, until the English finally torched the coastal settlement for the last time in 1758, this specific hillside site kept returning to the French drawing boards. There were elaborate architectural proposals made, with plans that appeared to cover most of the ruins under large fortresses.

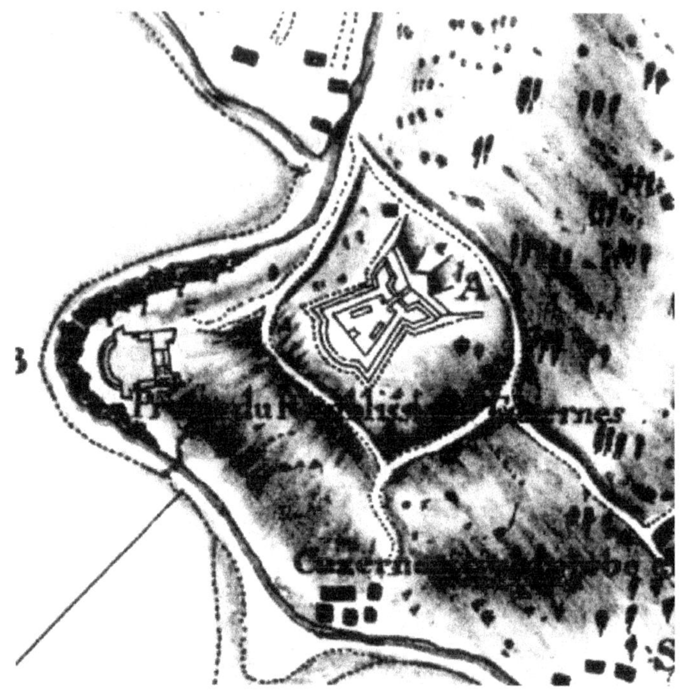

Detail of a French map (1731) with a proposed plan for the construction of a large fortress on Mount Grenville.

"Le Port Toulouse ou est representé en jaune le retablissement des cazernes, 1731." Archives Nationales d'Outre-Mer, ANOM, Aix-en-Provence, FR ANOM 03DFC264B.

On another map the French cartographers actually drew a square platform on the hillside. It appears as if they were drawing a building plan of some sort, with specific distances given to the coastline, but it was unlabelled. What was this thing they were drawing? Why were the surveyors so specific with the measurements to the shore unless the structure already existed? From an architectural viewpoint, this appears to be an as-built drawing.

The ruins on Mount Grenville are not French. There are no records of the French having left any construction at all on the side of Mount Grenville. Most importantly, it appears that the ruins were there when the French arrived.

Perhaps the ruins on Mount Grenville were an embarrassing problem for the French military and their claims to the area. The smaller

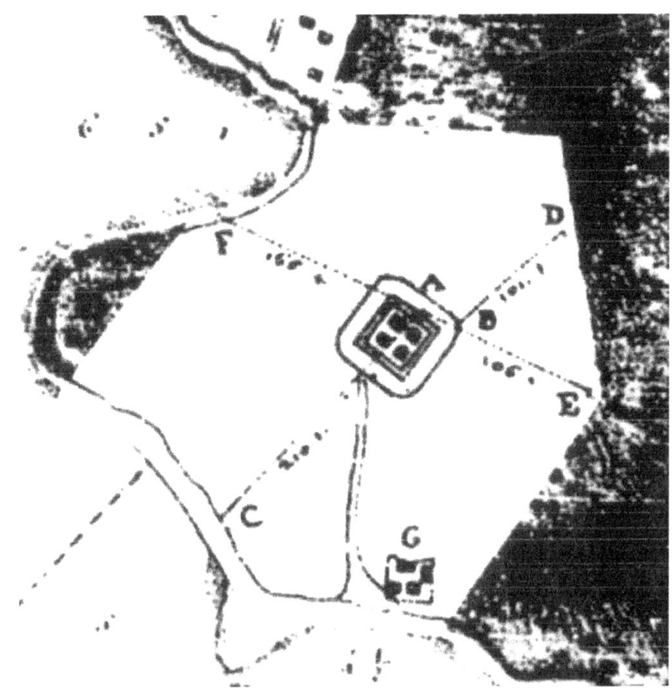

A detail of a French map of Mount Grenville (ca. 1730) showing a structure where the existing ruins are located with distance measurements given to the surrounding shoreline.

"Plan du Port Toulouse." Library and Archives Canada, MIKAN No. 4125760, NMC656.

platform on the shore that they had labelled as a ruined redoubt, even with its earthen perimeter walls and surrounding moat, could have been acknowledged with some degree of comfort as being French. For those curious enough to ask, the old redoubt could have appeared to have had its roots in either Nicolas Denys or the earlier *Compagnie de Cap-Breton*. With one or the other seeming to fill in the historical gaps, the French must have found it relatively easy to ignore any rumours of a strange, earlier history of the area. However, the larger construction up on the hill would have been much more problematic, a puzzle piece that did not fit so easily into France's image of the area's history. No early French trading company operating in the New World and dependent on ships would have built on a hillside away from the shore. Yet something was there. The French, building an empire in the New World, found it impossible to erase the uncomfortable memory of something, or someone, who had come before, had settled before, and had built before in a manner and in a location that Europeans wouldn't.

After the French left in the mid-eighteenth century, the English took possession of Cape Breton. In 1790, the newly appointed lieutenant governor of Cape Breton, William Macarmick, proposed, like the French had before him, an extravagant construction scheme for Mount Grenville. He wanted to level the summit and build a massive triangular fortress with corner bastions, thirty large cannon, twenty small cannon, and a garrison of nine hundred soldiers.[3] Again, like the French, the English were determined to build over anything that was there. Also like the French, Macarmick's elaborate proposal came to nothing. However, the English garrison did build something on Mount Grenville, seemingly on top of the ruins.

Lieutenant Colonel George Moore, the commander of Fort Grenville, or Fort Dorchester as it is also called, had approximately fifty soldiers under his command. The English construction on the summit of Mount Grenville was done by local volunteers, seemingly on the site that the French had marked earlier in the century. During the fall of 1793, a guardhouse was built to allow the garrison to winter at the site, but by the spring of 1794, eight or nine months later, both interest and money for the construction had disappeared. Macarmick, Moore's boss, claimed that a guardhouse, a magazine, and a redoubt had been substantially completed, but the hastily constructed buildings appear never to have been used.[4] In 1798, Lieutenant General James Ogilvie was sent to Cape Breton to investigate what was seen as Macarmick's disastrous administration of the island. It was only four years after the English garrison left, and Ogilvie reported that the fortifications were "all in ruins."[5] The British Army's Core of Engineers, in their reports from 1853 and 1867 on the remaining defenses on Cape Breton, reported no construction whatever at Saint Peters.[6]

Only a generation after the English may have spent the winter on Mount Grenville, Judge Haliburton's history showed the ruins, seemingly the same ones that the French surveyors had shown on their maps a century before. Haliburton's "Old Redoubt" on Mount Grenville is similar to the platform the French had drawn in the eighteenth century. His map appears to match the early French maps. Haliburton was saying the same thing the French had said: here is a strange, old earth platform and we don't know what it is.

In 1869 the Canadian historian Richard Brown included a short explanation of the English garrison at Fort Dorchester in his *A History of the Island of Cape Breton*. He wrote, "Lieutenant-Colonel Moore, the Commanding Officer of the Southern District, was dispatched to occupy a redoubt at 'the important post of Mount Grenville', near St. Peters, armed with eight guns. The remains of the redoubt, which commanded the isthmus of St. Peters and access to the Bras d'Or lakes, may still be seen."[7] Brown's history marked the beginning of much of the current confusion surrounding these Mount Grenville ruins.

Enter William Ganong again. Ganong, who edited and translated Denys's book in 1908, claimed that he had been informed by local sources that the Mount Grenville ruins had been left behind by the English garrison in 1794. With Brown's suggestion that the remains of a redoubt could still be seen, and with Ganong's claim garnered from local recollection told over a century after the English had camped there, the ancient platform officially became Fort Dorchester, the English ruins of 1793. Again, the Mi'kmaq legends of early mounds were ignored.

Not surprisingly, Ganong became a definitive voice on the history of Mount Grenville. In the same footnote in which he had discredited any suggestion that the lower ruins had been left by anyone but Denys, Ganong also tried to erase the enigma surrounding the ruins on the side of Mount Grenville. He reported, "The other 'Old Redoubt' on the mountain, the remains of which are still visible, is a much later work, locally said to have been erected by Hon. Geo. Moore, by order of the British Government, but never used."[8] Like he had done with the lower ruins on the shore and its attribution to Denys, Ganong made a simple bold statement that was open to neither interpretation nor criticism. His claim suggested that, along with the ruins of a few wooden buildings, the substantial raised earth platform on which the ruins had been built was English in origin. The British did it, so claimed Ganong. Others now quote Ganong.

Could the redoubt that Macarmick claimed had been built by volunteers for Moore's small garrison during the winter of 1793 be the same ruins on the mountainside referred to thirty years later by Judge Haliburton and shown on his map? How could it be? The Mi'kmaq claimed it had been built centuries before. The French had drawn the platform on their maps before the English arrived. Something was clearly there when the French first settled the area, yet, against all logic, Ganong decreed that the ancient raised earth platform on Mount Grenville was actually built by Moore during the winter of 1793.

In 1966 Mount Grenville was investigated by the Historic Sites and Monuments Board of Canada as a possible National Historic Site. There was no digging done. In the report written for that investigation, after reviewing in detail Moore's failed construction, the final sentence of the final paragraph of the report declared, "Remains of the redoubt are apparently still visible on Mount Grenville."[9] From what the records claim, the English garrison had left nothing more than the overgrown remains of a few simple wooden walls, built in a few months during winter and never used, buildings that in 1798 were reported all in ruins. They would have been somewhat haphazard buildings built on top of this much larger structure shown by the French surveyors. Nonetheless, by failing to clarify the distinction between these simple wooden ruins and the earth platform on which they were built, these histories give the impression that the ruins found on the summit of Mount Grenville, and shown on maps by both the French and by Judge Haliburton, were left by the English at the end of the eighteenth century.

Currently, a government sign giving the history of the Mount Grenville site has been erected on a small raised wooden seating area on the far side of the ruins, on one of the perimeter mounds, close to the steep slope overlooking the bay. The sign, an official description of the ruins, explains how the fort had been constructed "in 1793–94 at the request of William Macarmick, the Lieutenant-Governor of the British colony of Cape Breton Island." It explains that it "was the era of French Revolution and Macarmick feared that the Acadians of Isle Madame might rise up against British rule." This explanation also gives a very brief description of the ruins and a short history. It reads, "Fort

Dorchester was a square redoubt with 15 embrasures, a guardhouse, and a powder magazine. For several years there was a garrison of about fifty men here, then the crisis passed, and the fort was abandoned. The earth mounds are what remain of the walls of the fort; the hollows in the walls are where the gun embrasures were."

This claim, like Ganong's, and like his theory that Denys had built the lower ruins, makes little sense when looked at closely. The size and the mass of the platform suggest it was not English. It is difficult to imagine Moore's unpaid workforce, even if helped by his own garrison, building such a structure on a heavily treed hillside out of frozen ground. In addition, the map Haliburton used, drawn thirty years after Moore's occupation, makes no suggestion that the ruins were English. Haliburton must have understood the importance of the Mi'kmaq oral histories of an ancient mound built before the French. He realized the enigma the Mount Grenville ruins posed. He was writing only a generation after the English occupation, and he knew the area well. By suggesting it was a mysterious ruin, in the same way the ruins on the shore were shown, Haliburton must have realized this was not of Moore's hand.

The question of who built the ruins on Mount Grenville has proven as confusing as who built the ruins on the shore. There is even a suggestion from one historian that Nicolas Denys was responsible. In a history of the Saint Peters canal from 1973, written by the Canadian government's Department of Indian and Northern Affairs, the writer claimed that, "To the east of the Atlantic entrance [of the canal], atop Mount Granville, the foundations of Denys's second 'redoubt,' which dates back to the mid-17th century, guard the approach to St. Peters canal."[10] This may be an attempt to explain why the French drew the ruins on the eighteenth-century maps. The idea of Denys's ruins on the mountain overlooking the bay is an appealing image, but it is just plain wrong. It seems that historians have been trying to force this strange platform on Mount Grenville into a simple, straightforward, and European ruin. However, the history of Saint Peters is neither simple nor straightforward.

If it was not the English who left the ruins, nor the French before them, who was responsible for this platform on Mount Grenville? That is really the question at the core of the puzzle of Saint Peters. Officially at least, the case had been long closed. The area is now part of a Public Provincial Park and the information brochure and hiking map given to tourists visiting the park shows Mount Grenville as the site of the "Fort Dorchester Ruins."

With the English given responsibility for the ruins on Mount Grenville, and Denys and his crew given responsibility for the smaller ruins on the shore, the ancient mounds spoken of by the Mi'kmaq have been made to fit neatly into standard European history. However, given the documentation of both ruins, neither Denys nor the French nor the English built those platforms. There is a past in Saint Peters that has not only been forgotten, but perhaps consciously ignored.

The nineteenth-century Mi'kmaq remain the only source of clarity. The truth seems to lie in their simple and straightforward claim to Judge Haliburton. The ruins predate European settlement. The ruins are an awkward piece of history, a piece that has never fit into the way the island's history has been told. The ruins in Saint Peters have become, like the ruins on Cape Dauphin, an uncomfortable suggestion of an unspoken history.

Even more extraordinary than the two ruins is another mystery that appears in the documents covering the centuries of exploration and settlement. The first records and maps of the region claim that there was a passage through which ships could travel cut across this narrow neck of land — a manmade canal that allowed ships to sail from the Bay of Saint Peters and the Atlantic Ocean on one side to the Bras d'Or Lakes and the interior of the island on the other. It is to that remarkable claim that we now turn.

4

THE MARK OF AN ANCIENT CANAL

The suggestion that there had been an ancient canal across the isthmus separating the Bras d'Or Lakes from the bay and harbour of Saint Peters was what first began to stoke my interest in the history of the area. It seemed so unlikely that a canal would have existed in Saint Peters when Europeans first arrived, yet it was impossible to ignore the early records. There are documents and maps that suggest a passage had been built — a road of water on which ships could pass.

Beginning from the side of Mount Grenville, the squat mountain that rises gradually to the east of the isthmus, a low solid-granite ridge extends across the isthmus of Saint Peters from the east to the west. The stone ridge now has a wide, deep cut through it, believed to be made by the construction of the modern canal across the isthmus begun in the mid-nineteenth century. However, a passage of some sort must have existed across the isthmus when Europeans first began arriving in the New World, seemingly already cut through this stone ridge, because a passage is referenced in the earliest records and maps of the region, centuries before the construction of the modern canal. The first mention of such a passage I found was in a ship's log from the late sixteenth century.

A view of the existing canal across the Saint Peters isthmus looking north.

In April of 1597 two ships, the *Hopewell* and the *Chancewell*,[1] sailed out of Falmouth, England, on their way to the New World. Aboard one of these ships was a small party of four men who were looking for a place to begin a religious colony in the New World. They represented a group of English religious separatists who would eventually become known as the Pilgrim Fathers, and who finally settled on the east coast of what is now the United States in 1620, over two decades after this little-known first visit. The plan of the commander of the *Hopewell* and the *Chancewell* was to fish for walrus and cod while the four religious leaders scouted for land that might be appropriate for their new colony. Charles Leigh, the captain of one of the ships, the *Hopewell*, wrote an account of the journey.

Having left England on April 28, 1597, the two ships arrived on the Grand Banks, the rich fishing grounds off the eastern coast of Newfoundland and Cape Breton, on May 18. The *Hopewell* and the *Chancewell* lost each other in the thick fog along the coast. While searching for the lost *Chancewell* off the coast of Cape Breton Island, the *Hopewell* found a small boat with some of the men from the *Chancewell* along the eastern coast of the island near the northern mouth of the Bras d'Or Lakes. The *Chancewell*'s men guided the *Hopewell* back down into the Bras d'Or Lakes where their ship had been run aground.

According to Leigh, the *Chancewell* had found its way into "a great bay eighteen leagues within the Cape."[2] Here, at the end of the Bras d'Or, the *Chancewell* had come aground. According to Leigh's report, once the *Chancewell* was grounded, "there came aboard many shallops with sort of French men, who robbed and spoiled all they could lay hands on, pillaging the poor men even to their very shirts."[3] It is then that Leigh's observations become confusing. Leigh claims that, hoping to rescue the men of the *Chancewell*, the *Hopewell*, "put into the road where the *Chancewell* lay where there was also one ship of Sibiburo [Ciboure is a port in southwest France] whose men that hoped to pillage the Chancewell were run away into the wood...."[4] He writes of a road used by these ships, a road of water on which ships could travel. Leigh also mentioned this road later in the log. He wrote that on "the 29, betimes in the morning we departed from that road toward a great Biskaine, some 7 leagues off of 300 ton."[5]

According to the captain's log, the *Hopewell* found the *Chancewell* shipwrecked on a road that the ship had sailed onto while making its way down the Bras d'Or. A road. At the end of the sixteenth century, almost a half a century before Europeans started settling in this part of the world, there had been a road, seemingly made of water, reported in this area, a road upon which large, ocean-going ships had found themselves stranded. Moreover, it seemed like a busy place. From Leigh's report, the pillaging of stranded sailors was a popular sport. But what reason did the *Chancewell* have to sail down through the centre of the island, the full length of the Bras d'Or? They may have been searching for a way out, out to the ocean across the isthmus. It must have been an opening that they believed existed, that they had been told existed once, that was shown on the maps that they had trusted enough to have guided them across the Atlantic, through the fog of the Grand Banks fishing grounds, and down through the centre of the island.

This early claim that there was a road on which ships could sail through the far southern end of the Bras d'Or might be of little importance if the log written by the captain of the *Hopewell* was the only mention we had of an ancient passage across this isthmus. However, the maps that were drawn in the early years of European visits show what this road mentioned in the *Hopewell* log may have been.

During the first years of the 1600s, two French adventurers, Marc Lescarbot and Samuel de Champlain, both young men who lived in Acadia, drew maps of Cape Breton Island, the first to be drawn by people who had actually lived in the region. Both Lescarbot and Champlain mapped Cape Breton in the easily recognizable manner of a group of various sized islands, a large island to the northwest and a collection of smaller islands to the southeast. Neither of the maps showed a road at Saint Peters. Their maps suggested something much more remarkable.

They show an opening, a way for ships to sail through. Both men drew the deep inland sea — the Bras d'Or Lakes — running down the centre and separating the two sides of the island. Both Lescarbot and Champlain show the southern tip of the Bras d'Or Lakes opening out through the isthmus at Saint Peters. According to these early mapmakers, both men who mapped Cape Breton while living in the region, a ship arriving from Europe and the Northern Atlantic could sail through the Bras d'Or and out through the opposite end, out to Saint Peters Bay and the open ocean beyond.

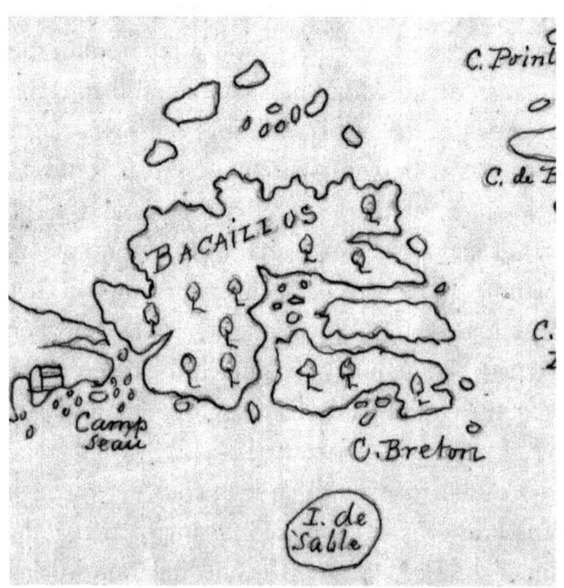

A detail of Marc Lescarbot's map of New France from the early seventeenth century, showing a passage through the isthmus at Saint Peters.

Marc Lescarbot, "Figure de la Terre-Neuve, Grande Rivière de Canada et Côtes de l'Océan en la Nouvelle France," 15.5 x 41.5 cm. Musée de la civilisation, fonds d'archives du Séminarie de Québec, T-4.

There is even an earlier map, drawn over a century before, that shows the same opening. The Christopher Columbus map of the known world, on which he drew for the first time what appears to be Cape Breton, had the same passage running across the isthmus at the southern end of the island.

Columbus's map, drawn in the early 1490s before Europeans had started exploring the coast, shows the outline of an island located in the North Atlantic recognizable as Cape Breton. Columbus called it the Island of Seven Cities, just as John Cabot would in 1497 when he landed on Cape Breton and claimed the island for England. It is one of the most interesting references in early New World history: an island in the wilderness, unexplored by Europeans, where the inhabitants had built seven cities. European legends started by sailors who had briefly visited the island, who had been shipwrecked or blown off course, and who had returned to their home ports to recount their adventures, told of the island's wonders. Remarkably, Columbus, just like Lescarbot and Champlain would more than a hundred years later, drew an opening at the southern tip of the island with the Bras d'Or Lakes emptying out into the Atlantic through Saint Peters Bay. That isthmus had been open once. There was a passage here through which ships could sail.

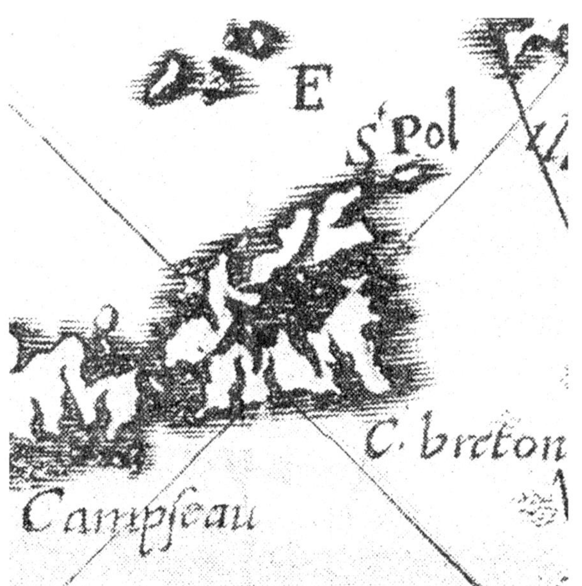

A detail of Samuel de Champlain's map of New France, 1613, showing a passage through the isthmus at Saint Peters.

Samuel de Champlain, "Carte geographique de la Nouvelle Franse," 1613. Library and Archives Canada/ Les voyages du sieur de Champlain, Xaintongeois, capitaine ordinaire pour le Roy en la marine collection/ e010764734.

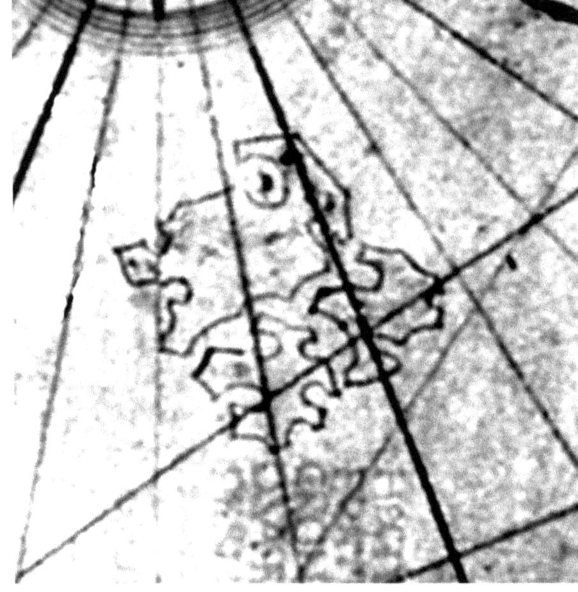

A detail of Columbus's map of the world (ca. 1490) showing the Island of Seven Cities with a passage through the southwest end of the island.

Christopher Columbus, "Columbus World Map," late 1400's, illuminated manuscript on vellum, 28 x 44 inches. Bibliothèque nationale de France, Paris.

Nicolas Sanson, geographer to the French king and a central figure in seventeenth-century French cartography, also drew a map of Cape Breton Island. On his 1656 map of *Le Canada ou Nouvelle France*, Sanson drew a narrow passage across the isthmus at the southwestern tip of the island as two parallel lines, as if it were manmade, as if it were a canal. On his map, this thin path of water cuts across the granite ridge of the isthmus connecting the Bras d'Or on the north side with Saint Peters Bay and the Atlantic on the opposite side. Vincenzo Coronelli, the Venetian monk considered one of Europe's most important seventeenth-century cartographers, drew a very similar map of Cape Breton in 1692. Using stories of the New World gathered from returning mariners and adventures, both Sanson and Coronelli filtered and distilled these descriptions into the clarity of two lines, into what appears to have been a canal. These cartographers chose to draw a clear and obvious connection between the inland lake to the north and the bay and the ocean beyond to the south; ships could easily sail into the Bras d'Or and out the opposite end.

Imagine Cape Breton Island maps from a sailor's perspective. These maps served as precious documents that informed the men who had just

A detail of a 1656 map by Nicolas Sanson showing a passage through the isthmus at Saint Peters.

Nicolas Sanson, "Le Canada, ou Nouvelle France, & c.," 1656. Library and Archives Canada/ Alexander E. MacDonald Canadiana collection/ n0021100.

A detail of Vincenzo Coronelli's map of 1692 showing Cape Breton Island and a passage through the isthmus at Saint Peters.

Vicenzo Coronelli, "Canada Orientale nell' America Settentrional," 1692, 46.0 x 61.5 cm. Bibliothèque nationale du Québec.

finished a dangerous, cold journey across the North Atlantic. The trips would have been made in the early spring, when the waters of the North Atlantic were icy. The crew finally reached Cape Breton Island, the first land seen. Generations of mapmakers claimed that their ships could safely and easily continue to sail through the centre of the island, down to and out through the isthmus and to the ocean beyond. By using the Bras d'Or, they could easily bypass Cape Breton's rocky southern coast and sail instead with calm, direct access to both the coast of America to the south and the Bay of St. Lawrence to the north.

These maps were made by important cartographers — Columbus, Lescarbot, Champlain, Sanson, Coronelli — giving critical information to a ship's captain sailing toward the coast of Cape Breton. If the maps were wrong, they would have been amended quickly. But they weren't. The opening across the isthmus remained on maps for centuries. A ship's captain was able to trust these maps. His decision to go through the centre of the island and avoid the dangerous outer coast would have been a critical choice. He could not afford to sail down into the Bras d'Or only to find a solid isthmus blocking his ship's path and have to turn around and retrace his path. These early mapmakers had claimed that there was a way to navigate out through the Bras d'Or, a passage to Saint Peters Bay and the ocean and coast beyond. When Europeans began arriving in the New World, there had been a canal here. It must have been what the *Chancewell* went looking for, the road on which they found themselves stranded.

A couple of additional early maps, along with the records of the *Hopewell* and the *Chancewell* help provide a clue to how this ancient canal may have changed over time. On Champlain's early map of Cape Breton, drawn in 1613, the passage across the isthmus was depicted as neither clear nor obvious, but it was there nonetheless. There was still a way through. Moreover, to reinforce that claim, Champlain wrote in his 1606 description of Cape Breton that there were two entrances to the Bras d'Or Lakes, one from the north and one from the south.[6] According to Champlain, there was a way through the isthmus, a way large and deep enough for ships to sail through. However, this passage across the isthmus was aging. By the time Champlain's later map was published in 1632, the opening had closed over. It had become solid land again, filled in by rocks from Mount Grenville, as the later attempts at a canal would be. Sometime between 1613 and 1632, Champlain, who lived in New France until his death in 1635, discovered that this passage had become unstable, untrustworthy, and unusable, as canals do without maintenance. Coronelli would make the same correction in 1696.

In the seventeenth century, after these early maps were published that showed a canal of some sort across the isthmus, Nicolas Denys claimed in his memoirs that he had had a road built from Saint Peters Bay to the shore of the Bras d'Or Lakes. He wrote, "I have had a road made through this distance in order to transport boats, by dragging, from one water to the other, and to avoid the circuit which it would be necessary to make by way of the sea."[7] It appears the Denys's road was meant to haul boats, seemingly drawn along as they were in many early canals, with ropes pulled by men or animals from a road that ran by the canal's side. His claim supports the existence of an earlier canal. Denys's road across the isthmus eventually became known as the Haulover or Portage Road. Traces of it appeared on maps into the early twentieth century bordering the modern canal.

A detail of a later Champlain map of New France, 1632, with the isthmus at Saint Peters shown as solid land.

Samuel de Champlain, "Carte le la Nouvelle France," 1632. Library and Archives Canada/Alexander E. MacDonald Canadiana collection/e010694118.

From the early maps and records, it is clear there had been a passage across this isthmus before Denys arrived, a corridor that Denys was able to make useful. It seems that this enterprising fisherman and fur trader was still able to drag ships through the passage, but only smaller ships. Later records claim that Denys had to abandon one of his largest ships on the Bras d'Or side of the canal.[8] During the sixteenth and seventeen centuries, this passage deteriorated. It became useful by dragging, then not at all. A dry canal becomes little more than a wet road. Around the end of the seventeenth century, the canal had become shallow, seemingly regulated by the water level of the tides which in this region vary several feet between high and low, a tide that changes at different times on the Bras d'Or side and the ocean side.

When the French military arrived in 1713, Saint Peters had been abandoned by Nicolas Denys for over forty years. The French military were in Saint Peters searching for a site for a major coastal fortress, and their reports were to be used by the government administration in Paris to see what was out there in this new wilderness. One of the reports of Saint Peters claimed there was a road across the isthmus of Saint Peters. "*C'est un chemin*," (It is a road) the report announced. Moreover, the report claimed this road the French found across the isthmus was fifteen to eighteen feet wide, "*quinze à dix-huit pied.*"[9] An eighteenth-century French *pied* was a bit more than an English foot, or 12.789 inches. That would make the road reported in 1713 between sixteen and nineteen feet or approximately five to six metres wide. The French maps show the road as having had solid and thick walls, seemingly of stone, lining the sides. This was no small project.

The reports that the French sent from Saint Peters boasted that, "so practical is this road that every day one can make pass *chaloupes* [small boats capable of carrying a crew of five or six and sometimes fitted with a single sail] and even *charoys* from the Bras d'Or to Saint Peters." A *charoy* is a low rolling cart used to transport large ships in shallow water. It is clear from their description that in the early eighteenth century the French were taking large ships across the isthmus. The solid rock of the isthmus had had a passage cut through it.

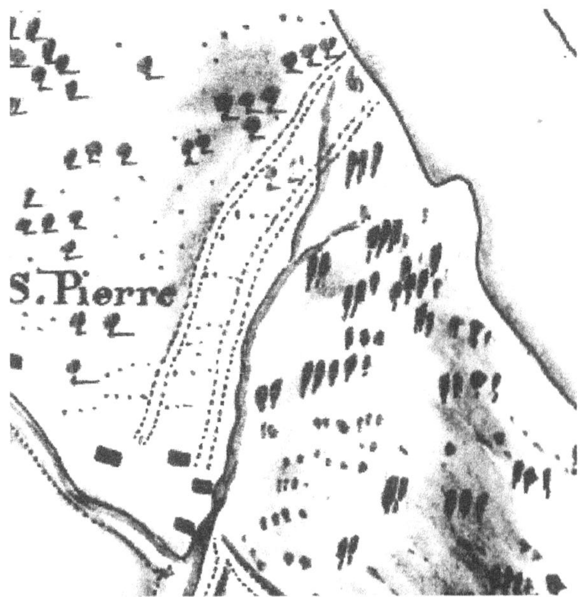

A detail from an early eighteenth-century French map of Saint Peters showing the remains of a wide road across the isthmus from the shore of the Bras d'Or Lakes to the shore of Saint Peters Bay.

"Le Port Toulouse ou est representé en jaune le retablissement des cazernes." Archives Nationales d'Outre-Mer, ANOM, Aix-en-Provence, FR ANOM 03DFC264B.

A detail from an early eighteenth-century French map of Saint Peters showing the remains of a wide road across the isthmus from the shore of the Bras d'Or Lakes to the shore of Saint Peters Bay.

"Plan du Port Toulouse." Library and Archives Canada, MIKAN No. 4125760, NMC656.

According to the French surveys, when they arrived in the early eighteenth century, the passage had been well made enough to still be useful. At one time, it must have had a finished surface that was both flat and hard. These ships were not being dragged over rough boulders or over hills. This was considered a relatively easy passage. The French claimed that their largest ships could be rolled along the eight hundred metre distance between the two shores of the isthmus using only "the arms of men alone without added force."[10]

After the French left Cape Breton in the middle of the eighteenth century, the remains of whatever canal had once been there were forgotten. The canal was mentioned only as a curious adjunct to traditional colonial history.

Ensign Prenties, the sailor who was shipwrecked on the coast of Cape Breton in 1780, observed and recorded the canal at Saint Peters. According to Prenties, the French "had formed a design of cutting through this narrow neck of land, and opening a communication on that side between the ocean and the lake, in order to bring their large ships of war to lie during the winter in the lake of St. Peters."[11] To Prenties the cut was obvious and unambiguous. He had seen it. But the French were not responsible. They were not the ones who had cut through the stone of the isthmus. Their records are clear. The French military had discovered this communication, this road on which ships could travel across the isthmus, already existing when they took control of the island in 1713. Nor would Denys have been responsible for a cut of this depth and width through the stone of the isthmus. He used it but he didn't build it.

At the very end of the eighteenth century, the Reverend James McGregor, a Presbyterian minister travelling through Cape Breton Island in 1799, reported that the road across the isthmus between Saint Peters and the Bras d'Or Lakes could still be used to drag small vessels under the power of a team of oxen.[12] Presumably they were using the Haulover Road to lead the vessels through the canal below. This ancient, mysterious canal across the isthmus was deteriorating, but it was still there and still usable to transport ships at the very end of the eighteenth century. It was the same passage that Columbus, Lescarbot, Champlain,

Sanson, and Coronelli had shown on their maps centuries before. By the time Reverend McGregor made his observation, the canal had been in use for at least three hundred years.

Whatever was there appears to have been ignored and destroyed by the builders of the modern canal that was begun in the mid-nineteenth century. The ancient canal had fallen into such disrepair that nature must have easily blanketed it, obscuring what it once must have been. We can only suppose that by the mid-nineteenth century, heavily covered in growth, the cut may have looked natural. What little was left could easily have been attributed to the French, just as Prenties had thought only seventy-five years earlier. It appears to have been ignored. In the most complete history of the modern construction of the canal, *St. Peters Canal: A Narrative and Structural History*,[13] an official government report written for the Canadian Department of Indian and Northern Affairs in 1973, the ruins of an earlier canal are not mentioned.

This report describes the first drawn-out construction of the canal, which lasted from 1854 until the canal was finally opened for ships in August of 1869. It appears to have been, in every way, a fiasco. An 1860 provincial government report prepared by a committee investigating the project claimed the methods of construction were disorganized and unscientific, there was no large-scale earth-moving equipment available, and the business and scheduling aspects of the job were in shambles.[14] In 1864, ten years into construction, the project had to be resurveyed.

A year later, in 1865, the canal project was restarted under new management. The new construction company soon had twenty-one horse-drawn carts on site and had opened two local quarries to provide cut masonry and cut gravel for the canal.

Very soon after the canal's grand opening in 1869, serious structural problems began appearing. The side embankments began to erode, filling up the bottom of the canal and making it difficult to navigate. In a letter to the Privy Council dated March 15, 1870, the Honourable Edward Kenny, a key player in Canada's confederation only three years before and a Member of Parliament for Halifax, declared simply, "I am sorry to tell you that our canal is falling in."[15] By all reports, the canal was a disaster, poorly planned and poorly built. This long construction process underlines the difficulties that faced even the modern, nineteenth-century canal builders. Whoever had built the original canal shown on the early maps must have been highly skilled and well organized.

The first lockmaster of the canal complained that crews had to wait for high tide to tow their vessels through.[16] This may provide an insight into what happened to the earlier canal. The difficulties of the nineteenth-century canal help explain how, centuries before, large ships would have become stuck while attempting to cross — a shallow, ruined canal becomes an intermittent passageway dependent on the tide.

In 1871, renovations to the recently opened Saint Peters Canal began. Over the next fifty years, the canal would be excavated, rebuilt, and realigned. Masonry was added to the new canal, and a great deal of masonry was removed. The masonry that was removed during this period was deposited on the shore of Saint Peters Bay, immediately to the west of the canal. Cut stones that may have lined the original canal may also be among the many hundreds that are scattered here.

The sides of the modern canal have been built of various materials in various sections: at times metal, at times heavily stained and darkened wooden posts, at times rough rock. Most importantly, however, in the middle of the isthmus there is the ridge of stone coming out from the west side of Mount Grenville. It has been sliced through, hollowed out,

Stones excavated from the isthmus at Saint Peters in the late nineteenth century during construction of the modern canal.

and excavated to below sea level to accommodate construction of the canal and to allow the water to easily and deeply run through it at one time. The modern canal appears to be in the same position as the ancient canal, both cut through the low granite ridge that runs across the isthmus. The eighteenth-century maps drawn by the French military surveyors show a small river running through this opening. The same is the case with the map of the isthmus that the first historian of the province, Judge Haliburton, included in his history of Cape Breton, published before the construction of the modern canal.

Haliburton's map shows marshland where the earliest mapmakers had shown a waterway and the French had shown an almost dry road that ships could still cross. A marsh is a flat thing. The small rivers that run along the canal on the French maps go from one side of the isthmus to the other, from one coast to the other, both stopping just short of the Bras d'Or. When the French arrived, this granite ridge was cut, its base excavated to below sea level so that ships could easily sail through. If the stone across the isthmus had not been cut when the French surveyors drew their maps, the water could not have flowed across it. Rivers do not run uphill. Ships do not climb hills. A waterway is controlled by gravity.

There had to have been an opening in this stone ridge. It is the only way to explain the French surveyors' river and Haliburton's marsh. It explains Ensign Prenties's claim that the French "had formed a design of cutting through this narrow neck of land, and opening a communication." It explains why the French military showed a road going through, a road on which ships could sail. The stone of Mount Grenville that juts across the isthmus had to have been cut before the French arrived, before Judge Haliburton's map, before the modern construction. The nineteenth-century builders may have added to the opening and made it wider, but they did not make the original cut through the side of Mount Grenville. As shown on the very earliest maps of the island, this cut was already there.

5

A CANNON FROM THE PAST

After my Cape Dauphin book was published, various people who had read it or who had heard of the theory suggested that I investigate the nineteenth-century reports of an old cannon that had been unearthed on the shore near Louisbourg, the eighteenth-century French fortress that had been built on the east coast of Cape Breton. The cannon appeared to predate the typical cannon that had been left from the French occupation of the island, and some people thought it might have a bearing on the Seven Cities theory. During my search for information on this cannon, I discovered that there had been a second old cannon found on the island, this one in Saint Peters. The two cannon, the one from Louisbourg and the one from Saint Peters, are very similar, but they also appear to be different in ways that suggest they both tell separate and distinct stories. It is insightful to compare the two cannon because their differences serve to highlight the difficulties that arise in any discussion of the region's early history.

The cannon found at Louisbourg was described by George Patterson, the nineteenth-century historian who had also written about the ruins in Saint Peters. In 1890 Patterson wrote a lengthy article in the *Transactions in the Royal Society of Canada* in which he suggested that not only was there a strange, unexplained history in Cape Breton — a lost chapter he called it — but that this mysterious history was due to early settlement by the Portuguese. The title of his article is clear, "The Portuguese on the North-East coast of America, and the first European attempt at Colonization there. A Lost Chapter in History." In his article Patterson claimed,

> On the shore of Louisburg Harbour, opposite to what is known as Sally Bush Pond, about half a mile west of the site of the old Grand Battery, Mr. Thomas Cannington, about fifty years ago, found embedded in the mud an old hooped cannon. It was composed of bars of forged iron, bound together by iron bands, and was a breech-loader as the old cannon of that construction were. At the same time was also found an old anchor.... These all plainly indicate the wreck of some vessel or vessels at the spot.[1]

Patterson, believing that this cannon found in Louisbourg had been left by early visitors, went on to claim that, "history tells us that such guns were not used after 1540."[2] Patterson theorized that the wreck must been earlier than 1540, and that the only ships carrying such guns would have either been warships or ships carrying settlers and the materials they would need to build a new colony. Patterson went on to theorize that, because no European country was sending warships to the New World and no fisherman would be carrying such guns, the cannon must have been left behind by a very early group of settlers. To Patterson the only alternative was the Portuguese.

The year after Patterson's article, in an attempt to disprove the Portuguese theory and dispel any mystery of a lost chapter weaving its way through New World history, another nineteenth-century Canadian historian, J.G. Bourinot, published a different theory of the Louisbourg cannon along with a detailed ink drawing.

Like Patterson's earlier article, Bourinot's response was also published in the *Transactions of the Royal Society of Canada*.[3] Bourinot argued that the cannon found in Louisbourg was certainly not ancient and therefore had not been left by early visitors. Indeed, the cannon was not at all very unusual. Bourinot explained:

An 1891 illustration of the ancient cannon found at Louisbourg Harbour.

J.G. Bourinot, "Cape Breton and Its Memorials of the French Regime," *Proceedings and Transactions of the Royal Society of Canada for the Year 1890*, 8 (1891), 284. Toronto Reference Library, Baldwin Collection.

> Nearly fifty years ago there was one interesting "treasure trove" in the form of an old gun, which is clearly a memorial of several centuries ago. The hooped cannon, of which I give a sketch on this page, was dug up in the mud of the western shore of the harbour, nearly half a mile to the west of the ruins of the Grand Battery. A distinguished Nova Scotian archaeologist [Patterson] has thought this memorial worthy of an elaborate paper, in which he indulges in a good deal of interesting speculation as to its original ownership. Its workmanship shows it to have been one of those forged pieces of ordnance common in the early part of the sixteenth century, and not infrequently used until, and perhaps even after, the beginning of the seventeenth century, when cast metal guns came generally into use.[4]

Bourinot then described the gun much as Patterson had. It was made of "bars of malleable iron, encircled by ten rings or hoops in accordance with the fashion of those early times." He gives the length and the diameter. According to his description and drawing, at the rear of the gun was a "chamber for the reception of a breech block, which was kept in its place by iron bolts, and was placed in or taken out of its chamber by either a leather or iron handle. The gun otherwise is in excellent preservation, despite the corroding rust that has eaten into the iron that was forged by a cunning gunsmith centuries ago in some foundry across the seas."[5] It is important to note that Patterson, like Bourinot, had also described the found cannon as a "breech loader."[6]

The Portuguese made such cannon, called *petriera*, almost identical to Bourinot's illustration, and, as Patterson claimed, this type of gun went out of general use by the mid-sixteenth century. Because of that fact alone, it was Patterson's conclusion that the cannon found in Louisbourg had been lost by a group of early European vessels. In opposition to Patterson's theory that this was an indication of an earlier, unrecorded history, Bourinot claimed that the cannon easily could have been left behind in Louisbourg at a much later date, even into the early seventeenth century. Bourinot's dating brings the English and the French into the probable history, erasing in large part Patterson's belief that there was a mystery to be solved. With the debate between Patterson and Bourinot finished, for historians following the story, there was every reason to believe that the cannon found in Louisbourg was probably seventeenth-century European. That ended the mystery. There was no lost chapter in our history.

However, Patterson also wrote about a second seemingly similar cannon found in Saint Peters. Patterson also sensed the Saint Peters cannon, like the Louisbourg cannon, was an important but misunderstood piece of some earlier history. To him, it was an artifact from the same mysterious background as the Louisbourg cannon, the same lost chapter. However, the two cannon are not the same. The Saint Peters cannon appears to differ from the Louisbourg cannon on three critical points.

Writing about the discovery of the Saint Peters cannon in the same *Transactions* article in which he described the Louisbourg cannon, Patterson claimed, "About fifty years ago, some parties in pursuit of money, digging at one angle, unearthed a hooped cannon, such as we have described. The hoops were so corroded that, after lying for some time at the door of Mr. Handley, a resident of the place, it went to pieces, and the bars went to the forge of a blacksmith, who used them in this trade, and pronounced them of the best iron he had ever worked."[7]

This same cannon found in the ruins at Saint Peters was also described in 1885 by R.G. Haliburton, the historian son of Judge Haliburton, as having been "formed of bars of iron fastened with iron bands or hoops, those toward the breech being the strongest."[8] The cannon found at Saint Peters seems very similar to the one found in Louisbourg, but it is also quite different and possibly much older.

The rear of the cannon is one important difference. Haliburton described no breech loading mechanism in the Saint Peters cannon. It does not appear to have been like Bourinot's drawing. The breech loading mechanism, that section shaped like a two-pronged fork that pivots at the back end of the barrel to allow loading, had been a mid- to late-fifteenth-century development in cannon design. Given that this was a technical innovation that was common at least until late in the sixteenth century, the breech loading cannon found in Louisbourg must fit within that period, and so appears to have been left during the early years of European discovery. However, the one found in Saint Peters does not appear to have had a breech loading mechanism at the rear. It was not described with one. This cannon seems to have been much simpler in design, originating from before the mid-fifteenth century when breech blocks were invented. This cannon was abandoned in the Saint Peters ruins before Europeans are believed to have settled on the island.

Two other elements suggest that this cannon was from a different time than the later Louisbourg cannon. The cannon found in Saint Peters had not been lost on shore in a shipwreck as the Louisbourg one appears to have been, but had been found buried inland in the shoreline ruins of Saint Peters, apparently set in place and used from that position, possibly by the "rovers of the sea" who were thought to have built the fortress. Even more tellingly, the Saint Peters cannon was made from an unusually high-quality iron. It was so unusual that the nineteenth-century blacksmith made a special note of it, claiming it was the best he had ever seen.

Who was making these early bar-and-hoop cannon out of such high quality iron? Not surprisingly, the earliest bar-and-hoop cannon were, like gunpowder, invented and first used extensively in ancient China. To historians like Patterson, Bourinot, and Haliburton, a Chinese answer to the mystery of the Saint Peters cannon would not have been in the realm of the possible; it simply would not have occurred to them. However, knowing now that large Chinese ships were sailing the oceans before the European Age of Discovery, it is worth looking at this type of cannon more closely.

The form of these bar-and-hoop cannon, a long cylinder banded along its length by equally spaced rings, developed out of the Chinese use of large-diameter bamboo for the barrels of their earliest guns. The regularly spaced hoops of the cannon represent the raised bamboo nodes.

As Chinese metallurgy advanced, these bamboo "fire-barrels" evolved into more substantial cast- and wrought-iron forms.

By the time gunpowder and guns became common in Europe in the mid-fifteenth century, China already had a long history in the use of advanced artillery. According to Joseph Needham, "to put the matter in a nutshell, several hundred specimens of metal-barrel cannon, large and small, as also hand-guns, have survived in China from the +14th century (even indeed the +13th) and are preserved mostly in Chinese museums."[9]

These simple bar-and-hoop cannon were common in China before European soldiers knew what they were, and well before the breech block mechanism was introduced. Much of what Europe was to learn about artillery, it learned from China. This adds great significance to the report that the Saint Peters gun was of such a remarkable quality. Chinese cannon makers, because of their early advances in the science of metallurgy, had developed an extremely high quality iron: five to seven parts cast iron and one part wrought iron.[10] This would account for the local blacksmith's unusual claim that the iron of the cannon found in the Saint Peters ruins was the best he had ever worked.

There is also both written and archaeological evidence that these early cannon, in a wide range of sizes and of the highest-quality iron, were carried on Chinese ships dating at least back into the fourteenth century. These guns were standard naval ordnance, and we know that Chinese ships, including the great Treasure Fleets of the early decades of the fifteen century, would have carried such cannon on board.[11] Given the archaic form of the Saint Peters cannon, the high quality of the metal

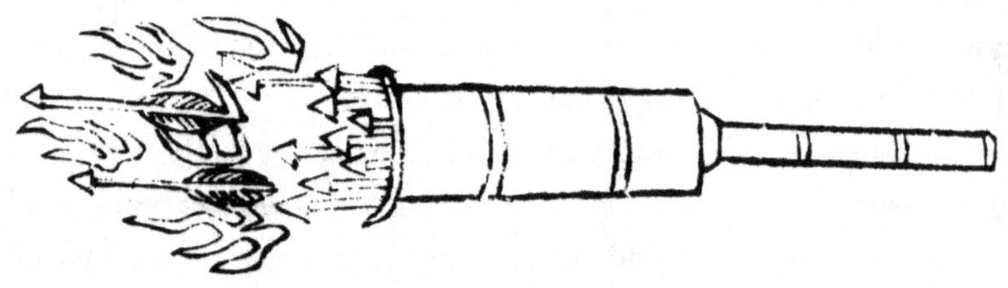

An early Chinese bamboo "fire tube," which used gunpowder to fire arrows.

Joseph Needham, *Science and Civilisation in China*, 5, VII (Cambridge: Cambridge University Press, 1986), 244.

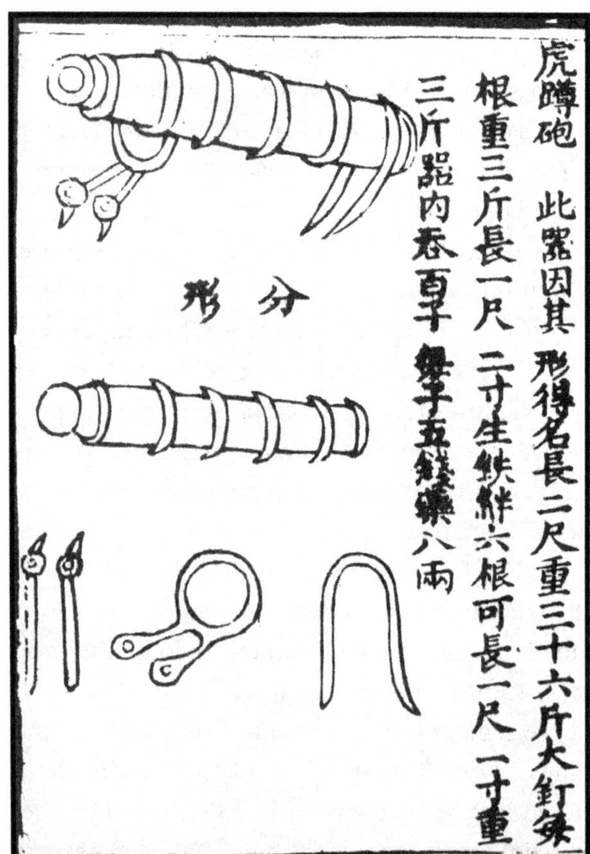

A small Chinese metal cannon from around 1350.

Joseph Needham, *Science and Civilisation in China*, 5, VII (Cambridge: Cambridge University Press, 1986), 279.

reported, and with a history of Chinese naval artillery that has to be considered, a Chinese source for the Saint Peters cannon is a real possibility.

These elements of the Saint Peters cannon suggest a much different history than that of the European cannon found in Louisbourg. On one hand, Patterson's and Bourinot's nineteenth-century explanations of the Louisbourg cannon were clear and logical, but on the other hand, the question of the earlier Saint Peters cannon remains unanswered. Bourinot did not comment on the Saint Peters cannon, though he knew it had existed. A description of it had been published by R.G. Haliburton in 1885, and Patterson's description had been published in the same *Transactions* article in which he had described the Louisbourg cannon, the article which Bourinot was debating. Did Bourinot realize that it was of a much older period? Its mention may have clouded the clarity of his easy dismissal of Patterson's theory of Portuguese settlers. That was the dilemma that these nineteenth-century historians faced in Cape Breton. Who had left what, and when? There was some unknown at which they were grasping, at which we still grasp.

That is why the two cannon and their differences are so important. They help shed light on the way in which we have looked at the early history of the New World. The nineteenth-century historians who sensed the mystery of the Saint Peters cannon and called attention to it were ignored. Once Bourinot made his claim that the one cannon, the Louisbourg cannon with the breech block mechanism, was European and not a mystery at all, the cannon discovered in Saint Peters was painted with the same brush. That it was found in the ruins of the small fortress on the shore, possibly left by mysterious rovers of the sea, became of little importance. The reports of the earlier cannon faded and were forgotten.

With this cannon now added to the mysterious history of Saint Peters, and when the various elements of the site are seen together as a single group, a remarkable picture begins to appear. The canal, a deep cut across the isthmus shown by the French military surveyors to have had wide, solid walls built on either side, was known to handle large ships. It is evidence of a substantial commitment to the region. The ruined structure on the shore was a relatively small construction that may have guarded and controlled the canal traffic. The larger ruins on Mount Grenville, a flat earth platform carved out of the wilderness and elevated with a commanding view of the bay and the ocean beyond, would have once served as the base for buildings of some importance. The position suggests that this was a significant settlement that wished to be seen and admired.

The Mount Grenville ruins imply that Saint Peters was more than just a transportation link for a temporary community. It may have served as an administrative centre for the island. These "white men before the French" brought with them a sense of permanence. They understood the power of the built form, that architecture could elicit a sense of respect, even awe. These early visitors were not only settlers, but they appear also to have been acting as diplomats for their remarkable civilization. Even the small and seemingly insignificant cannon, in its construction and in the composition of its iron, reflects a highly evolved technology that speaks of a level of scientific understanding that would have surprised even the most sophisticated fifteenth-century European. That the various elements of the Saint Peters site, when seen in total, appear so advanced for the period may be why the great mystery of the site was misunderstood, a lost chapter in the history of New World discovery. Above all, this lost chapter that historians have sensed for centuries was certainly never thought to have originated in the Far East.

Part Two:

ROVERS OF THE SEA

6

THE ADVENTURES OF DAVID INGRAM

The theory that the Chinese came to Cape Breton Island in the early fifteenth century is not an unsubstantiated idea contrived out of nothingness. This theory has grown out of claims made since the mid-sixteenth century, claims that point directly to the possibility of an early Chinese occupation of the island. Those claims are made in original documents accepted as genuine by historians of the New World, and they clearly and specifically mention early Chinese settlement and an ongoing Chinese influence in the region of Cape Breton. Moreover, Cape Breton was believed to be the Island of Seven Cities. These records can no longer be denied.

Early explorers, sailors, and settlers had found something remarkable on Cape Breton Island. First, there was John Cabot. In 1497, it was reported that Cabot declared he had discovered the island we now call Cape Breton, and, giving very specific sailing directions to its southernmost point, he claimed it was the Island of Seven Cities, the famous island referred to in fifteenth-century European legends.[1] A half century later, in 1542, a sailor named Jean Alfonce, navigator for Jacques Cartier's voyages of discovery, referred to Cape Breton as the land of the Chinese. Alfonce, in his published sailing directions for the region, called Cape

Breton Island *la Tarterie*,[2] the place of the Tartars, a term then used to refer to the Chinese. Two centuries later, in the mid-eighteenth century, Pierre Maillard, a Christian missionary who wrote a description of his life among the Mi'kmaq, asked if there might be "an affinity between their language [the Mi'kmaq] and that of the Orientalists, as the Chinese or Tartars."[3] Like Jean Alfonce, it was the Chinese that Maillard spoke of. In the mid-nineteenth century Silas Tertius Rand, a noted language scholar who studied the Aboriginal peoples of Nova Scotia for most of his life, wrote that the Mi'kmaq used in their writing not "letters but characters, after the manner of the Chinese."[4] Again, it was the Chinese influence that Rand was making note of.

There is even a very specific claim made by the Mi'kmaq in the sixteenth century that Chinese ships had visited them. The claim was recorded in a first-person account of a trek across North America from the Gulf of Mexico to Cape Breton Island written by a young shipwrecked Englishman. Not only is it a remarkable record of great courage, but the story also alleges that the Chinese had visited the region before the earliest days of European discovery.

In August 1567, a twenty-six-year-old English sailor named David Ingram left the coast of England aboard a fleet of six ships. The fleet's plan was to follow the regular slave trade route from England to Africa, from Africa across the Atlantic to the Caribbean, and then back to England. Twelve months after leaving England, in the late summer of 1568, with trading nearly complete, the fleet reached the Gulf of Mexico. There they were attacked by the Spanish navy off the port of Veracruz. Four of the six English ships were lost, and the shipwrecked crews were forced to crowd on to the remaining two ships. The commander of the fleet, John Hawkins, just thirty-four years old, had two hundred men onboard his small ship, *Minion*, and it became dangerously overcrowded. Before Commander Hawkins would attempt the crossing back to England, he had to lessen the ship's load by half.

In October of 1568, Commander Hawkins left a hundred men from the *Minion* ashore on the eastern coast of Mexico with a promise that he would return for them the following spring. Once Hawkins's ships had sailed out of sight, the hundred sailors who had volunteered to stay behind decided to take matters into their own hands. Rather than wait the eight months for an uncertain rescue, the men chose two very different paths. Fifty of the men chose to walk south along the Mexican coast, heading towards the nearest Spanish colony less than two days away, while the other fifty men chose to hike north, through the wilderness of uncharted North America toward the coast of Cape Breton, nearly five thousand kilometres away. The stark difference in the two choices is part of what makes the story so remarkable.

Those who went south knew that they would soon be met by armed Spanish soldiers, captured, and marched overland to prisons in Mexico City. For these shipwrecked sailors there was the sure safety of a Spanish prison, though most would end up serving terms of hard labour. In contrast, those who decided to head north, including the young David Ingram, were in search of the European fishing fleets that would arrive in the spring to net cod on the Grand Banks, as ships had for a generation. Ingram and his group believed that if they arrived on the coast near Cape Breton before the end of the following summer, before the fishing fleets returned to Europe, they would find a ship to take them home to England. It would be a dangerous journey overland across an unknown landscape, but their goal was freedom.

Within two days of heading north toward Cape Breton, these fifty sailors were attacked by a local Aboriginal tribe. Three of the men were killed, including the group's leader. Fear must have swept through them. After more than twelve months at sea, losing a naval battle and their ships to the Spanish, and being attacked in the wilderness, the now-leaderless group decided to split in half. One group decided to turn back south along the coast with hopes of joining the other men who had decided to go to the Spanish garrison. The second group, numbering just twenty-four, decided to remain steadfast in their hope of finding the European fishing grounds off the Cape Breton coast and a ship to freedom. Ingram was chosen to be the new leader.

This second group reached their goal, though they lost all but three of their original twenty-four. Their trip, nearly five thousand kilometres overland from the Gulf of Mexico to the southern coast of Nova Scotia, "traveling towards Cape Britton,"[5] as David Ingram was to report later, took them eleven months. They arrived in Nova Scotia just in time to get the last fishing boat back to Europe, a French ship that had stayed late to trade with the Mi'kmaq. They were now free and safe. David Ingram and his companions, after being forced each day to make unimaginably difficult decisions, sailed back to the freedom of England.

Thirteen years after returning to England, in 1582, Ingram was asked to describe his journey to the British Secretary of State. The British government was interested in establishing colonies along the Eastern Seaboard of North America, and they were searching for information on the condition of the new continent. The British government and those interested in settling the new continent needed a vision from the ground. It is why the religious leaders sailing on the *Hopewell* and the *Chancewell* would visit the coast in 1597. The British Secretary of State believed Ingram could provide information on the new continent, so the government went to him. However, Ingram proved to be not very helpful. He knew little about the safest harbours or the best farmland. Even though he was able to describe to them things that no westerner had ever seen — herds of buffalo, the prairies, tornadoes — Ingram and his small group had travelled mostly overland, not along the coast, and never rested long in one place. The information he was able to give them just was not good enough.

However, in addition to recounting his unusual journey, Ingram made an astounding claim. He reported that he and his companions arrived on what appears to have been the northern coast of Nova Scotia, the only region in northeastern North America that matches Ingram's description of having found a "maine sea on the Northside of America,"[6] a north facing coast that looks out to a horizon of open water. They then travelled "the space of two whole days"[7] presumably to the end of their journey "within fiftie leagues or there abouts of Cape Britton."[8] There they met the Aboriginal people of this region. Ingram then claims that these people were drawing Chinese ships on the ground. Ingram reported that they had "signified unto him, that they had seene shippes on that coast, and did draw upon the ground the shape and figure of shippes, and of their sailes and flagges."[9] Ingram claimed in his report that all the Aboriginal people had shown him, "especially proveth the passage of the Northwest, and is agreeable to the experience of Vasques de Coronado, which found a shippe of China or Cataia upon the Northwest of America."[10] To Ingram, there was no doubt. The way in which they had drawn the unique shape of the ships, their unique sails, and their unique flags had proven to Ingram that these were Chinese ships. The Aboriginal people of this region could only have been the Mi'kmaq. This remarkable observation by Ingram, reported near the very end of this narrative, reads as if it were not only completely plausible, but even unsurprising.

Ingram was clear. These were not European ships the Mi'kmaq were drawing. This was the mid-sixteenth century and a European ship on this coast would have been old news to the Mi'kmaq and to Ingram. Ingram made the point that these were ships of "China or Cataia" that the Mi'kmaq were drawing. They were convincing enough in the shape, the sails, and the flags described by the Mi'kmaq to prove to Ingram that the Northwest Passage had been open and freely navigated in the recent past. Ingram believed that Chinese ships were sailing over the top of North America.

The story also highlights the power of the Mi'kmaq oral history. The Chinese are believed to have stopped their international sailing by the mid- to late fifteenth century, more than half a century before Ingram's journey and the Mi'kmaq stories. That these ships, so clearly Chinese that Ingram was able to recognize them, had been etched so unmistakably in the Mi'kmaq oral history demonstrates the mastery of their storytellers. These keepers of the Mi'kmaq oral history tried to say the same thing to Judge Haliburton in the nineteenth century when they pointed to the two mounds built before the French. The Mi'kmaq had been visited before by settlers who came before the Europeans. It is undeniable; it is in their legends and in their history. They had been visited by "white men before the French." The Ingram report gives a face to that description. It adds substance to the theory that the Chinese were visiting the East Coast of North America before the European Age of Discovery.

Although Ingram's account was not useful for British settlement plans, in 1589 it was seen as important enough to be published by Richard Hakluyt, the sixteenth-century English chronicler of early voyages and discoveries. Ingram's narrative appeared in Hakluyt's *The Principall Navigations Voiages and Discoveries of the English Nation*, and was the first European description of a journey made overland through the interior of North America.

However, even as important as it was, in 1599, just ten years after it was published, it was omitted from further printings of Hakluyt. For unknown reasons it appears to have disappeared from almost all notice until it was reprinted in 1966 from Hakluyt's original book.

It is not clear why Ingram's report was omitted from publication after the 1599 edition of Hakluyt. In many ways the report was exact in its descriptions of uniquely North American wildlife and geography, as seen objectively through European eyes. Unfortunately however, Ingram mentioned seeing horses, which were believed by Europeans to have been imported only by the Spanish and exclusive to the few Spanish settlements in Mexico. To English historians, it would have been impossible for Ingram to have seen horses elsewhere on the continent outside of Spanish held territory. Ingram also reported seeing elephants, which would have seemed preposterous. Moreover, there was the embarrassing matter of the Chinese ships visiting the Mi'kmaq. However, if this report of Chinese ships is correct, and the Chinese had established settlements in the Americas, Ingram's mention of horses and elephants would also make sense. Both were available to the Chinese, the first from Mongolia and the second through trade with Africa, and both could have been used as work animals in the new Chinese settlements. Both are mentioned in the fifteenth-century records of the Treasure Fleets.[11] However, his report was dismissed, seemingly because of what were considered lies at the time — his "incredibilities" as they were called in 1625 by Hakluyt's successor, Samuel Purchas.[12]

The general feeling remains, as Purchas claimed in 1625, that due to all of Ingram's supposed falsehoods, there is nothing in his story to be believed. Historians have little time for Ingram. However, with everything that Ingram had been through, he had little need to create elaborate stories from his imagination in order to impress his listeners. David Ingram had no reason to lie. The truth was staggering enough.

Nonetheless, Ingram was censored. Seemingly, it was not the horses and elephants that did it. Europeans were only just discovering what the New World had to offer, so it is unlikely that unusual animals would have been heretical enough to have such an important document completely silenced. The removal of Ingram's report from publication suggests that a critical choice was made by the most important early British historians of the New World. Any suggestion of China or things Chinese was erased or ignored. A century after the Treasure Fleets had stopped their remarkable voyages, and just as European sailors had begun to enter the world stage as adventurers and discoverers, perhaps the British found it impossible to believe that such advances in ship building, navigation, cartography, and naval organization had already evolved far in advance of anything that had occurred in Europe — and on the other side of the globe. However, we now know that these remarkable Chinese fleets not only existed, but we are beginning to understand their gargantuan scale, a scale that perhaps was impossible to imagine for those reading the stories of David Ingram in the late sixteenth century. Incredibilities indeed. It is to these incredible fleets and what we know of their size and of their accomplishments that we now turn.

7
THE TREASURE FLEETS

In order to fully appreciate the importance of China's Treasure Fleets to the recent theories of early New World settlement, it is necessary to understand that these massive fleets do not stand alone as an isolated and unique period in Chinese history. These remarkable fleets of the fifteenth century grew out of a long maritime tradition in China that far surpassed anything being imagined in Europe at the time. We now know that China could have been visiting the Americas for centuries.

China's first permanent navy was established in 1132.[1] A late twelfth-century Chinese document describes the "ships which sail the southern sea and south are like houses. When their sails are spread they are like great clouds in the sky. Their rudders are several tens of feet long. A single ship carries several hundred men, and has in the stores a year's supply of grain. Pigs are fed and wine is fermented on board."[2] By the early thirteenth century there were hundreds of such ships in the Chinese navy and over fifty thousand conscripted sailors,[3] and while military and diplomatic concerns were part of this evolving maritime strength, trade, too, had become a central feature of the growing sea power. The ocean was a lucrative place of business. Between the end of the eleventh century and the middle of the twelfth century, profit from overseas trade had quadrupled. The vital importance attached to this growing trade by the Chinese government was made clear by the Emperor Gaozong (1127–62) of the Song Dynasty (960–1279) when he claimed that "profits from maritime commerce are very great. If properly managed they can amount to millions. Is this not better than taxing the people?"[4]

The size of the fleets and of the ships continued to multiply. In 1281, Kublai Khan, grandson of Genghis Khan and emperor of the Mongol or Yuan Dynasty (1246–1368), was able to organize an enormous Chinese armada against Japan,[5] one of the largest naval forces ever assembled. The numbers associated with this armada are simply staggering — 4,500 ships and 150,000 men — and they show how well equipped and well prepared China was to build, organize, and maintain a series of massive ocean-going fleets during the great flowering of the Ming dynasty.

By the early fifteenth century, Chinese shipyards were launching the largest wooden ships ever built. Resembling floating islands, dense with tall tree-like masts, these flat-decked, nine-masted ships could carry a crew of up to five hundred. Depending on what measurement is used to translate the Chinese foot *(chi)* of the period, these ships are believed to have measured between 117 and 134 metres long and between 48 and 55 metres wide, with a displacement of between approximately 24,000 and 31,000 tons.[6] There is simply no comparison to ships being built elsewhere at the time. European countries would not build their first three-masted ships until the second half of the fifteenth century.[7] John Cabot's ship *Matthew* measured 22 by 6 metres and displaced 80 tons. The largest ships in David Ingram's 1597 slave trading fleet displaced 300 tons. The total crew of all six ships was just four hundred men. Of the two ships carrying the four Pilgrim Fathers to Cape Breton in 1597, the larger *Hopewell* was less than 30 metres long and displaced 120 tons. It is clear that in the early years of the European Age of Discovery, no ship being built or even imagined in Europe, and certainly no fleet being assembled there, compared to what China had been sailing for centuries.

The Ming dynasty and the time of the Emperor Zhu Di (1402–24), who christened his reign "Yongle" meaning "lasting joy,"[8] marked the beginning of the Treasure Fleets. These massive ocean voyages continue to stand as a symbol of China's maritime greatness, but they should also serve to remind us that well before the fifteenth century China had already long been a land of sailors, navigators, mapmakers, explorers, and overseas traders. With the construction of the Treasure Fleets, it was the Yongle emperor's intent to spread a continued sense of awe in China's achievements, in the country's power, and in its great wealth. These fleets were meant not as a means of conquest or trade, but instead served primarily to represent China's greatness in each of the ports the fleet entered and to each of the government officials the fleets' ambassadors visited. The Chinese dignitaries bestowed gifts and accepted tribute in return. The commercial transactions that certainly existed were seen as secondary to China's great theatrical presentation of her splendid accomplishments.

Each of the seven Treasure Fleets consisted of hundreds of ships. Leading each of the fleets were sixty or so of the nine-masted Treasure Ships. In addition, each Treasure Ship was supported by different types of smaller vessels. There were horse ships, which besides carrying horses for both land travel and trade, were loaded with tribute goods that served as gifts of diplomacy at the various ports of call. There were supply ships that carried the crew's food, ships that carried building and supply materials, troop ships that carried soldiers, and even water tankers that supplied fresh water for the crew while they were at sea.

Each of the seven Treasure Fleets was organized by the commander Zheng He (1371–1433), a eunuch considered one of the Emperor's favourites. Accounts from the period also claim he was of massive stature — seven feet tall and five feet around[9] — but given the varying sizes of the foot or *chi* at the time, in modern English measurements he may have been closer to six feet tall and four feet around. This may be a more realistic size, but it is still impressive enough to have remained an important element in the development of the legends which have grown up around Zheng He and his accomplishments.

It should be noted that the appointment of a eunuch to such a powerful and important post was not unusual. Eunuchs had a long history in Chinese culture, their roles within the imperial court having been established during the Han Dynasty (206 BC–220 AD). The eunuchs had full access to the emperor and his concubines, they oversaw the imperial household, and they acted as intermediaries between civil officials and members of the emperor's inner circle. Surprisingly, maritime trade was also their traditional domain.[10] Eunuchs acted as the commanders of Chinese fleets beginning in the first century BC, and so the Yongle emperor's appointment of Zheng He to lead the Treasure Fleets would have been expected and welcomed. Zheng He's appointment would have been seen simply as a sign of continuity and respect for the past.

The crews of each of the seven Treasure Fleets were as impressive in their size and organization as were the vessels on which they sailed. Under Commander Zheng He, there was a group of directors and ambassadors who, like Zheng He, would have been eunuchs. Eunuch leaders also commanded the various military regiments that accompanied the fleet. In addition to these eunuch directors, there were hundreds of assistant directors, ambassadors, imperial representatives, and military commanders on each voyage. There were thousands of navigators, sailors, and repair personnel, as well as secretaries, business managers, accountants, astrologers, doctors, and pharmacologists. These were finely crafted and highly managed self-sufficient floating cities with the aim of establishing China's superiority throughout the world. Imagine one of these fleets sailing into a small overseas port: dozens of nine-masted ships and hundreds of their support vessels, thousands of white robed crew members[11] filling the decks, and ambassadors with their refined manners and ornate foreign rituals bringing rare and luxurious gifts.

The first Treasure Fleet sailed out of Nanjing harbour in the fall of 1405 with 255 ships, 62 of them Treasure Ships leading the fleet, with a total crew of 27,800.[12] This first fleet was followed by six more fleets of a similar size, each sent out every few years until the final fleet of 1431. The existing records claim that they travelled throughout the Indian Ocean, along the coastlines of India and Arabia, up into the Red Sea, and at least as far west as the southeast coast of Africa down to the Strait of Madagascar. Throughout their travels, the Chinese collected the new and unusual, rarities and treasures, gems and minerals, medicinal plants and peculiar wildlife. In Africa, they captured a host of exotic animals, from antelopes to zebras, carting the entire menagerie safely back to the

Yongle emperor. The emperor took a particular delight in the gentle, stately giraffes. Along the way, several of the fleets separated into smaller squadrons, each sailing in a different direction, each commanded by a team of eunuchs. Though we do not know if any of the seven fleets or any of these smaller squadrons sailed further than the east coast of Africa, a Chinese/Korean map presented to Zhu Di in 1403[13] clearly depicts Africa's western coastline, so there is reason to believe that Chinese ships had rounded the Cape of Good Hope even before the Treasure Fleets.

A ship that has rounded the Cape of Good Hope into the Atlantic Ocean only need raise its sails and point its bow northward, in the direction of the current, to reach Cape Breton Island. Without doing much actual sailing, the ship will be carried along the natural flow of the Benguela Current that runs north up along the west coast of Africa. The ship can then sail west across the Atlantic carried by the Equatorial Current and then northward again by the powerful Gulf Stream flowing up from the Caribbean along the eastern coast of North America. This natural flow of the ocean will efficiently deposit a ship on Cape Breton's doorstep. Here, just off the island's southeast coast, the Gulf Stream meets the cold Labrador Current flowing in the opposite direction, the Gulf Stream slows down, and it turns back out into the Atlantic. It is a transition point for sailors and a natural place to lay anchor. Moreover, the waters off Cape Breton were once known to have one of the world's largest edible fish populations. The coast was thick with fish. For the Chinese fleets, given the distance travelled and the size of their crew, the island could have easily become a welcome port of call.

Unfortunately, where the Chinese ventured beyond the west coast of Africa remains only conjecture. By the middle of the fifteenth century there was a significant shift in China's international policies, a turning inward. The many extravagances and financial excesses of the Treasure Fleets were seen as reason to begin to cancel all shipping beyond China's shores. The many gains made through these voyages were seen as no match for the fleets' wasteful expenditures, money that could have been better spent on China's growing domestic problems. Added to this sense of waste was the Confucian sensibility shared by many of the civil officials that merchants and distant voyages were not to be trusted, that trade was fundamentally an unkind and lowly activity, and that the government had no place in such commercial adventures.

There was also an anti-eunuch sentiment that had been growing inside the country. The eunuchs, who had close access to the imperial court and to the emperor, had become powerful and wealthy. Like the Treasure Fleets they commanded, the eunuchs were thought to be extravagant and indulgent, and so became linked to all that was seen as wasteful about China's maritime expeditions. This sense of mistrust increased in 1435 when the eunuchs took control of the secret police and began to dominate the army.[14] Already seen as devious and secretive, this only added to the widely held sense of mistrust and suspicion with which they had come to be viewed.

This growing anti-maritime and anti-eunuch sensibility become stronger, eventually leading to the cancellation of the Treasure Fleets after the seventh voyage returned in 1433. In the years that followed, it also led to the destruction of the records of many of China's overseas voyages. In 1477 the vice-president of the Ministry of War is known to have destroyed many of Zheng He's documents claiming they were "deceitful exaggerations of bizarre things far removed from the testimony of people's eyes and ears."[15] He reported to his superiors that the documents had been lost. The Ming dynasty stopped looking outwards toward the opportunities that lay beyond the distant horizon. China's new priority was the defense of its borders. The history of Chinese sailing, of the country's great maritime adventures, and particularly the memory of Zheng He's remarkable Treasure Fleets, was either destroyed or rewritten. By the end of the fifteenth century it was made a capital offence to build seagoing ships with more than two masts. By 1525, ships of this kind were destroyed, and to go out to sea in such a ship was considered a serious crime.[16] The massive shipyards that had produced the large Treasure Ships were shut down, and the highly advanced Chinese ship building technology that had evolved over centuries was soon eroded away until it was forgotten. The growing fear and anger directed towards the eunuchs meant that the memories of Zheng He and his maritime commanders soon devolved into a superficial and incomplete mention in the history of the period. Memory of the Treasure Fleets faded. By the sixteenth century, just as the European Age of Discovery was beginning, little remained of China's maritime greatness.

When the Yongle emperor sent out the Treasure Fleets in the early fifteenth century, China was the richest, most populous, and most organized country in the world. What history now faces is the undeniable logic that China could have reached the shores of the Americas. China certainly had the ships, the crews, and the navigational skills, all to a far greater degree than those of the early European voyages of discovery. China also had the desire for knowledge, for power, for diplomacy, and for gain. There was every reason to reach the ends of the world. However, after centuries of success on the seas, there was a growing list of internal problems. There was aggression at the borders, the collection of taxes had begun to fall into disarray, there was a rapidly growing population and food production had begun to suffer. There was war, famine, and plague. The country began to spiral downward. Eventually the great maritime accomplishments of an ancient China would become of little relevance to the telling of world history.

8
A CULTURE FORGOTTEN

The western scholars who wrote the history of Cape Breton, men like Haliburton, Patterson, Bourinot, and Ganong, were all highly knowledgeable and insightful, yet the scope of their ideas regarding the early history of the region may now seem narrow. To these historians, the ruins in Saint Peters were restricted to the French or the English or the Portuguese. They believed that the white settlers of whom the Mi'kmaq had spoken could only have been from a small handful of European countries. That was all that was possible to nineteenth-century historians, even to twentieth-century ones. However, this has changed. With the opening up of China and its history, the West is being forced to acknowledge China's centuries of greatness that preceded the European Renaissance and the Age of Discovery.

Looking at the claim the Mi'kmaq made to Judge Haliburton in the nineteenth century — that the ruins in Saint Peters had been left by early settlers — we must now acknowledge that these could be Chinese ruins. The Chinese were "white men" to the Mi'kmaq, and we now know that they were sailing "before the French." Nineteenth-century historians knew that China existed, of course, but adding China to the Saint Peters puzzle never occurred to them. By the nineteenth century, the idea that China had once ruled the oceans with the world's largest and most technically advanced navy had been lost to scholars of New World history.

But why was this? What had happened to China to make historians and the West turn their backs? When historians like Haliburton and Ganong were studying reports of strange archaic ruins, when the Mi'kmaq told them stories of past visitors, and when they examined the unexplainable, China had not even occurred to them, not even as a distant possibility. The report made by David Ingram was ignored. The remarkable quality of the cannon iron was of little importance, except as a curiosity.

It is not difficult to see that by the nineteenth century China had become uninteresting to most historians in the West, even ones with a mystery on their hands. When they were pondering the dilemma of Saint Peters — and they pondered that dilemma for almost a century — they did not even consider China. China and her long history had dissolved into invisibility.

There are many reasons for this invisibility, but one of the most obvious and disturbing aspects of China's nineteenth-century history was one we seldom hear about now — the meteoric rise of drug use. The widespread use of opium in China helped destroy the country. By the nineteenth century, millions of Chinese had been seduced and weakened, addicted to opium smoke. The country stopped functioning efficiently. By the middle of the 1800s there were an estimated twelve million opium addicts in China.[1] These were addicts who needed the drug daily in order to function. By the early twentieth century, that figure had grown to forty million.[2]

The story of opium use started with the fall of the Ming dynasty and its ruling class. In the middle of the seventeenth century, the Ming Dynasty was overthrown by the armies of Manchuria, a region in Northeast China, who established the Qing Dynasty. The Manchu rulers, as a way of marking their power and control, forced Chinese men to shave their heads in the front and grow a long pigtail, they were not allowed to marry Manchurian women, nor could they carry weapons like the Manchurians did. The Chinese became angry and frustrated with the demands of this new foreign leadership.

Meanwhile, on the other side of the world, the British were building a navy and searching for power. With a view towards trading opportunities in Asia, they established the British East India Company, and by the 1700s the East India Company had started to buy from China the sort of things that one would expect: silk, porcelain, tea, silver. The problem was that what the British were buying from the Chinese was of far greater value than what they were able to sell to China in return. The Chinese had little need for British products. In 1793 a British ambassador was sent to the Chinese court to argue the cause of equal trade but was told that China did not need his British goods.

The British were beginning to lose out financially. They were buying from China but not selling anything in return, and the Chinese goods were far too attractive to stop importing them, especially tea. By 1800, Britain was importing over nine million kilograms of tea annually to keep up with the demand. The balance of trade was dangerously on the side of China, so Britain went looking for something China would buy. It seems they thought that if there wasn't a market, they would make one.

The British turned to the very lucrative business of narcotics. For most of the eighteenth century, opium was used only as an effective pain-relief medication in China. However, at the end of the eighteenth century and the beginning the nineteenth, with few other options to sell, the British made opium their number one import into China. Then the French, Americans, Greeks, and Spanish got involved. Even the Dutch, Swedish, and Danish all shipped opium into China when they realized the profit that could be made. In a few short years, opium went from being used strictly as a pharmaceutical in China to clouding the entire nation in a haze of apathy and neglect.

The British brought the opium in through the major ports. They didn't have to hide it. They simply shipped it from India where it was cheap to produce. The drug was grown in poppy fields run by the British through their East India Company. By owning the source, processing the raw material themselves, and selling it on their own terms to a country that had been demoralized, the British were able to addict a weakened population.

In the late eighteenth and early nineteenth centuries, even with strict laws controlling it, opium use swept through China, especially in large cities. Young Chinese urban males were the first users. Initially, the smoking of opium was a fashionable habit of the wealthy, and the young and the rich provided the avenue through which opium use spread. In many ways it mirrors the use of illegal drugs in our own culture. There was an efficient system of supply established. Along with that came a certain level of social acceptance. Opium use increased to the detriment of the country's population, and in 1799 the Chinese government stepped in and made importation of the drug illegal. The large suppliers were targeted, along with the users and their local dealers. However, the laws had no effect.

In order to give some idea of the amount of opium being consumed at the time, it is worth looking at the numbers. In 1729, China imported 200 chests of opium.[3] A chest of opium contained approximately 77 kilograms,[4] so the 1729 shipment would have been around 15,500 kilograms. This was mainly for medical use. By 1767, that had increased to 1,000 chests, or 77,000 kilograms.[5] By 1830, Britain was importing 30,000 chests of opium into China, over 2,000,000 kilograms.[6] In 1859 that number had increased to 58,000 chests, or almost 5,000,000 kilograms, and by 1879 to over 100,000 chests. By the end of the nineteenth century, nearly 8,000,000 kilograms of pure opium was being imported yearly into China by the West.[7]

Once the opium was unloaded on the docks, local gangs took care of the distribution. Dealers gave their customers guns to resist the police. Large areas of the inner cities became dangerous. There was violence. That was how it began: urban youth, drugs, gangs, guns, and violence. As opium spread, crime related to the trade spread, entire towns became addicted, babies were born opium addicts, and families were ruined. Nothing seemed to stop it. In 1888 it was estimated that 70 percent of the adult male population of China were opium users.[8] In the coastal cities, where the drug was most available, that figure was as high as 90 percent.[9] It was becoming clear to China that opium was helping destroy the country, every law possible had proven futile, and the future of China was beginning to look desperate. By mid-century, Chinese jails and sanitariums were at capacity. There was no end in sight.

When the British questioned the trade's morality, profits always turned out to be more important than virtue. All the while, Chinese law continued to ban the drug, there were high level discussions among the country's bureaucracy arguing the benefits of legalization and taxation, and the Emperor, having witnessed three of his sons killed by opium addiction, implored the Chinese people to stop the "flowing poison." It was undermining the very core of the nation.

In 1838 the Chinese government sent a sorrowful letter to England's Queen Victoria imploring her to end the drug trade. The letter began, "The Way of Heaven is fairness to all. It does not suffer us to harm others in order to benefit ourselves."[10] How gentle a plea it was. The Queen claimed to have never received the letter. Instead, for reasons unexplained, it was published in *The Times* of London. With painful clarity, the Chinese explained the hopeless situation in which they found themselves. "Formerly, the number of opium smokers was small, but now the vice has spread far and wide and the poison penetrated deeper and deeper."[11] China realized that it was being ruined by opium: there was lawlessness involved in both its supply and its use; the health of its citizens was deteriorating; the civil service was being corrupted; there was decay in the Imperial Court; and the long held sense of national morality and cohesiveness was dissolving into smoke.

England kept importing the drug into the country. China's pleas were ignored. When Chinese authorities physically tried to stop the shipments, Britain kept them coming, always more. In 1839, the Chinese destroyed 20,000 cases of opium, over 1,000,000 kilograms, a single ship's cargo. The British got angry and fought back. Britain started the First Opium War. The English government sent 47 ships, 16 of them warships, along with 10,000 men. Nothing was going to stop such a lucrative business.

The balance of trade had shifted. The British had won. Silver was used as payment for the opium so its price shot up. Chinese peasants, who earned their pay in copper but paid their taxes in silver, were soon falling into poverty. With an impoverished peasantry, a drug-addicted cross section of the population, and aggressive trading partners who would not take no for an answer, by the middle of the nineteenth century China was rapidly becoming a destitute wasteland. It had lost all importance on the international stage. It had fallen so far, gotten so dark, it is no wonder Western historians like Haliburton could find nothing left of interest.

That is one reason why the nineteenth-century opium story is so important. To the West and to historians who were writing the first histories of the New World, China and its remarkable history no longer existed.

After the First Opium War ended in 1842, the Chinese were forced to sign the Treaty of Nanking. The Chinese government was required to pay a massive indemnity to the British, and Chinese ports were opened to foreign vessels. This meant that the dwindling Chinese economy, with a culture already in rapid decline, was being given away to foreigners. Because of China's opium addiction, the West was able to demand enormous concessions. As a result of the First Opium War, Britain was given Hong Kong. They drained China of its silver.

Once Britain had its teeth into China, other western countries started to take their own sizable bites out of the country. Nations like France, Germany, and the United States opened their own ports on Chinese soil. These were small foreign cities with their own laws. When these ports opened, the country's agents took control of the collection of duties, bypassing Chinese bureaucracy completely. China was no longer master of its own affairs. Well into the twentieth century, foreigners played a central role in the way China's economy was organized, an economy that continued to deteriorate as foreigners continued to manipulate it. Even the mail service was run by foreigners. All this while the evils and ills of ancient Chinese ways were preached freely and openly by foreign missionaries.

China was in a grave depression. Its economy was controlled by an aggressive colonization program run by foreign powers, many waving a cross of salvation. There was widespread drug abuse. There were religious rebellions and peasant revolts at regular intervals, floods, droughts, famine, and a rapid increase in the population. It was a spiral that China only recently — not until the middle of the last century — began to escape. Sadly, it was fueled in great part by the West.

The Chinese tried to fight back. Rebel groups formed. A group calling themselves the Righteous and Harmonious Fists, or the Boxers as they were known by Europeans, formed late in the century. They wanted a return of China to the Chinese, and they had the backing of the central government — or whatever was left of it. In the summer of 1900 the Boxers tried to take back much of the land being controlled by foreign powers, even holding the residents hostage. A dozen countries organized against the Boxers. There was a combined force of twenty thousand foreign troops sent into China. China lost again. Peking was sacked by the Germans, Chinese officials were executed, and massive costs in silver were levied on the Emperor. A poor country was becoming even more destitute.

China had become lifeless. A Chinese opium addict described the effects of the drug as being like a plant that had been "covered by a huge stone: rain and dew can't get in to provide nourishment, and the plant has no way to sprout and grow. There is only fatigue and emaciation."[12] There were drug addicts in the Chinese army, in the courts, in the government. There were users in every city, town, and village. Throughout China the wealthy had become poor and the poor had become destitute. Opium addiction wasted days, weeks, and years of effective labour. It had become a way of life, and it helped destroy the ancient China of Confucius, Mencius, and Lao Tzu. Addiction helped squander everything the country ever was. The country was destroyed from outside by foreign greed and from within by a society that had lost control. In 1890, after a century of illegal drug use, China ended all remaining pretensions to control. The Emperor revoked all laws against buying, selling, production, or use of opium. The drug had been legalized. Within a century, narcotics had won.

In all this, the British were clearly aware of their actions. The drug trade had been publicly condemned in front of the British Parliament. An 1842 editorial in *The Times*, written following the First Opium War, claimed, "We owe some moral compensation to China for pillaging her towns and slaughtering her citizens, in a quarrel which could never have arisen if we had not been guilty of this national crime."[13]

For the most part, however, China was seen as not worth saving. Even a British Royal Commission in 1893 reported that China, from the rich streets of its capital to the impoverished back alleys of its ports, was fully to blame for its own addiction. The Chinese were seen as the evil ones. The churches even agreed. In the 1882 book *The Truth about Opium Smoking*, the Reverend W. H. Collins was quoted as saying that "the Chinese were all of them more or less morally weak, as you would expect to find in any heathen nation."[14] Another nineteenth-century churchman, Reverend R.H. Graves, dismissed the Chinese as "ease loving Asiatics."[15] Opium addiction and the destruction of their country were seen as being their own fault. According to an 1853 medical book *The Opium Trade in India and China*, written by an American physician, it was widely believed that, "the Chinese people have naturally excessive acquisitiveness and fondness for those temporary enjoyments which do not require great efforts of body or mind."[16]

Unfortunately, that is all most of the West knew of China and the Chinese. Other than the thirteenth-century memoirs of Marco Polo or the occasional letter from the Jesuit missionaries, Europe got its first introduction to China in the nineteenth century, mostly from newspaper articles and books that were usually in full support of the opium trade. If that was what was believed in the halls of science, religion, and politics, it was clear why historians like Haliburton and Ganong would have ignored China.

Drug use in China remained rampant throughout the early twentieth century. Prohibitions did not work. Drug programs did not work. In 1936 over a hundred hospitals were opened to provide care for China's addicts.[17] The addiction continued. It stopped only when the Communist leaders came to power in 1949. The new government made the growth, sale, and use of opium illegal, and put real force behind the laws. Detoxification hospitals treated the addicts. Drug dealers and those who relapsed after detox were imprisoned. By 1960, within a generation of those new laws, the government was able to declare that drug addiction had been eradicated. Sadly, to achieve that claim, it took over a hundred years and the near destruction of the oldest civilization on earth.

A memoir written by a young Chinese opium user in 1878 described how the opium addicts who surrounded him were like flowers that bloomed in winter,[18] something once beautiful now made lifeless and left to wither. This was what China had become during the nineteenth century, a once great society ruined, unimportant, and uninteresting to the West and to its historians who were looking for answers to what was seen as a mysterious lost chapter in the story of early settlement in the Americas.

9

HISTORY THROUGH A NEW LENS

Over and over again, when each of the elements of the Saint Peters puzzle was studied during the past centuries, the possibility of a visit to this region by the early Chinese fleets was never considered, even remotely. Traditional Western history has attempted to explain all the pieces of this mystery separately, using different and sometimes overlapping — and often confusing — stories. The ancient canal shown on the oldest of European maps was never believed to have existed, yet Columbus, Lescarbot, Champlain, Sanson, and Coronelli, who all mapped it as an open waterway, would have argued otherwise.

Then there is the difficult issue of the two ruins that seem to have been built before the French arrived. The small fort on the shore is now thought to have been built by Nicolas Denys, a seventeenth-century French fisherman, yet Denys never claimed to have built the fort. He built his fort farther to the east along the shore at the base of Mount Grenville on Jerome Point. And the mysterious ruins near the summit of Mount Grenville are said to have been left behind by a group of late eighteenth-century English soldiers who carried themselves and their supplies up the side of the steep, heavily treed slope to build a raised solid earthen platform in a single winter, only to leave it behind, empty, in the spring. Yet there was disagreement even on this. The ruins appear to have been shown on earlier French maps, and it has even been argued that Nicolas Denys may have built them. The only consistency in these stories is the sense that something is missing.

Through all of this, the Mi'kmaq have been trying to tell a different story, a more complete story. They once told of an ancient memory, a history they had lived before the French began arriving in the middle of the seventeenth century. Their stories must have seemed unimaginable to the first Europeans, more myth and distant legend than reality, yet to the Mi'kmaq these ancient visitors had been very real people, "white men before the French." These visitors left a significant impression on the landscape, on the Aboriginal culture, and on our history.

Even though never considered until now, the Chinese would have been seen by the Mi'kmaq as foreigners, as "white men," and they were certainly sailing "before the French." We now know that the great Chinese fleets could have sailed to the eastern shore of North America, and that there were riches here that would have enticed them to stay. Logic begins to suggest that the mysterious ruins in Saint Peters, like those on Cape Dauphin, were originally built by the Chinese in the early fifteenth century or possibly before. The suggestion on early maps of an ancient canal is the most telling sign of all. By the early 1400s — the time of the Treasure Fleets — China already had a long history of canal construction, with the longest, most widely used, and most well-constructed system of canals in the world. After a massive reconstruction of the Grand Canal had been completed in the early part of the fifteenth century,[1] a highly trained workforce would have been available to sail on the Treasure Fleets. Building a canal anywhere in the world, even in the most remote wilderness, would have been both viable and reasonable for these ancient mariners.

The existence of an ancient canal is no longer unimaginable. The first European cartographers were not mistaken when they drew the ruins of a passage across this narrow neck of land. By the time the French arrived, almost three hundred years after it had been built to link Saint Peters Bay with the interior of the island, the canal had deteriorated into a broken-down road across the isthmus, useful at high tide for small boats or ships loaded onto carts and pulled across, but no longer able to handle vessels of any significant size. It had become unpredictable. The captain of the *Chancewell* tried to cross it, as Nicolas Denys would too. Both men's ships became stuck when the tide changed. This passage, shown on eighteenth-century French maps of the isthmus, even though in ruins, was wide and walled, and still in the eighteenth century it looked like a canal. It was obvious to the young Ensign Prenties that this "communication" across the isthmus had once been able to handle large ships of war.

These white men before the French, builders of canals in the wilderness, who else could they have been but the Chinese? Ancient Egyptians, Greeks, Romans, Persians, Knights, Pirates? History seems to be grasping at any idea to explain the mysterious past of the region. However, the theory that the Chinese settled here, outrageous as it may seem, correctly places into a single, clear, logical, and accountable history all these perplexing stories that have been misshapen and recast over time. And what a rich history this past may prove to be.

When Canadian historians like Haliburton and Ganong were searching for answers to the mysterious ruins they had found, China would have been farthest from their minds. As Lord Elgin, the British High Commissioner to China in the mid-nineteenth century, wrote in his personal diary, "There is certainly not much to regret in the old civilization which we are thus scattering to the winds. A dense population, timorous and pauperized, such would seem to be its chief product."[2] This was all the West knew of China. The memory of a once great past had long been forgotten. Records of the maritime adventures had been destroyed, and a century of opium use had done the rest. Nonetheless, we know that such greatness had once existed. What the Chinese left behind on the shores of Cape Breton may help tell the story of that greatness, of when and why they came.

Why the Chinese came to Cape Breton and why they built on the scale they did continues to puzzle. These expeditions of the fifteenth-century Treasure Fleets were seen by the Chinese Emperor and by his governing bodies as being primarily diplomatic exercises. The extravagant size of the fleet was a proclamation of China's wealth and prestige among the nations, and these regular voyages were seen as a way of establishing China's position throughout the world. However, the Chinese are known to have explored and traded as well.[3] The records that remain tell of the acquisition of wild animals[4] and the harvesting of goods they needed.[5] Moreover, there were centuries of Chinese ocean travel preceding the Treasure Fleets. These were commercial adventures as much as voyages of discovery.

Cape Breton could have been both a commercial venture was well as a coordination point for future discovery, and the Saint Peters ruins may have played a key role in both. Cape Breton is located at a crucial point in world shipping, a juncture of tides and weather and geography that has made the island a hinge of ocean politics and discovery. For further exploration of North America, Cape Breton Island is a key location. It was seen as the opening to the Saint Lawrence River and to the centre of the continent, the Gateway to the New World. Moreover, the island had all the makings of a successful commercial venture. Nova Scotia was rich in gold.[6] The nineteenth-century gold rush in the region is remembered by town names such as Goldenville,[7] a name that stands as testament to the significance of the local gold mining industry. And China, throughout her long history, has valued gold: it was a form of coinage; it was used in the production of ornamental objects for the wealthy; it was even used in the decoration of buildings.[8] China would not have been blind to the riches of Nova Scotia.

The mining of gold in the mainland of Nova Scotia depended on the river system that runs through the gold district in the centre of the province. That river system leads to the eastern end of the peninsula and directly across the narrow Strait of Canso to Cape Breton Island and the Bay of Saint Peters. The canal in Saint Peters may have been a relatively simple way for the Chinese mines to transport their gold through the Bras d'Or Lakes to be smelted on Cape Dauphin. Cape Dauphin has a deep water port useful for large ocean-going vessels, so from the east coast of Cape Breton, gold bullion could be shipped safely and easily back home to China.

Moreover, there is the suggestion in the early history of Cape Breton that the interior of the island may have been used for just such gold transport. The early European explorers and mapmakers referred to the interior lake system that stretches down the full length of the island as the *Bras d'Or*, the Arm of Gold. These lakes are still called the Bras d'Or

Lakes, but the reasoning behind the name has never been explained. It has always been a bit of a local mystery. Was it because of the warm golden colour of the cliffs that frame the entrance to the lake? Or was this long narrow collection of lakes once a waterway through the island where small Chinese ore boats could carry raw gold within the protected shores of the interior from Saint Peters canal to Cape Dauphin? To the first European visitors who called this lake system the Bras d'Or, perhaps it was an old story they had heard, a memory of something once spoken of and now forgotten, a lost chapter.

China is today stretching beyond its borders again. The change is recent and vast. China is now mining for resources in dozens of countries. Many of those countries are places where the West has had little luck, countries where other nations simply will not venture, and wherever the Chinese go they bring with them construction projects on a massive scale. China has helped build roads in Senegal, a telecommunications system in Kenya, railways in Angola and Zambia. It builds ports, power dams, and electrical grids; hospitals and schools and government buildings. The list of the country's projects is as long as it is varied. No country is too difficult, no situation without its merits. China's modern expansion may be the best indication of a centuries-old Chinese way of searching for riches far outside its borders.

To the ancient Chinese, this tiny island on the East Coast of Canada had much to offer. The island functioned as a key location to further exploration of the continent. Given its location at a transition point in the ocean's currents, it was relatively easy to reach for anyone sailing in the Atlantic. Moreover, it was rich in minerals, it had a near constant supply of luxurious furs valued by the Chinese upper classes, and there was food in abundance. But there is something more here. It was best described by Joseph Needham in his description of the Treasure Fleets of the early fifteenth century. Needham wrote that it was China's goal "to impress upon foreign countries even beyond the limits of the known world the idea of China as the leading political and cultural power."[9] Six centuries later, the Mi'kmaq still speak of early visitors to their nation with great respect. Above all, perhaps that is what ancient China left in Cape Breton, an insight into a forgotten greatness.

With documents such as David Ingram's report that the Mi'kmaq were drawing Chinese ships, or Jean Alfonce's description of Cape Breton as the land of the Chinese, or the suggestions by language scholars that the Mi'kmaq were writing with Chinese-like characters, we are witnessing a list of claims which all point to a lost chapter of not only New World history but Chinese history as well. It has been pondered, hinted at, and feared, but these quiet voices from history — strong, clear, persistent voices — are becoming impossible to ignore.

However, there are other interests and other historical theories now at play in the region. These other voices are speaking loudly and convincingly of the possibility of a very different group of early visitors to Nova Scotia. We are being told that there may have been an unexpected and very unusual pre-Columbian discoverer of North America. In any discussion of our earliest history, these recent claims have also become impossible to ignore.

Part Three:

HISTORY DERAILED

10
HISTORY TAKES A TURN

While researching China's early maritime adventures, I read through various articles on early Chinese military technology. Some showed images of small Chinese walled structures called fortified manors.[1] These fortified manors were simple, perfectly square enclosures that could protect a few small buildings built within their walls. Each had two entrances on opposite sides of a central open space. These square Chinese fortified manors appeared to be very similar to the eighteenth-century French surveyors' written description of the small ruins on the shore at Saint Peters, the walled enclosure that Nicolas Denys used for his storehouse and offices. It made me think that when Denys first arrived in the region he may have looked for locations for his fishing and trading business that already had walled and fortified structures in place, buildings that could have been used as secure storage areas. As a businessman, such pre-existing structures would have saved him time and money. I began to search for other places Denys had settled in the region, so I could compare those ruins with what I had found in Saint Peters.

Denys's nearest settlement to Saint Peters had been built just across the Strait of Canso, the narrow expanse of water that separates Cape Breton from the mainland, on a bay called Chedabucto Bay, at a place now called Guysborough. Even before a fire destroyed much of Saint Peters in 1669, Denys had moved his primary settlement to Guysborough, and because it had become a significant settlement for Denys, I suspected there would still be ruins to see. I planned a visit to Guysborough to see if the ruins Denys had left behind there were anything like the ruins of Saint Peters.

I thought that perhaps Guysborough could give me some insight into what I was seeing on the shore of Saint Peters Bay. The visit was to be a casual couple of days tacked on to a trip to Cape Breton. However, what I was to find would shock me. A radical new gloss on the region's history has developed there that would send my research on an unsettling voyage into stories of a sixteenth-century Italian family's lost letters, strange legends of the Knights Templar, holy bloodlines, and a mysterious new image — a flag — that to some now appears to be representing the early history of the region.

It was the summer of 2010, and my fascination with the ancient ruins that might be left in Guysborough had been simmering for months. My research had begun to reveal that the region had a rich history. To the Mi'kmaq, Guysborough was known as *Sedabooktook,* meaning "running far back." The Mi'kmaq name describes its position at the far west of the long, thin Chedabucto Bay. The head of the bay is also the mouth of an important river that gives easy access to an inland water system joining together the central heartland of the province. Given its connection to both the coast and the region's interior, as well as it being a short paddling distance across the Strait of Canso to Cape Breton, Chedabucto had developed into a Mi'kmaq settlement before the arrival of Europeans. I also suspected that its position at the access point for the inland water system, and therefore the gold fields of the province, could have been reason for the Chinese to find the region of economic importance.

Chedabucto had been significant enough in the seventeenth century that Nicolas Denys built a successful settlement there.[2] That is what interested me. I wanted to compare the ruins in Saint Peters, the ones on the shore now said to have been left by Denys, with what he was known to have built in Guysborough. Like Saint Peters, it appears that Chedabucto Bay enticed Denys because of its location and its importance to the Mi'kmaq, but could there have been earlier walled structures already in place that

Denys knew he could use? For whatever reason, in 1660 Denys began work on a new settlement on a spit of land at the mouth of Chedabucto Bay. Soon, he was operating a successful fishing and trading business with a crew of about 120 men. He was also growing his own food on twenty acres of cleared forest. In the mid-seventeenth century this was a significant settlement. Denys described how at Chedabucto he had employed his workforce to "enclose and fortify all [his] dwellings with two little bastions, which, furnished with eight pieces of cannon and some swivel-guns, with an enclosure of barrels filled with earth, put [him] in a state of defense."[3]

Chedabucto must have been important to the Jesuits as well. They sent a priest to work there, Father Martin de Lyonne. De Lyonne had arrived in Canada in the summer of 1643, an energetic, well-educated Jesuit in his late twenties. He spent the next two decades ministering at the various fishing and trading stations throughout the eastern region. He must have settled in Chedabucto soon after Denys because he is known to have died there in mid-January of 1661, a victim of a scurvy epidemic that killed much of the settlement.[4]

The crops that Denys planted in Chedabucto may have been a response to that epidemic. Although not a farmer, Denys was smart enough to realize the need for fresh produce to combat disease. Ever since European settlers began arriving in the New World in the early part of the seventeenth century, the death toll from scurvy had made it clear that it would be difficult to live year-round in such an isolated environment without either a hinterland that could deliver food or the ability to grow one's own. Denys appears to have learned from the 1661 epidemic. The clearing of twenty acres of forest and the successful planting of crops to provide a large population with fresh produce and grains would have been a significant undertaking in the middle of this seventeenth-century wilderness.

Another local land owner, a French entrepreneur named La Giraudière, was envious of Denys's success. Being able to grow your own food and provide for your settlement was a richness coveted by those who witnessed Denys's self-sufficiency. In 1667 La Giraudière attacked Denys's fort without notice. The defenses fell quickly. Denys abandoned the site entirely and his coveted fields were allowed to "return to their primitive state," as Denys lamented years later.

In 1682, with Denys's prized property in ruins, this area of Chedabucto was given by the French king to another businessman, Sieur Clerbaud Bergier, a Huguenot. Bergier was primarily there for the fishing business, which was some of the best along this coast, and, like Denys before him, he also cleared fields and planted new crops. He not only grew grains like wheat, barley, and rye, but he raised his own vegetables and had fruit trees producing. Among the various buildings he constructed was a wind-powered sawmill and a chapel to St. Louis, patron saint of Chedabucto.[5] By 1687 the population of Chedabucto had grown to 150.

The following year, Chedabucto was attacked by a group of English pirates out of Boston. It was looted but not fully destroyed, and was almost immediately rebuilt by the French. This was its third major building period. Its final destruction at the hands of the English occurred two years later, in 1690, when Sir William Philips burnt the place down. The settlement was so solidly constructed that it took five days to demolish.[6]

The written records from the period suggested that the buildings on this small spit of land at the head of the bay were relatively extensive. Aside from the storerooms and the fortifications, Denys was believed to have built at least one building eighteen metres in length, and had the foundations laid for a second. Bergier, besides building new storerooms, fortifications, and housing, and adding the chapel and the sawmill, also built two large structures eighteen metres long by just under nine metres wide. Much of this construction was reported to have been of stone.

After Bergier's settlement was destroyed by Philips, the fort was partially rebuilt by the French. However, the area soon became unimportant, and although a census in 1693 listed no inhabitants, the Acadians appear to have maintained a presence at Chedabucto, where they continued to be used as pawns between the English and French governments. In 1764, there were fourteen Acadian families still there.[7] In the 1770s, more Acadian families arrived from Étang des Berges, a small brackish lake on the sandy north shore of Prince Edward Island that the Acadians had settled for a generation after leaving the Beaubassin area. Chedabucto may have acted like a way station between the time they were forced off their land in Prince Edward Island by the English, driven to seek shelter with the Mi'kmaq in the forest, and their eventual resettlement in

Cape Breton by the French. Although nothing seems to have been easy for them, at least they were consistently given help and comfort by the Mi'kmaq. The two groups considered each other brothers.

In 1777, English settlers began arriving in Nova Scotia. The date coincides closely with the Acadians settling in Cape Breton. This type of abrupt move had happened to the Acadians before. When the English arrived, the Acadians were forced to leave. In this case, the new English immigrants were Empire Loyalists, including some thirty-five hundred free African Americans, fleeing the south and its simmering hostilities.[8] This first contingent of settlers helped found modern Guysborough, named after the commander of the British in North America, Sir Guy Carleton. The new Guysborough was built not far from the old settlement of Chedabucto on the point of land at the head of the bay, but not on it. The ruins of the old French settlements were left alone. A License of Occupation of the Chedabucto site was given to James Wyatt on January 24, 1786 with the condition that "none of the works on said tract shall be leveled or pulled down."[9] Over the next two centuries the ruins remained untouched. When I read that condition in the records, I sensed that there might still be something significant to see on the site.

There were also two seventeenth- and eighteenth-century gravesites in Guysborough. These were Acadian graves, possibly the graves of some of my ancestors. When the English began arriving in the late 1770's, they were still visible.[10] One was just to the west of the site of the original Denys settlement, and the second, still marked by a large cross when the Loyalists arrived, was on a hillside overlooking the water at the head of a nearby cove. Crosses, and graves, and Bergier's chapel: I began to imagine what still remained. There was clearly something to be seen.

I was not sure how much of these ruins were still intact. I didn't even know what to look for. I could find no plan of either Denys's or Bergier's settlements, but I knew there must be something somewhere. Ganong, in his notes to the English translation of Denys's memoirs published in 1909, wrote of the Chedabucto site at the mouth of the harbour that "earth ramparts, stone heaps, hollows, and well, which are still visible, are without doubt remains of Bergiers' Fort Louis in 1685."[11] Ganong had written this description only a hundred years ago, and save for the shipping industry farther up the coast nearer the causeway connecting the mainland of Nova Scotia to Cape Breton Island, not a great deal has happened in Guysborough during the last century.

Modern Guysborough is built along the edge of the long narrow Chedabucto Bay, named after the original Mi'kmaq settlement. The town has a single main street, an extension of the highway, lined with crisp looking painted wooden houses. It is a pretty coastal town, well washed with the fresh, clean smell of salt water. I arrived to investigate the ruins late on a Thursday afternoon. My first stop was to have been the small Guysborough Museum, housed in the old courthouse, but unfortunately it had closed early that day. My plans were a bit off from the start.

I decided to try the library, which was a few blocks back from the museum, and open and welcoming. It was also busy, a good sign. I asked the librarian about the Denys ruins. There was a pause as she looked up from her desk. "Those have disappeared, built on years ago," she answered trying to remember where they were. "Back in the seventies — I think it was the seventies — they built a house on that site. I think they ploughed it over for a lawn."

I felt like history had been destroyed. The graveyards were gone too it seemed. For the librarian, it was something that happened a long time ago, perhaps a bit embarrassing, but unimportant until someone came looking for them. History is not highly valued on the East Coast. We often take our legacy for granted without appreciating how unusual it is. To have the ruins ploughed over was as bad as I could have imagined. They had been destroyed. I felt profoundly disappointed. I walked out of the library and headed to my hotel, unsure what to do next.

I had made a reservation at an early nineteenth-century house that had been turned into a small hotel. It had been built for a man named DesBarres, a relatively famous name in Nova Scotia history. DesBarres was a local judge and the grandson of J.F.W. DesBarres, a surveyor and cartographer, who in 1774 produced and published *Atlantic Neptune*, an atlas of New England, Nova Scotia, Cape Breton, and the St. Lawrence. His atlas is one of the high points of early Canadian cartography, and I wanted to see what maps the hotel might have.

The DesBarres Manor was plain from the outside, simpler but larger than I had expected. It was three storeys high, wooden-shingled with small sash windows arranged neatly in rows. The interior was a bit more ornate with impressive woodwork in the main rooms.

As I was waiting to check-in I started looking at the framed DesBarres maps hanging on the walls. The young woman at the reception desk asked if I was interested in history. When I said I was, she responded with, "You might want to see the Sinclair things while you're here. There are two."

"Sinclair things?" I asked. I had no idea what she meant.

"Yes, there are two monuments to Henry Sinclair, the Scotsman." She looked at me as if I should know who she was talking about. "They say he discovered America a hundred years before Columbus. I don't know, but that's what some people around here say. There's one in Boylston Park, the provincial park as you come into town. That one is more recent. The other one, the earlier one, is out on the highway at the other end of town, a place called Halfway Cove. It was built back in the eighties. You can't miss it."

I thanked her while I tried not to act surprised. Two monuments to Henry Sinclair and no French ruins. What had I found?

In my years of research into early New World settlements along the East Coast, I had never seen any significant historical discussion of Henry Sinclair and his early discovery of America. What I had read suggested that the story was more fiction than reality. A little-known Earl Henry Sinclair had actually existed in Northern Scotland in the late fourteenth century. Very recently, he has been given credit by some for founding the New World a century before Columbus. The story goes that he sailed around the North Atlantic with two Italians from Venice, but there are no records of what he accomplished. Sinclair left no written history of ever having made these voyages. All I remembered from the little I had read of him was that very few people take the story seriously.

The first time I heard Henry Sinclair's name mentioned was by an archaeologist who had been curious about my research and the idea that the ancient Chinese may have reached Cape Breton. He called me at home early one evening and after a brief introduction asked if I thought Henry Sinclair had settled in Nova Scotia and if the ruins I found might have been left by him. Here was a stranger asking me about a fourteenth-century

Scotsman settling in the New World. I told him I knew nothing about the man. I was also a bit astounded at the idea of pre-Columbian Scottish settlement in Nova Scotia. I thought I would have read about it.

The second time the Sinclair stories were mentioned was by another archaeologist, this time while walking down a mountain road near the Cape Dauphin site on the east coast of Cape Breton. The archaeologist picked up a small fragment of cut stone and asked if I thought Henry Sinclair could have left this behind. I was a bit surprised. "No, I don't really have much time for the Henry Sinclair story," I replied, as best I could not wanting to seem too puzzled that the question was coming from an archaeologist. I felt slightly confused. After two Nova Scotian archaeologists came to me asking the same question, I wondered why they seemed so caught up in the story.

It was the third time that Henry Sinclair's name was mentioned that stayed with me, for it originated from an unexpected source: the Mi'kmaq. I was waiting in the Halifax airport for the film crew that had been in Nova Scotia filming parts of the documentary on the Seven Cities research. The documentary makers had been interviewing the Mi'kmaq for most of the day. I had not been invited to that part of the filming because the producers had already gotten the sense that the Mi'kmaq were not happy with my theory of early Chinese settlement. The producers thought it was best if I stayed away so as not to "add fuel to the fire," as they said. When the group entered the airport lounge, the first question the director asked me was about Henry Sinclair. "What do you know about this Sinclair story?" he asked. I told him I knew very little about Sinclair but that historians do not take the story very seriously. "Well they do, the Mi'kmaq, they take it very seriously," he responded with that same sense of childish awe that I had seen in the archaeologists. "They really believe in him, this Henry Sinclair fellow. They think he came to visit them from Scotland." First archaeologists, then Mi'kmaq leaders, and now mention of monuments in Guysborough: I was beginning to realize how significant this story had become.

After checking in to the hotel and getting settled, I went looking for the two "Sinclair things" that the women at the reception desk had mentioned. Given that this legend is seen by most as being on the far outskirts of accepted history, I expected little more of these two memorials than a discreet commemorative plaque nailed to a tree. I was interested though, because it was difficult to imagine celebrating an event for which there are no records, nor any reputable history. I imagined the two markers mentioned by the hotel worker were the sort of thing that could be seen quickly in the evening, so I headed out to find them.

On the narrow winding road along the coast toward Halfway Cove, several miles east of Guysborough, I found an official looking sign that read, "Scenic Look Off 800 m." Just below, there was a second sign that read, "Sinclair Interpretation Site." The Sinclair site was the next turn off the highway toward the shore. My first surprise was that this Interpretation Site appeared to be less a simple commemorative plaque and more a historical monument of some importance.

The site of the Sinclair monument is an open, flat gravel lot with a magnificent view across the water. There are several plain looking low granite boulders laid out in a curve. The area referred to as the Sinclair Interpretation Site is a group of four different signs: two on wooden panels (one that looks very worse for the weather), a low granite marker that looks like a gravestone with a list of names carved in it, and a six-foot-tall piece of roughly shaped granite, a bit like a squat obelisk pointing skyward, with a metal plaque attached to its face. These four elements are randomly placed a few steps away from each other along a metal guardrail that acts as the edge of the parking lot. The shore is just beyond. The various signs appear as if they have been added piecemeal over time, but the materials — the stones, the carved granite, the bronze plaque — attempt to give the site a sense of the monumental.

After surveying the site, I read the first of the wooden panels. Its title — "The Voyage of Prince Henry Sinclair to the New World in 1398. The Saga Begins." — suggested that this sign was the place to start. The panel was dense with text. I remember thinking that I had not planned to make such a commitment to this strange story. I had come out of curiosity, not real interest. Now I was faced with reading a long historical essay. However, I had driven this far, and it seemed that everything I needed to know about Henry Sinclair was about to be explained.

The first paragraph made it clear that this was no small matter, however plain the various elements of this Interpretation Site may have seemed. It read, "On June 2, 1398, Henry Sinclair allegedly set foot in North America on the sandbar of Guysborough Harbour. His fleet consisted of 12 ships with between 200-300 men on board, a considerable force designed to be self-sufficient made up of sailors, soldiers, sail-makers, carpenters, armourers and farming monks." I paused, having had no previous idea how this alleged journey of Henry Sinclair had been assembled. Ships, men, farming monks: this story was being told as if it had been a major voyage of discovery. I read on, my curiosity aroused. This story claimed, among other things, that once Sinclair landed in Guysborough he sent all his ships away and kept only the row boats. He then built his own ship, hence the sail-makers. The panel also claimed that Sinclair met the "friendly Mik'Maq people." The interpretive panel even suggested that Sinclair, "may have built himself a small castle," referring to "some interesting foundations to suggest an early stone building" in the backyard of a house on a hilltop 250 kilometres to the west.

The panel went on to claim that Sinclair explored the Eastern Seaboard in his newly built ship, and then sailed the North Atlantic back to Scotland. He died in Scotland a few years later and is now buried in Rosslyn Chapel, outside of Edinburgh. The chapel is regularly discussed in legends of the Knights Templar. The Knights Templar are said to have brought the Holy Grail to Rosslyn. According to this monument, Henry Sinclair's body lies there with other members of the "lordly line of high St. Clairs."

I moved on to the second sign in the sequence, the six-foot-tall grey granite rock pointing towards the sky. Bolted to it, on the face toward the parking lot, was a bronze metal plaque with carved lettering. It too was thick with text. It began, "Over the years there has been much controversy over who lays claim to being the first European explorer to set foot in the 'New World.' A persistent theory supports a 1398 voyage by a Scottish Earl Henry St. Clair of Orkney, based on the 'Zeno Narrative,' whose authenticity has been challenged by most historians. The St. Clair Saga persists." Finally some background, a reference, I thought. The *Zeno Narrative*, or the *Zeno Stories*, is where all this seems to have started. The *Zeno Stories* is a collection of letters supposedly from a fourteenth-century Italian, but not published until the sixteenth century by one of his ancestors. They were written to appear as an early travel narrative of the northern Atlantic. I had already studied the Zeno letters while researching stories of early voyages to the Americas, but I could remember nothing about a fourteenth-century Scottish earl.

The panel continued, "This monument presents the claim for Prince Henry's supposed voyage as described in Frederick J. Pohl's authoritative book: *Prince Henry Sinclair His Expedition to the New World 1398.*" This would give me something to work with, I thought. It seemed that "Frederick J. Pohl's authoritative book" was a critical text in the making of Henry Sinclair's history. First the *Zeno Stories*, now this. I was beginning to be very curious about this entire thing. Where had all this come from?

The plaque also claimed, "Henry spent a year exploring Nova Scotia with the kind cooperation of the Mi'kmaq people." The Mi'kmaq were clearly part of something here, either that or they knew nothing about these claims. It was hard to tell from what I had read so far. The sign ended with a quote, "A prince as worthy of immortal memory as any that ever lived for his great bravery and remarkable goodness." With mention of having been buried with the "lordly line of high St. Clairs" and then this, it seemed that someone was trying to make Henry Sinclair into some kind of saint.

The third interpretive panel looked most like a carved gravestone. It was a low block of light grey granite with its upper face canted at an angle skyward towards the viewer. The carved text read, "To the loyal and dedicated board of the Prince Henry Sinclair Society of North America, Inc." Eleven names were listed. I took note of one name in particular and what it represented, "Chief Kerry Prosper, 1st Nations Afton Band." He was the leader of the local Mi'kmaq, and he was being thanked for being a member of the board of the Prince Henry Sinclair Society of North America. I stood back for a moment in the long shadows of the evening sun. History was being reinterpreted in front of me by this Sinclair Society, heralding an unknown Scottish earl, on what appeared to be public land, with the support of the local Mi'kmaq leader.

The last of the four interpretive panels was text printed on wood again, similar to the first panel. On this panel there was no sense that this theory was improbable. The text gave every suggestion that Henry Sinclair's voyage was solid fact. No longer a question, this panel claimed that, "Chronicles of Prince Henry Sinclair's historic voyage of 1398 are indelibly hewn in stone on both sides of the Atlantic. There are other corroborating factors which point to the voyage having been made. The following summary gives some of those factors."

The panel then listed ten "corroborating factors" of Sinclair's supposed voyage. The only substance of the claim seemed to have been generated by the *Zeno Stories*. However, the panel also listed the "Indian Language" and "its assimilation of Norse and Gaelic words" as a factor in the Sinclair proof. The Mi'kmaq were clearly part of the story. Another piece of evidence the writers of the panel claimed was "Indian Legends." It appeared that the great Mi'kmaq story of Glooscap was being reinterpreted by this Henry Sinclair monument.

The Mi'kmaq believe Glooscap was a pre-Columbian visitor to Nova Scotia who had lived among them some time before the European Age of Discovery. The Mi'kmaq claim that Glooscap built a ship during his visit, leaving them and sailing away "to the other side of the North Pole,"[12] to a place where he could "never be reached."[13] This Sinclair monument was claiming that Henry Sinclair had built a ship, therefore this was another reason why Henry Sinclair must have been Glooscap. I thought the logic was stretched beyond common sense, until I realized what I had just read. The head of the local Mi'kmaq was thanked for helping erect this monument, his name carved in stone. It appeared that some of the Mi'kmaq leaders were in agreement with this interpretation of their history.

Now I really became fascinated. The Glooscap legend is extremely important in New World history because it describes pre-Columbian contact between the Mi'kmaq and a non-native visitor. Understanding who Glooscap was and his role within the Aboriginal community is critical to the way in which our very earliest history is understood. The adoption of Glooscap by this Sinclair story was troubling.

The final paragraph was also strangely unnerving, as if the logic and rationale behind advocating this new history was neither clear nor open, but instead had some ulterior religious motive. It read, "The knowledge of Prince Henry Sinclair's voyage has been known about for hundreds of years but in the subsequent battle for land (and souls) Rome decided to promote the claims of Spain and Portugal (Treaty of Tordesillas, 1494). Henry, although known as 'the Holy' Sinclair, did not have the ear of Rome and he was, alas, consigned to the dustbin of history." I sensed there was an air of unpleasantness in this closing note, as if some ancient religious bitterness was simmering just under the surface of this historical concoction.

I drove back into Guysborough. My mind started to picture what I had just read: a Scottish earl comes to Nova Scotia, lives for a winter among the Mi'kmaq, builds his own ship over the winter months, sails, ropes, anchor, and all, navigates the Eastern Seaboard, and sails back to Scotland in the spring. This was a serious claim. Whoever was promoting this history had made a public monument out of it. Even some of the Mi'kmaq believed it. The town appeared to support it.

The next morning I drove out of town to visit the second Sinclair monument at the Boylston Provincial Park. I followed the road up the hill with its long wide curves through the forest just as I had been instructed to by someone at the hotel. At the summit, the road led directly to what appeared to be a monument prominently located in front of the camp office. It was an odd-looking construction, a boat sticking out of the ground, straight up vertically, surrounded by a large, well-tended field of grass.

Getting out of the car and looking more closely, I could see that it was shaped like a small wooden boat that had been tipped upward and buried stern first into the hillside. With the bow pointing toward the sky, what would have been the flat wooden deck faced the viewer and had two plaques affixed to it. The upper plaque showed the profile of a man with a thick mustache and flowing hair wearing a kind of helmet. The name "Sinclair" was written under the profile. Under Sinclair was written only "Nova Scotia – 1398." Below this large title, a second plaque gave the history of Henry Sinclair. There were maps and illustrations. There was a drawing of a multi-sail and impressively rigged wooden ship labelled "Sinclair's Ship." Was this what he allegedly built? The ship's mainsail was emblazoned with a large red cross.

The text was long. It began, "The Sinclair Expedition to North America." The first paragraph was almost identical to the plaque I had seen the evening before. This one read, "Over the years there has been much controversy over who lays claim to being the first European explorer to set foot in North America. A persistent theory supports a 1398 voyage by a Norwegian Earl, Henry Sinclair of Orkney. Based on the Zeno Narrative, whose authenticity has been challenged by some historians, the Sinclair saga persists. This memorial recognizes the claim for Prince Henry's voyage."

A change that had been made in the text was very insightful. Aside from the confusion over whether Prince Henry was a Norwegian or Scottish Earl, the plaque I had seen the evening before at Halfway Cove described the *Zeno Stories* as a work "whose authenticity has been challenged by most historians." That was true, I remembered thinking at the time. At least whoever wrote that admitted this was an unaccepted, extreme view of history challenged by the vast majority of historians. However, this more recent monument at Boylston Park had changed the wording slightly. The text now claimed that the authenticity of the *Zeno Stories* has been challenged by only "some historians." As I read it a second time, I realized how clever a change it was. Just *some* historians, maybe just a few. It seemed someone was trying to sell the Sinclair story.

The text on this monument laid out the Sinclair theory as if it were fact. Of the *Zeno Stories*, the monument claimed "some researchers have concluded" that Henry Sinclair was the sailing prince referred to in these fourteenth-century Zeno letters, a wild, warlike prince who tamed the north seas. It was becoming clear that those responsible for this monument were relying heavily on the *Zeno Stories* to give some substance to their story. However, the *Zeno Stories* hold a dubious place in traditional history. The stories have been called one of the most confusing narratives ever written. Little of it is considered factual. Some consider the *Zeno Stories* a hoax. The Sinclair Society's claim that "some researchers" have made historical conclusions by reinterpreted the *Zeno Stories* is not a very positive foundation on which to build a monument, I thought. Two monuments, I reminded myself.

The Boylston monument also claimed, like the monument at Halfway Cove, that the Mi'kmaq legend of Glooscap was evidence of Sinclair's visit. I tried to remember any such claim made by historians, or by the Mi'kmaq, in any history, in any of the early manuscripts. There was no such claim that I could remember, and no mention of Henry Sinclair. Those responsible for these monuments were using the Mi'kmaq to support their theory. The text was serious enough to make most people visiting the monument think there was something to this Henry Sinclair story.

There was a sponsorship plaque located off to the side of the monument, just off the grassy rise. It read, "The Nova Scotia and the Canadian Clan Sinclair gratefully acknowledge the following supporters who made possible the Celebration 1998 Program and this Interpretation Memorial." So this monument was built in 1998, just thirteen years after the earlier monument at Halfway Cove. Under the title, "Public Sector," a number of Nova Scotia government agencies were thanked, including the Department of Natural Resources and the Department of Economic Development and Tourism. The provincial government was clearly involved and supportive. Those thanked under "Private Sector" ranged from an offshore energy corporation to a grocery store, a car rental, and a brewery. It was obvious that this Sinclair theory was believed locally and provincially by the mighty and small. I was beginning to sense that there was a real issue to be faced in how our history was being reinterpreted. This was not a small problem. It involved the history of Nova Scotia, of the Mi'kmaq, and of early exploration to the New World.

Driving back along the coastal road towards Cape Breton, I began to realize that the two monuments I had seen were trying very hard to give substance to the Sinclair legend. It was also clear from the writing and from seeing the local Mi'kmaq Chief thanked for his contribution to the project, that some of the Mi'kmaq had recently cast Henry Sinclair in the role of their legendary teacher Glooscap. I began to realize that, strange as it sounded to me, with the Aboriginal people and the government both on side, history was truly being rewritten.

That thought stayed with me for the rest of the weekend. I sensed the story was important because it appeared from visiting the two monuments that this new theory of pre-Columbian contact had been recently elevated to a position of prominence by the strong support it had received locally. Some leading figures in the Mi'kmaq community and at least a couple of departments of the provincial government supported the claims being made by the Sinclair Society, claims that many would consider outrageous. There must be something to this, I thought. The *Zeno Stories* had been mentioned, and so I knew there would be a place to start the research. I headed back to Toronto with the intent of finding out how the Zeno family had gotten to the New World.

11
NICOLO ZENO OF VENICE

The claims made on the two Sinclair monuments in Guysborough depend solely on one small book written in Venice in the mid-sixteenth century. It is usually referred to as the *Zeno Narrative*, the *Zeno Stories*, or just simply the Zeno letters, but its full title is: *Annals of the Journey in Persia of Messirs Caterino Zeno, the Knight, and of the wars carried on in the Persian Empire in the times of Ussun Cassano. Two books. And of the Discovery of the Islands of Frislanda, Eslanda, Engrouelanda, Estotilanda, and Iscaria, made under the North Pole, by the two brothers Zeni, Messire Nicolo, the Knight, and Messire Antonio. One book. With a detailed map of all the said parts of the North discovered by them. With permission and privilege. Venice by Francesco Marcolini, 1558.*

The book is organized into three sections, all of them written in 1558 by Nicolo Zeno the Younger, a Venetian geographer. This Nicolo Zeno is termed the Younger to distinguish him from his ancestor Nicolo Zeno the Knight, about whom part of the Zeno book is written. Their names are identical. It can get confusing. To add to this mix, the first two sections of the book, its main portion, are a collection of stories about yet another Zeno, one of Nicolo the Younger's other ancestors, this one in Persia. However, it is the later third of this small book, a section only twenty-seven-and-a-half pages long, that is the reason for its importance.

It is this section of the Zeno book, the stories of Nicolo the Knight and his brother Antonio, that has fascinated historians and mapmakers for centuries, and it is this section that has led directly to the two monuments in Nova Scotia, to their inscriptions and assertions, and to the belief among at least some Mi'kmaq that Henry Sinclair had lived with them in Nova Scotia during the late fourteenth century — that he was their legendary Glooscap.

Nicolo the Younger, the writer of the book, claims that his two ancestors sailed from Venice to the northern Atlantic during the 1380s. He credits them with discovering certain islands "under the North Pole." While living in the north, they supposedly wrote letters back to their family in Venice describing their travels. Nicolo the Younger claims the letters were saved by the family, and the Zeno book is said to be a compilation of these letters.

However, the letters do not exist. Nicolo the Younger wrote the *Zeno Stories* when he was forty-three years old, based on the letters he claims he found when he was a boy. He also admits that being young and foolish he had torn up the original letters, not realizing what they were. The book, he asserts, is simply a reconstruction of these letters from memory, letters that he had destroyed almost forty years before. Unfortunately, we have no way of knowing if any of the claims are true or if the letters were ever written. They do not exist now. They may never have.

Nonetheless, throughout the book Nicolo the Younger presents his stories with a seriousness that makes him believable. They are structured as if the original letters had been written in the late fourteenth century by his adventuring ancestors back to their family in Venice. However, because the letters can no longer be examined — and this is the painful truth of the stories — a doubt hangs over every word. We are left wondering what is real and what is imaginary.

Nicolo the Younger's stories of the supposed travels of Nicolo the Knight and Antonio begin with a phrase from the original title, "Concerning the Discovery of the Islands of Frislanda, Esland, Engroueland, Estotilanda, and Icaria made by the two brothers Zeni Messire Nicolo, the Knight, and Messire Antonio. One book, with a map of the said Islands." Nicolo the Younger then briefly traces his family's history through a dozen or so generations, showing the direct family connections from father to son. He connects Nicolo the Knight and Antonio his brother, the supposed explorers of the late fourteenth century, to himself, the writer of these stories in 1558, five generations and more than 150 years later. To make his ancestry even clearer, he adds a diagram of his family tree.

The Zeno ancestry is populated with larger-than-life figures from the world of noble Venetians. The great importance of an old family and the rarefied position they held in sixteenth-century Venetian society is made clear by the author. They were well known and well respected. Nicolo the Younger tells of governors and good works, of doges, senators, and counselors, and of famous men with honorific titles like Zeno the Dragon and Carlo the Lion. In sixteenth-century Venice Nicolo the Younger was an important political figure with an interest in the study of geography, mathematics, and history. He was also powerful. He was a member of the Council of Ten, one of the primary governing bodies of the city.

Nicolo the Knight and Antonio were both brothers of Carlo the Lion. Carlo Zeno, the Lion, had distinguished himself and brought honours to the Zeno family in a naval battle fought in 1380 against Genoa. For centuries afterwards, Venetians held the name Carlo the Lion in awe because it was believed that he had saved the Republic, a victory that helped keep Venice master of the seas. His brother, Nicolo the Knight, also fought in these battles, often alongside Carlo, but Nicolo received neither the honour nor the lasting glory of his brother.

Nicolo the Younger claims the first letter he found was written after Nicolo the Knight arrived in the north, and was addressed to his brother Antonio who was still living in Venice. The year, according to Nicolo the Younger, was 1380. In this letter, a letter that Nicolo the Younger says he tore up as a child but remembers enough to reconstruct, Nicolo the Knight is described as "being a man of high spirits" who decided to see the world "to make himself acquainted with the various customs and languages of men, in order that, when occasion arose, he might be better able to do service to his country, and to acquire for himself fame and honour." Given the family position in Venetian society — and that Nicolo the Knight's brother was Carlo the Lion, the great Venetian naval hero — there must have been a weight of responsibility for Nicolo the Younger to give his ancestor, the high-spirited one, the mantle of greatness as well.

In 1380, so Nicolo the Younger claims, Nicolo the Knight sailed north in search of adventure on a ship he had had built for the voyage. Nicolo the Younger goes on to claim that Nicolo the Knight became shipwrecked on a large island in the North Atlantic called Frislanda, where he and his men were saved from the wild Frislandians by a great prince named Zichmni. So ends the first letter.

In the second letter, Nicolo the Younger describes Zichmni, the man who saved his ancestor from the Frislandians. He was said to be "war like and valiant, and above all, most famous in maritime affairs." He had a small fleet of "thirteen ships (two only propelled with oars, the rest small vessels, and one ship)." In this letter Nicolo the Younger explains how his ancestor became invaluable to Zichmni's war efforts and to the navigation of his small, ill-trained navy. The story tells of battles large and small, of the conquest of Frislanda, and of Zichmni's knighting of the brave and skillful Nicolo, now Nicolo the Knight — at least according to the Zeno family. So ends the second letter.

Nicolo the Younger then adds a lengthy paragraph explaining that Nicolo the Knight invited his brother Antonio to join him in the north. Antonio sailed north and Zichmni made him captain of his fleet. The three together — Nicolo the Knight, Antonio, and Zichmni — waged war against more imaginary islands in the North Atlantic. We are told of Nicolo the Knight's voyage to a monastery in the far north of Greenland. (Throughout the *Zeno Stories,* Greenland is referred to in a variety of ways: Grolanda, Engrouiland, or Engrouelant.) The monastery is described in detail. He claims it was heated by a nearby volcano with gardens that never died and water that never froze.

After four years in the North, so claims Nicolo the Younger, as a result of the severe cold in Greenland, Nicolo the Knight sickened and died. That would have been 1384. We are told that Antonio stayed with Zichmni in Frislanda for an additional ten years.

Nicolo the Younger's next essay is written as if it was a letter from Antonio, now living with Zichmni as captain of his fleet, back to his brother Carlo, the famous Lion, in Venice. It is a description, as told to Antonio by a group of fishermen who had been blown off course in the northern Atlantic, of a new coast on the west side of the Atlantic, and of two newly discovered lands called Estotilanda and Drogio. It is now believed that Estotilanda and Drogio were meant to suggest North America, the New World. This was hardly news in 1558. However, Nicolo the Younger's claim that the story of this discovery had been included in letters dated from the late fourteenth century makes the story very suspicious. It is impossible to check his claims.

Nicolo the Younger's next reconstruction describes a supposed voyage that Antonio and Zichmni attempted to make to this place called Estotilanda. On their way, however, after a difficult, stormy period at sea, they are forced to land near the southern tip of Greenland, a place they call Trin. The local inhabitants are described as "small of stature," "timid," and "half savage." We are told they lived in caves. According to Nicolo the Younger, Zichmni decides to stay and build a city at Trin, but his exhausted crew rebels against the idea. After appointing Antonio captain of the fleet, Zichmni sends them all back to Frislanda. Zichmni stays behind at Trin with only the rowboats and a few of his men. Nicolo the Younger then surmises, from his memory of "a clause in another letter," that this strange character Zichmni "did his best to explore the whole country, together with the rivers in various parts of Greenland."

In the final essay reconstructed or imagined by Nicolo the Younger, Antonio is said to claim that there existed a separate book that he had written describing his adventures in the north, "concerning the men, the animals, and the neighbouring countries." This book was said to outline "the life of Nicolo the Knight, our brother, with the discoveries made by him" and to describe Zichmni, the man who made Nicolo a knight, as a "Prince certainly as worthy of immortal remembrance as any other who has ever lived in this world." Nicolo the Younger also claims Antonio's book described "discoveries in Greenland on both sides" as well as a description of Zichmni's Greenland city of Trin. Unfortunately, like the torn letters, this book that Nicolo the Younger claims that Antonio claims that he had written has never been found.

After twenty-seven pages describing a world full of daring battle, wind-worn ships, distant monasteries, newly founded cities, and a life of excitement "under the North Pole," the final paragraph, just half a page, has Nicolo the Younger finally giving us the truth: all these letters had been torn up by him as a young child. He regrets it, but asserts he has been able to remember and reconstruct enough of what his ancestors wrote to "make reparation to this present age."

That is the *Zeno Stories*, the small book that in very recent years has formed the basis for a retelling of New World history. As shown in the next chapter, the story persisted through the centuries. In the late eighteenth century, a British writer suggested that the Zichmni of the Zeno stories was actually Henry Sinclair of Scotland. The *Zeno Stories*, the Zichmni character, and the eighteenth-century claim that Zichmni was Henry Sinclair appear to be the sole reasons for the two monuments in Guysborough, as well as the apparent basis for the claim that Henry Sinclair landed on the shores of North America in 1398. The element critical to those claims in this long story, from the torn mediaeval letters to these modern monuments, is that Nicolo the Younger's reconstructions are based on a child's memory embellished by fantasy. Or they could be entirely the fiction of an adult. That may be the key to either a misinterpretation or a complicated deception.

12
EVOLUTION OF A MYTH

Nicolo the Younger had two very important allies in the telling of this story, his publisher Francesco Marcolini, who was a leading printer in Venice at a time when Venice was printing more books than any other European city, and Marcolini's rich patron, Daniel Barbaro, who was a young Venetian of wealth and privilege and a relative of the Zeno family. Daniel Barbaro was also a star. He has been described as the finest mind of his time. He was an ambassador, a cardinal, and a scholar. He was an expert on perspective and wrote the first description of the *camera obscura*, the first suggestion of the modern camera. His translation of Vitruvius's *Ten Books on Architecture* was the first in Italian. His portrait was painted by both Titian and Veronese. Palladio built his family's villa. It was to this man, one of the greatest thinkers of the Venetian Renaissance, from one of the great families of the period, that Marcolini, the printer and publisher of the book, dedicated the *Zeno Stories*. That dedication tied the two names — Nicolo Zeno and Daniel Barbaro — together, a strong deterrent to all those who would doubt the merits of Nicolo's stories.

Marcolini began his dedication to Barbaro, in text as large as he had set the title, "To the most Reverend my Lord Messire Daniel Barbaro." He then explained that, in publishing these stories of Nicolo the Younger's ancestors, he had "wished to adorn the beginning of the work with the celebrated name of your most Reverend Lordship, more especially on account of the brotherhood in love which your most Reverend Lordship has with the Magnificent Messire Nicolo Zeno."[1] The sentence is very confusing, given that there are two Nicolo Zeno's in the mix: Nicolo the Younger, the author of the book, and Nicolo the Knight, about whom it is written. However, the "brotherhood of love" which Daniel Barbaro is said to have with a Zeno named Nicolo is probably not with a man who had been dead for over a century and a half. No, Marcolini's comment is directed at Nicolo the Younger, and it highlights the very significant relationship that existed between him and Daniel Barbaro. Not only were they related, they shared a "brotherhood of love," they were close comrades, the best of friends. This relationship helps explain one of the mysteries that has followed the *Zeno Stories* for the past four and a half centuries.

In 1560, when he was just forty-seven years old, Daniel Barbaro was appointed historian of the Venetian Republic. In his official position he made no mention of Nicolo the Knight or of the *Zeno Stories*. If the Zeno voyages were real, Barbaro would have celebrated them, but he did not. As historian of Venice he ignored them. Why would Daniel Barbaro have allowed his name to be added to the publication of Nicolo's stories if he thought they were rubbish? The answer may be as simple as their relationship, their "brotherhood of love." Daniel and Nicolo travelled in the same circles. Marcolini's dedication explains why Daniel Barbaro appeared to support the *Zeno Stories* while knowing, or at least suspecting, that the book was a deception. And in 1558, who would have thought that an insignificant little story would cause such a storm. Perhaps Barbaro hoped they all would be forgotten.

This connection between Daniel Barbaro and Nicolo Zeno is important for another small but critical element of the story. The only contemporary mention of the fabulous Zeno letters in sixteenth-century Venice appears to have been a handwritten note that was found in a never-finished genealogy that Marco Barbaro, Daniel Barbaro's brother, was working on until his death in 1569. The short note was attached to Antonio's Zeno's entry in the manuscript. However, it is not clear who wrote it or when it was added, but later supporters of the *Zeno Stories* often quote this note in support of the voyages. The added note claimed that Antonio "wrote with this brother Nicolo the Knight the voyages of the islands under the Artic Pole, and of those discoveries of 1390, and that by order of Zichno [sic], king of Frisland, he went to the continent of Estotiland in North America. He dwelt fourteene years in Frisland, four with his brother, and ten alone."[2] The note gave no other information, no reference, and no evidence. In no other manuscript, in no other book, in no other record before Nicolo the Younger published his *Zeno Stories* in 1558, was any mention made of the great northern adventures of the Zeno family.

Besides the relationship between Daniel Barbaro and Nicolo Zeno, another reason the *Zeno Stories* were seen as important when first published was because of the map that Nicolo the Younger included with the book. He explains how he had once found a map "all rotten and many years old" that he redrew and had copied for his book so that the reader could more easily trace his ancestors' travels throughout the north. However, there is no original map, only the one drawn in 1558. This map Nicolo the Younger drew has become known as the *Zeno Map*. It depicts all the places, both real and imaginary, that Nicolo the Younger claims his ancestors had visited during their northern travels. Nicolo the Younger's map has helped serve as a compilation of all that was or was not known of the northern Atlantic in 1558 when the map was first published. Parts of it were copied by later geographers up until the end of the seventeenth century.

As a politician and geographer in mid-sixteenth-century Venice, Nicolo the Younger would have been at the crossroads of the world's greatest navigators. Maps were his stock and trade. The *Zeno Map*, or parts of it, could have been copied from any number of other maps available to him. Its great mystery, however, is that it represented one thing extremely well. The outline of Greenland on the *Zeno Map* is exceedingly accurate.[3]

Someone had to have mapped Greenland before the European Age of Discovery. The only fundamental error is the north-south axis. It is rotated about forty-five degrees clockwise because of the extreme compass variation that far north. When those variations are taken into account and corrected, the map shifts and broadens to reveal roughly the outline of modern Greenland. Whoever had mapped the coast had to have used a compass skillfully, only failing to calculate the variation so close to the pole.

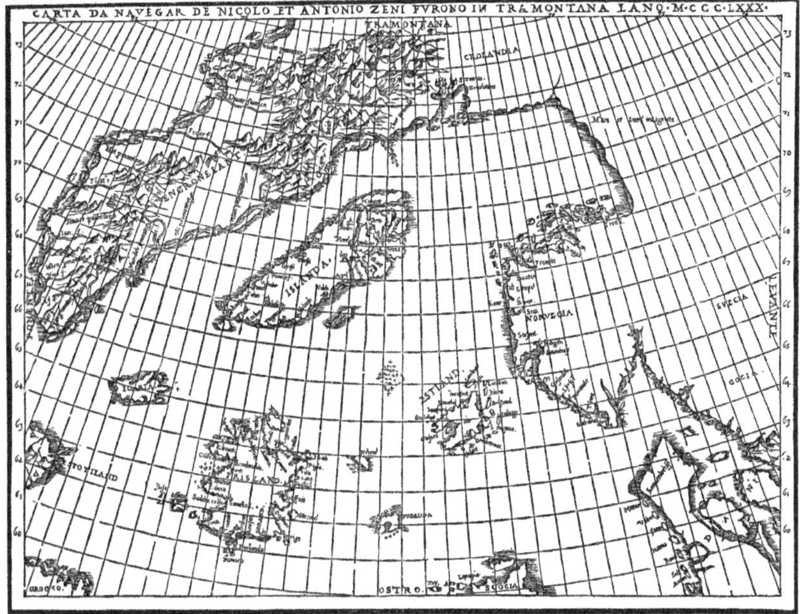

The *Zeno Map*, 1558.

"Zeno Map." Niccolò Zeno, *The voyages of the Venetian brothers, Nicolò & Antonio Zeno to the northern seas, in the XIVth century, comprising the latest known accounts of the lost colony of Greenland; and of the Northmen in America before Columbus* (London: The Hakluyt Society, 1873). Toronto Reference Library, Baldwin Collection.

This was no small job. Greenland has forty-five thousand kilometres of coastline, major bays to navigate and measure, and small islands to plot. Whoever mapped it, besides being proficient in the use of a compass, had a fleet of coordinated ships, a large crew of trained cartographers, and the time to produce such a survey. The *Zeno Map* is obviously not from the hands of Nicolo the Knight or his brother Antonio, even if they did make it to Greenland. Zichmni, if he ever existed, was said to have found himself on Greenland with only a few small boats.

Nonetheless, Nicolo the Younger had seen the outline of the Greenland map somewhere. His authority in Venice on things geographical would have meant that a map had crossed his desk at some time, and he either showed it to Marcolini or remembered enough to redraw it himself and then have Marcolini engrave it for his book. The *Zeno Map* is far from perfect, but for 1558, in relation to Greenland, it was as good as cartography got. It was part of the reason the map became valuable to navigators and was copied by so many well-known mapmakers.

What is most important about the *Zeno Map*, with regards to the story of Henry Sinclair, is that the map helped keep the Zeno tales alive for generations. There were the *Zeno Stories*; but, as a separate element, there was also this remarkable map, and because of the map people began to notice. We do not know who actually drew the map, but soon after it was published in 1558, it became important in itself. The stories, the letters, and the comments that Nicolo the Younger had written about his ancestors' supposed northern travels used the clear and well-presented *Zeno Map* as evidence of their truth. According to Nicolo, the reason the region was so well known and so well drawn, particularly Greenland, was because Zichmni, "did his best to explore the whole country, together with the rivers in various parts."[4] This map gave substance to Nicolo's fantastic stories.

It is easy to be seduced by the northern regions shown on the *Zeno Map*. The outlines are clear and easy to read. Unlike so many maps of this period, the *Zeno Map* looks almost modern. Moreover, in 1558 when it was drawn, it was quickly embraced as the only map of the north that was alleged to have been drawn from actual surveys. Nicolo the Younger claimed that his ancestors had visited these places. He labelled the map, "The Map of the Navigators Nicolo and Antonio Zeni," and dated it 1380, as if it had been surveyed and drawn by them. Whether it was Nicolo's intention or not, the map, which Nicolo claimed he had found in his family's house all torn and aged, was believed to have originated from his ancestors' travels. Not only were they lauded as adventurers, because of Nicolo the Younger's map his ancestors were seen as expert surveyors and cartographers as well.

Even though there were other maps of the North in circulation at the time, they were simply not as well-known as the one drawn by Nicolo the Younger. He was from a noble family and was considered to be a leading geographer of Venice. Without the Zeno name, Nicolo's book with its map and stories might have been nothing more than a short footnote in the history of sixteenth-century Venetian publishing. However, with the name of a noble family attached, a Venetian one at that, the *Zeno Stories* and its map were embraced in the late sixteenth century by the leading historians and cartographers in the intellectual centres of Europe. This was a good map of the Far North, a region about which very little was known. Moreover, Nicolo claimed that this part of the world had been surveyed and mapped by the noble Zeno family of Venice. That made it noteworthy. Its clarity, along with the hunger that Europe felt for a view of the North, brought the stories attached to it into a position of respect, even awe, among those writers, historians, cartographers, and intellectuals who would mould the history of the next centuries.

A giant step forward in the widespread popularity of the map throughout Europe was made by a Venetian intellectual named Ruscelli in 1561, soon after the *Zeno Map* was first published. Although Ruscelli's first love was the then new and mysterious art of alchemy, he also published commentaries on the Italian language and the rules of Italian poetry, on history, arms, and warfare, and, most important for Nicolo the Younger's map of the North, he published a new Venetian version of *Geographia* by Ptolemy, the Greco-Egyptian cartographer who had worked at the famous Library of Alexandria during the first century. Ruscelli's *Geographia* was written in Italian, not in Latin as was standard at the time. The Italian publication made this edition of Ptolemy's early maps more accessible to a wider audience. In it, Ruscelli used the *Zeno Map* to represent his generation's most advanced knowledge of the northern regions.

Ruscelli's maps were popular, not just because they were clear, easy to read, and annotated in Italian rather than Latin, but because they came with a very significant stamp of approval, a trademark of sorts. They had originated in Venice, the chief centre of map production and geographical knowledge in Europe. One of the primary roles that Venice played in the sixteenth century was as a synthesizer of geographic information and, in turn, as distributor of maps for the rest of the continent. As maps became popular, Venice and its cartographers became known and respected for trading in the most diverse and far reaching new representations of the rapidly evolving world image. With the largest merchant fleet in Europe, Venice acted as a commercial trading centre not just in silks and spices but in ideas, and the new geography was a hot commodity.

Ruscelli's new Ptolemy, including the *Zeno Map*, rode this wave of international respect and popularity. As we now know, there were other, earlier and even better maps of the North circulating in Europe at the time (see chapter 14), but Ruscelli was a successful author and a respected thinker and this was a map reported to have been drawn by members of a noble family. Moreover, it was Venetian. It could be trusted. It was accepted as authentic and important. And in many ways it was. It helped serve as a record of what was known of the northern regions in the mid-sixteenth century.

After Ruscelli republished the *Zeno Map*, the attached *Zeno Stories* also aroused interest among geographers. With the map now trusted as genuine, these travel stories of the North, letters supposedly written by the same Venetian family that had produced the map, were embraced by European intellectuals and adventurers. There was a thirst for knowledge of the unknown, and for the following centuries trust and belief in the *Zeno Stories* helped illuminate a small piece of the northern darkness. In spite of the complete absence of factual supporting material, Nicolo's 1558 book was the beginning of an international love affair with what many assumed to be a great and noble story.

Enter one of the world's first travel writers, Giovanni Ramusio. Like Ruscelli, Ramusio worked in Venice during the mid-sixteenth century. A well-respected writer and thinker, he was the first to collect, translate, organize, and publish firsthand accounts, documents, and records relating to the exploration of regions of the world still unknown in the West. His book, *Navigationi e viaggi*, was fundamentally a massive guide book, the first of its kind.

Ramusio organized *Navigationi e viaggi* into three volumes. The first volume, Africa, India, and Brazil — what Ramusio called the South — was published in 1550. More editions of this first volume were published throughout the rest of the century. The next volume, documents relating to the New World or the West, was published by Ramusio in 1556, again with subsequent editions. Ramusio died in 1557, at the age of seventy-two, the year after publishing his volume on the New World. The final volume of his collection, that section dealing with the Asian and Scandinavian regions — the North — was published in 1559, two years after his death. Zeno the Younger had published his stories and map the year before, in 1558, but neither his stories nor his map were included in Ramusio's last volume.

Seventeen years after Ramusio's death, in 1574, a new edition of this volume on the North was published by Ramusio's printer, Tommaso Giunti. Significantly, it was published using Ramusio's name. This time the northern volume included the *Zeno Stories*. This meant that, as of 1574, the *Zeno Stories* appeared to have the blessing of Ramusio, one of the most important geographers of late sixteenth-century Venice. Moreover, with Ramusio's name attached, it meant that the *Zeno Stories* appeared to have been filtered by Ramusio's critical examination. That may or may not have been the case. We don't know if Rumusio had read any of the *Zeno Stories,* or even if he knew they had been written. Nonetheless, by the end of the century it appeared to a new generation of geographers that the *Zeno Stories* had been published by one of the leading thinkers of the period, even though he had been dead for seventeen years. The stories now had the Ramusio brand. Who would doubt them? Now the *Zeno Stories*, like the *Zeno Map*, were seen as genuine.

As the stories were being circulated, the map continued to find its way into publications. After it was published by Ruscelli in 1561, the *Zeno Map* was included in another edition of Ptolemy's *Geographia* in 1562, this time in Latin, published by another Venetian, a printer and bookseller named Moletius. To give the map added authority, Moletius gave credence to the *Zeno Stories* from which the map had been copied. The stories, he wrote, had been printed "in the Italian language by the most distinguished Nicolo Zeno." And who would question a "most distinguished" Venetian on matters of geography? Clearly Moletius wanted to believe the *Zeno Map* and the *Zeno Stories*. He even dedicated his edition of Ptolemy to the son of Nicolo the Younger.[5] Venice was a small world.

Moletius translated his edition of Ptolemy, including the *Zeno Map*, into German. That translation is critical to the story because a copy of Moletius's German Ptolemy made its way to the library of one of the world's most famous and widely copied early cartographers, Gerardus Mercator.

On Mercator's world map of 1569, on which he used his newly devised system of longitude and latitude drawn as straight lines, the northern region appears taken almost directly from the *Zeno Map*. It has been slightly rearranged to make the various land masses fit, but Mercator's copy of Moletius's Ptolemy provided the outlines. The message was clear.

Mercator, the father of modern cartography, had seen fit to use the *Zeno Map* on the strength of its Venetian heritage. The world was about to follow suit. For the next hundred years, new maps showed the North as Nicolo Zeno had published it in 1558.

Ortelius, a close friend of Mercator and one of the most respected cartographers of the sixteenth century, also used the *Zeno Map* in his atlas. Like Mercator, Ortelius was able to justify his northern cartography because it came from the Zeno family in Venice. In his atlas of maps from 1570, *Theatrum Orbis Terrarum*, Ortelius used the *Zeno Stories* as evidence that the layout of the northern regions was trustworthy. He wrote:

> Howbeit I finde, that the North part of America (which lieth nearest unto Europe, and to some of our European isles, namely, Groenland, Island, and Frisland; and is called Estotiland) was long since discovered by certaine Frislandish fishers, driven by tempest upon that coast: and afterward about the yere 1390, that it was revisited anew by Antonie Zeno, a gentleman of Venice: and that by the authority of Zichmi [sic], the King of the said ilse of Frisland, a Prince in those time very valiant, and over all that sea, for his wars and victories most renowned. Concerning this his expedition there are extant in Italian certain Collections or brief extracts drawn by Francis Marcolino out of the letters of Nicolai and Antione Zeno gentlemen of Venice, who lived in those parts. Out of which Collections I add this that follows touching the description of this region. Estotiland (he says) abounds with all things necessary for mankind.[6]

This explanation has all the elements of the evolving Zeno legend. Frislanda and its king, Prince Zichmni, are still there; the imposing but imaginary island of Frislanda would take a while for cartographers to get rid of. Most important, Ortelius gives the reader the unquestioned assurance that his information came from the source. He claimed "there are extant in Italian certain collections or brief extracts drawn by Francis Marcolino out of the letters of Nicolai and Antione Zeno, gentlemen of Venice." It sounds as if the letters written by Nicolo the Younger in 1558 were verifiable fourteenth-century originals. They were not. They did not exist. Nonetheless, in the face of this assurance, there was no reason to doubt the Ortelius reference, the map, or the *Zeno Stories*. The fishermen's visit to Estotilanda (America) also reappears in Ortelius's explanation. Even more important, Antonio Zeno was given the credit for having revisited Estotilanda anew. That visit to the New World does not appear in the original stories, yet repeats the same error about Antonio's supposed visit to the New World made on the short handwritten note that had been added to Marco Barbaro's never-published genealogy. This visit to America was also becoming part of the Zeno myth. The seeds of confusion and obfuscation were starting to grow.

With Mercator and Ortelius in support of the *Zeno Map*, and with the justification given that the original documents could be found in Venice, the map soon became the standard depiction of the Far North, with Zichmni's Frislanda and all.

An equally rapid rise to fame and influence happened with the *Zeno Stories*. Ramusio's *Navigationi e viaggi* was translated and spread throughout Europe. Mercator had a copy in his library. Moreover, in 1582 an English translation of Ramusio's *Zeno Stories* was published by Richard Hakluyt in his *Divers Voyages Touching the Discoverie of America and the Ilands Adjacent unto the Same, Made First of All by Our Englishmen and Afterwards by the Frenchmen and Britons: With Two Mappes Annexed Hereunto*. Hakluyt, who originally published David Ingram's account of America, was the foremost English collector, editor, and publisher of early voyages to the New World, particularly by the English, and this edition of *Divers Voyages* proved to be an extremely significant collection of documents relating to international voyages of discovery. With the *Zeno Stories* included, Hakluyt's book gave the stories a stamp of authenticity among English speaking historians.

However, it appears that Hakluyt anticipated doubts regarding the truth of the *Zeno Stories*. Along with his translation, Hakluyt included this note:

> For the more credite and confirmation of the former history of Messer Nicolas and Messer Antonio Zeni (which for some few

> respects may perhaps be called in question) I have here annexed the judgment of that famous Cosmographer Abraham Ortelius, or rather the yielding and submitting of this judgement thereunto: who in his Theatrum Orbis, fol.6, next before the map of Mar del Zur, boroweth proof and authority out of this relation, to show that the Northeast part of America called Estotiland, and in the original always affirmed to be an Island, was about the year 1390 discovered by the aforesaid Venetian Gentleman Messer Antonio Zeno, about 100 years before ever Christopher Columbus set sail for Western Regions, and that the Northern Seas were even then sailed by our European Pilots....[7]

One can almost hear the question in Hakluyt's own voice when he writes, "which for some few respects may perhaps be called in question." Some. Few. Perhaps? There is trepidation, even suspicion. Is it right to publish these stories, he must have asked himself. Hakluyt appears to have suspected something was wrong, so he shifted the confirmation of proof to Ortelius, or at least to the "yielding and submitting" of Ortelius's judgement.

Yet still, the stories were published. And to make matters worse, at one point in the *Zeno Stories* Hakluyt incorrectly translated the way in which the wind had changed, from the northeast rather than from the southwest, and in turn incorrectly changed the course of Zichmni's ship. In the original Italian of Nicolo the Younger, it was a southwest wind in the open Atlantic that turned Zichmni's ship back to Greenland, a wind blowing *from* the southwest. This southwest wind blew the ship into Trin Bay at the southern tip of Greenland.[8] However, Hakluyt translated this as the wind changing to blow *toward* the southwest instead.[9] It was a small error, a preposition only, but it meant sailing toward the New World rather than away from it, and it allowed many to repaint the confusion of Nicolo the Younger's stories for their own goals. It allowed them to claim Zichmni had sailed towards the Americas. He hadn't. This mistaken wind direction allowed many to suppose Henry Sinclair, in the form of Prince Zichmni, might have reached the east coast of North America. This error in translation has only added to the confusion.

In 1688, Coronelli, the seventeenth-century cartographer and monk from Venice, drew a New World globe that addressed the Zeno question in two different areas. In the region of Labrador, that area of eastern Canada north of present day Newfoundland, Coronelli wrote, "Estotilanda, or the New Bretaigne and Terre de Labrador discovered by Antonio Zeno, a Venetian Patrician in 1390, before the other countries of America were known."[10] Coronelli also has Antonio Zeno discovering America. However, Nicolo the Younger never wrote that Antonio or Zichmni had reached America. His wind directions have the Zeno ship blown away from the Americas and back to Greenland. With Coronelli, as with others, there is a growing sense of confusion as to what the original *Zeno Stories* actually claimed. Nonetheless, the discoverer is still that "Venetian Patrician," so there is also a continued trust in the book's noble source. However, a sense of doubt, that new aspect of the *Zeno Stories*, was rapidly gaining ground.

On a second section of Coronelli's new globe, in the region once occupied by Zeno's Frislanda, the domain of Prince Zichmni, the mapmaker added that here, in this now empty sea, "many place the island Frislande, discovered 300 years ago by Nicolo Zeno, a Venetian noble, in the name of the King of Denmark, but as the sailors who have so often navigated this sea have never been able to find it, so these think, either that it must have been submerged or that the report of it is fabulous."[11] As always, mention of the Zeno's nobility is attached to the story. The Zeno family depended on their name. However, along with this continued element of trust, there was now a growing suspicion. Here was the clear realization that the Zeno's imaginary Frislanda, both on the map and in the stories, was a fiction. It could have disappeared, perhaps, but Coronelli admits that it just as well may have been a fable. As the North became better known, doubt continued to grow, and the *Zeno Map* disappeared into the fog of history.

As the map faded in importance, however, throughout the seventeenth and eighteenth centuries, the *Zeno Stories* continued to fascinate. There was always the same confusion in the claims, the same respect for the authority of the Venetian nobility, and the same growing doubt that had begun to frame the discussion.

In 1744, Pierre François Xavier de Charlevoix, the French historian who organized and wrote the first comprehensive history of New France, which was the area believed by some to have been the region of Estotiland visited by the fishermen mentioned by Nicolo the Younger, wrote briefly about the *Zeno Stories*. Charlevoix had travelled extensively throughout the continent, and his insight into the New World was considered accurate. He claimed that Estotilanda of the *Zeno Stories* "is now regarded as a fabulous country, that never existed except in the imagination of the brothers Zani, noble Venetians."[12] He admits that, "Others have since pretended that Estotiland, which was placed north or west of Labrador, was discovered in 1390, by fishermen of Frieseland. Anthony Zani, it is said, a noble Venetian, and his brother, Nicholas Zani, having sailed from the coast of Ireland, were driven by stress of weather on Frieseland, believed to be a part of Greenland, and there learned of this discovery. In their relation, they gave a magnificent description of Estotiland; but this account is evidently a romance."[13]

Charlevoix was clear that the stories were flights of the imagination. Nonetheless, he continued to respect the Zeno voice. The image of the noble Venetian, and the admiration and trust that image continued to evoke, was obvious in his history. It is this noble Zeno voice, a voice difficult to disbelieve, that continued to rouse each new generation of historians. It served to give a solid platform on which future writers could successfully present their translation of the *Zeno Stories* and bring Nicolo the Knight, Antonio, and Zichmni into the modern world.

13

THE *ZENO STORIES* COME OF AGE

Even with their fundamental errors, for hundreds of years the letters that Nicolo Zeno had written in the mid-sixteenth century continued to impress. The *Zeno Stories* was a mystery about a mysterious part of the world, the Far North, and it continued to have that critically important term "Noble Venetian" attached to it. Was there any harm done in believing that the Zeno brothers' exploits might be true? Mystery, danger, courage, nobility, and a map "all rotten and many years old": it had all the elements necessary for the telling of a great adventure story.

The person who most helped propel the *Zeno Stories* into the modern era was Johann Reinhold Forster, a pastor, naturalist, and historian. In 1772, because of a change in the scientific members of the crew of HMS *Resolution*, Forster was asked to accompany James Cook on his second voyage of exploration. Forster was to have published a book on the journey, but he fought with both his publisher and with Cook on his return, and the planned volume was cancelled. Living in poverty after his fiasco with Cook, Forster published pamphlets on a wide range of subjects: zoology, mineralogy, botany, and geography. In 1784, deep in debt, Forster resurrected the *Zeno Stories*, first in German, and then two years later with an English translation.

The essence of Forster's book, *History of the Voyages and Discoveries Made in the North*, was his unquestioned belief in the *Zeno Stories*. There is little doubt he was in awe of the Zeno family and their name. He wrote of them, "The family of the Zenos, in Venice, is very ancient, and is not only of the highest rank of nobility, but is likewise celebrated for the performance of great actions, as also by reason that the highest offices and dignities in the state had been filled from time immemorial, by men of merit belonging to this family."[1] Then he makes the reason for this adoration clear. He doesn't believe that such a family would allow such a lie to be told. The Zenos, Forster claimed, were

> one of the most considerable families in Venice; a family on which no one would have the boldness to palm stories of this kind, supposing them to be absolutely false. It must doubtless be well known, and be demonstrable from accounts to be found in original records and archives at Venice, that there were such people actually in being as these brothers, Carlo, Nicolo, and Antonio Zeno; that the Chevalier undertook a voyage to the North, and his brother Antonio followed him thither; that this same Antonio laid down all these voyages and countries on a map, which he brought with him to Venice, and which hung up in his house in Marcolini's time (where it was in the power of every one to see and examine it) as a sure pledge and an incontestable proof of the truth of this narrative. This being then the case, how is it possible for anyone to harbour the least doubt concerning the truth of these relations, such more absolutely to reject them as fabulous? Should, however, anyone persist in such incredulity, nothing farther can be opposed to him; as in this case there must be an end to all faith in history; and it would be but labour in vain to endeavour to convince one who purposely shuts his eyes against the truth....[2]

After that, who would dare doubt the *Zeno Stories*, and, in turn, the sincerity of Reverend Forster? According to Forster, it would be impossible to convince anyone "who purposely shuts his eyes against the truth." Forster believed the *Zeno Stories* wholeheartedly and wanted to ensure that his readers did too. To do otherwise was just wrong, or so Forster tried to convince us.

With his name attached to Captain Cook's historic voyage and with his belief in the *Zeno Stories* pushed on by his dogmatic intellectual forcefulness, Forster's book established itself as one of the most important Zeno texts in the modern era. Forster is still quoted by those who continue to support the truthfulness of the stories, or at least near truthfulness, even in the face of more modern research that proves most of their claims false.

Forster assured his readers that there were original documents in the archives of Venice that could prove these fabulous stories. He described how the original *Zeno Map* had hung in the family's house in Venice for all to see, "as a sure pledge and an incontestable proof of the truth of this narrative." Even though these original documents did not exist, and the map hanging on the wall in the Zeno home for inspection was a completely fictional image, Forster's book solidified the historical importance of the *Zeno Stories* as if, written by the "highest rank of nobility," they had undergone the careful scrutiny of researchers, archivists, and cartographers. That, of course, was not the case, but anyone who questioned the *Zeno Stories*, anyone who would "persist in such incredulity," was seen as shutting their eyes to the truth.

If you want to believe the *Zeno Stories*, Forster's book is very useful. He solved the problem of Frislanda, or at least got rid of it. According to Forster, the massive island of Frislanda had disappeared, destroyed by a volcano and swallowed by the sea. So much for the fabulous Frislanda. That got the Zenos off the hook slightly. However, he did not get rid of Frislanda's king, Prince Zichmni. Instead, he gave him a face. According to Forster, Zichmni was actually a little-known Scottish earl named Henry Sinclair.

This is the first mention of Henry Sinclair's involvement with the *Zeno Stories*. We know that Henry Sinclair was a real person; he held the position of Earl of the Orkney Islands during the late fourteenth century, but the Orkney Islands were not even important enough to Nicolo the Younger's stories for him to have drawn them on his map. Nicolo could have easily copied them from earlier maps if he had felt his story had needed them. Moreover, according to Nicolo the Younger, Prince Zichmni, the king of Frislanda, was at war with the King of Norway. However, history tells us that Henry Sinclair was actually a close ally of Norway. No war, no Frislanda. And all signs point toward there being no Zichmni, regardless. Even lacking any strong parallels between the fictional Zichmni and the little we know of the real Henry Sinclair — Henry Sinclair had no adventures in Greenland, there are no records of the building of new cities, there were no visits from Italian nobles — Forster, in his intimidating and dogmatic way, asserted the claim nonetheless. The basis for his assertion? Forster believed that the name Zichmni sounded like Sinclair. That is all. Does Zichmni sound like Sinclair? But who would doubt Forster, doubt the noble Venetians and shut one's eyes against the truth as Forster envisioned it?

In 1808, Placido Zurla, a Roman Catholic monk and highly respected Cardinal of Rome, added to the confusion of the *Zeno Stories* with a book he wrote on early Italian voyages. He completely rejected Forster's suggestion that Henry Sinclair was Zichmni, but Zurla was stuck in the belief that Nicolo the Younger had written the truth about his ancestors' northern travels, even with the serious errors he found.

In the Venetian archives, Zurla had discovered documents that showed Nicolo the Knight had been in Venice for most of the 1380s[3] and that his brother Antonio had been married there in 1384.[4] However, this period, the decade of the 1380s, was when Nicolo the Younger claimed the two brothers had been in the North with Zichmni. For most historians, this would have been the end of the *Zeno Stories*. Nonetheless, Zurla, a Venetian himself, obviously wanted to believe. According to Zurla's reckoning, Nicolo the Younger had simply made a mistake in the date, both in the letters he wrote and on the map he drew. Zurla concluded that it was not really 1380 when the Zeno ancestors had travelled to Frislanda, but rather 1390. Like the historians who came before him, Zurla gave the noble Venetians the benefit of the doubt. He readjusted the story, again. The history of the *Zeno Stories* was becoming a difficult exercise among the believers. Against all good sense, they continued to seek a logical foundation for their belief.

The next historian to comment on the *Zeno Stories* also remains one of the most important. His name was Richard Henry Major, curator of the map collection at the British Library during much of the second half of the nineteenth century. Like Forster and Zurla before him, Major was a firm believer in the truth of the *Zeno Stories*. Also like those who came before him, he rewrote and reinterpreted the most fantastic elements to make them fit the geographic and historical reality of the late fourteenth-century North. Even more than Forster's, Major's book remains the standard work on the subject and is usually held up as proof of Earl Henry's fourteenth-century exploits with the Zenos.

Again, in the nineteenth century it was an issue of belief. There was no proof of the *Zeno Stories*, and no original documents. There was nothing authentic about the stories, nor about the map, and Major realized this was a serious problem. He claimed, "The genuineness of the work lies at the root of the whole question ... the authenticity of the document is so preponderating an element in the case, that when once it is well established, the minor objections might be fairly left to shake themselves into their places as best they could."[5] The story was a fantasy with mismatched elements borrowed from older maps and older legends, so the authenticity of the document was impossible to prove. Nonetheless, according to Major, once we got over that problem, the minor inconsistencies in the story would work themselves out or fade into the unimportant background. Again, Major was borrowing a theological argument. Once you believed, everything fell into place.

Major argued that all the mistakes found in the *Zeno Stories* or on the *Zeno Map* could be corrected by rearranging Nicolo the Younger's geography. Major blamed Nicolo the Younger for having naively distorted the facts simply because he had had no idea of the North. The incongruities between the map and the stories and the errors in both, according to Major, only proved that Nicolo the Younger, "could not possibly have been the ingenious concocter of a narrative, the demonstrable truth of which, when checked by modern geography, he could thus ignorantly distort upon the face of a map."[6] However, there was no "demonstrable truth" to the narrative. According to Major, if Nicolo the Younger had known better, he would have written a better story and drawn a better map. It was clear that Major entered the Zeno discussion already believing.

Like those before him, Major also played the noble card again, asking whether a "nobleman of high and ancient lineage, the members of whose family had many of them so eminently distinguished themselves in the history of their country as to stand in no need of falsehoods to add to their glory, himself a Member of the Council of Ten, is to be branded as a concocter of falsehoods."[7] Major's most essential proof of the narrative was that a family like the Zenos would not tell a lie.

According to Major, Nicolo the Younger had simply made some mistakes. Major claimed that, "in the present case, exaggeration, employed only for the glorification of the occasion, has, from a foreigner's liability to misapprehend the true state of the case, led to the introduction of a false element into the story."[8] Apparently, it was because Nicolo the Younger was a foreigner, an Italian, that there were mistakes in the *Zeno Stories*. Those foreigners could not be trusted to "apprehend the true state of the case." Once Major rearranged the map and rewrote the geographical descriptions, and once he justified Nicolo's exaggerations as nothing more than "hyperbole so common amongst southern nations," Major was convinced that all the problems of the *Zeno Stories* had disappeared. Only to those who believe will the story be believable. Just as Forster had claimed, only those with faith could see the truth.

By the end of the nineteenth century, the *Zeno Stories* and the claim that Prince Zichmni of Frislanda was Henry Sinclair had begun to entice the Sinclair family, perhaps lured by the notion of ancestral greatness. In 1873, during the Chicago Exhibition, in response to the anniversary of Columbus's voyage and now believing that Henry Sinclair was the Zichmni of the *Zeno Stories*, Thomas Sinclair, a London journalist from northeastern Scotland who wrote on the history and genealogy of the region, presented an outline of the Forster and Major claims at a meeting of the newly formed Sinclair Society of North America, the Society de Sancto Claro. Thomas Sinclair was unequivocal, claiming that "Henry as a civilised man, in the modern sense of civilisation, was the one and only discoverer of America ... the important conclusion having been unmistakably reached. With this Zeno admiral, Prince Henry, first placed really civilized foot on that continent which is now the home and glory of more than fifty millions of the earth's pick of white men and women."[9] The Sinclairs were now on side. Their ancestor Henry had discovered America.

Unfortunately for the Sinclairs and their belief that Henry had gotten to America, Nicolo the Younger's stories had only brought his Zeno ancestors and the noble Prince Zichmni as far west as Greenland. Even as a fable, they went no farther. Zichmni landed at Trin, the city Nicolo claimed he founded. On the *Zeno Map*, Trin is located on the southern tip of Greenland. However, even though Nicolo the Younger had his heroes sailing no farther than Greenland, the story he told of the fishermen being lost in the New World, in the regions of Estotilanda and Drogio, was an open door to the additional claims that the Zeno brothers and Zichmni had also visited the New World a hundred years before Columbus.

With the *Zeno Stories* acting as a foundation, a new biography was created for the Sinclairs' ancestor. Thomas Sinclair's speech to the Sinclair Society set the tone for the next century. Henry Sinclair became "the Pre-Columbian discoverer of the fourteenth century." For proof, the family pointed to Forster and Major and to the mysterious documents and records in the Venetian archives. With the Scottish Sinclairs involved, the Zeno tales had a strong new voice, and with so much already written about the Zeno voyages during the eighteenth and nineteenth centuries, the Sinclairs could pick and choose as they needed to support their claims.

In 1898, Roland Saint-Clair, a New Zealander who had changed his name from Sinclair to Saint-Clair, published a family history, *The Saint Clairs of the Isles*. No previous historian of the Sinclairs or of northern Scotland had ever mentioned any grand adventures of Earl Henry. That did not stop Roland. In a chapter entitled "Orcadian Argonauts, or Voyages of the Zeni 1374–1404," Roland laid out the facts as he envisioned them. "Almost a century before Columbus commenced.... Henry I, 42nd Earl of the ancient, autonomous maritime principality of the Orkneys ... had commissioned his Admiral, Antonio Zeno, a Venetian navigator, scion of the renowned Ducal family of that name, to retrace the footsteps of the Scandinavian discoverers of the Western World."[10] As proof, Roland cited the Zeno's noble background and quoted Forster, "distinguished companion of Captain Cook" and Major, who he claimed had "completely established the genuineness of the discovery." Roland Saint Clair had little need to question the actual historical substance of Henry's new found fame. The credit to his ancestor had been accorded at the highest level of nobility and scholarship. Roland dedicated his book to the family's new hero, Henry Sinclair, whom he called Henry the Holy for the first time. This is the reference used on the Halfway Cove monument in Guysborough. By the end of the nineteenth century, at least according to Sinclair family history, Earl Henry had become a famous — and holy — discoverer.

14

THE BATTLE FOR HISTORY

Throughout the centuries that the *Zeno Stories* circulated in Europe and America, doubts were growing. Hakluyt's 1582 comment that the Zeno history "for some few respects may perhaps be called in question" highlighted the problem. The stories and the map were being questioned, doubted, and dismissed. A hundred years after Hakluyt, in 1688, the cartographer Coronelli reported that no sailor had been able to find the Zeno island of Frislanda and suggested that "the report of it is fabulous." In the next century, in 1744, the great French historian Charlevoix wrote that the land of Estotilanda had come to be regarded as "a fabulous country that never existed except in the imagination of the brothers Zani." It was becoming obvious that, even though there continued to be support for the *Zeno Stories* in some circles, respect for and belief in the stories and the map was being gradually chipped away by some of the world's leading historians and cartographers.

In 1835, with men like Forster, Zurla, and Major trying to give the *Zeno Stories* the shine of respectability, a voice of reason spoke up. Admiral Zahrtmann, hydrographer to the Royal Danish Navy, had had enough. As the person responsible for charting and mapping the northern ocean,

Zahrtmann knew the region better than anyone. Of the *Zeno Map* he wrote, "The whole chart bears the most palpable marks of having been compiled by a person who had never been at the places themselves, and who knew nothing of either the language or the history of the North...."[1] Zahrtmann was right. It appeared to him that Nicolo the Younger was borrowing from older maps, knew nothing of what he was copying, and making up the geography he needed as he wrote his story.

Zahrtmann believed that the *Zeno Map* was a sixteenth-century compilation of maps that had come before. He used the Zeno cartography of Scandinavia as an example. It was a region shown on the *Zeno Map,* but never visited in the *Zeno Stories.* Zahrtmann wrote, "the comparative correctness of the delineation of Denmark and Norway is the best proof that the chart was not drawn in 1380, but about the middle of the sixteenth century."[2] It was becoming clear that in spite of the work of Forster, Major, and Zurla, when the *Zeno Stories* were investigated by those who knew the region well, the falseness of the stories was beginning to show. As Zahrtmann declared in frustration, "As to the fabulous parts of the narrative, it is difficult to select one passage in preference to another for refutation, the whole being a tissue of fiction."[3]

Nicolo the Younger was right in claiming that his map had earlier precedents. We now know that the map Nicolo the Younger drew was traced from several other maps. He hadn't concocted the thing out of nowhere, but it was highly unlikely that his ancestors had anything to do with it. With the discovery in the late nineteenth century of several very early maps of the Northern regions, it is now clear that there were maps available in Italy that showed this region as depicted on Nicolo the Younger's map. Whether he actually found copies of these older maps at his family home, all torn and aged, we will never know, but it seems he had copied his map from these other non-Zeno sources.

The North had begun to appear on world maps in the early fifteenth century. Previous to that, the only maps that western Europe knew were the maps of Ptolemy, which simply left out any depiction of the North, because to the West it was an unknown and unimportant region. After the Ptolemy maps began reappearing in Europe around 1400, other maps began to materialize that were used by European mapmakers to supplement the limited knowledge of this unknown northern wasteland. The source of those maps can only be guessed at. Someone clearly had surveyed the North and had carefully and precisely delineated the coastlines of Greenland, Iceland, and Scandinavia. We may never know who had done the surveying or first produced the charts, but we have copies of the maps that were made from those charts to prove that the area had been measured and drawn before Europeans had the technology, the ships, or the trained manpower.

The early fifteenth-century Danish cartographer Claudius Clavus drew various maps showing land masses in the northern sea. The maps were only discovered in European archives in the late nineteenth century.[4] They were usually in the form of a copy of a copy, and usually attached as an addition to Ptolemaic maps of northwestern Europe. Though a Dane, Clavus had worked in Italy, so his maps would have been easily available to the Italian market, and especially in Venice.

One of these maps from 1427, known as the *Clavus Nancy Map*, after the French city of Nancy where it was discovered, depicted a Greenland coast in the northwestern region of the northern ocean, an island to Greenland's east called Iceland, and the coast of Norway at the far eastern edge of the ocean. The map is weak on detail and still very coarsely drawn, but it makes the clear point that the north had arrived on the drawing tables of European mapmakers, at least by 1427.

A second Clavus map of the North, drawn by two German cartographers working in Florence in the second half of the fifteenth century, showed a more exact outline of Greenland, albeit located too far east. The massive knuckle of land was called Engroneland — one of the early names for Greenland — like it would be on the *Zeno Map* over a century later, and the various rivers and promontories along the western coast were given names like those that would be used on the *Zeno Map*.

The names on this map are evidence that this second *Clavus Map* was one of the early maps used by Nicolo the Younger to draw his *Zeno Map*. Strangely, the names used by Clavus, and subsequently by Zeno, came from a Danish children's rhyme, "There dwells a man in Greenland stream," popular at the time.[5] Apparently, in lieu of actual place names, Clavus had used the Danish words of the rhyme to fill up Greenland's western coast. Nicolo the Younger, no doubt believing the names to be authentic locations, simply copied the Clavus labels onto his 1558 map, making it appear that the Zeno brothers and Zichmni had surveyed the region and visited these nursery rhyme towns.

One of the most important early maps of the North is the *Zamoiski Map* from the mid-fifteenth century.[6] Like the Clavus maps, it too was found in a Latin codex of Ptolemy's *Geographia*, this one in Warsaw in 1888. Originating from Italy, the map was a gift from the Pope in Rome to the Polish Chancellor Zamoiski. The names along the western shore of Greenland are almost identical to the *Clavus Map*. The Zamoiski cartographer had copied from Clavus, or copied from a copy of Clavus. This *Zamoiski Map*, and others like it, became the model on which later fifteenth- and sixteenth-century maps, including the *Zeno Map*, based their outlines of the region.

Putting Clavus's fictitious nursery rhyme names aside, the actual outline of these landmasses was often remarkably accurate. On the *Olaus Magnus Map* of 1539, the island of Iceland and the Scandinavian coast are highly articulated, even though there had been no direct effort to

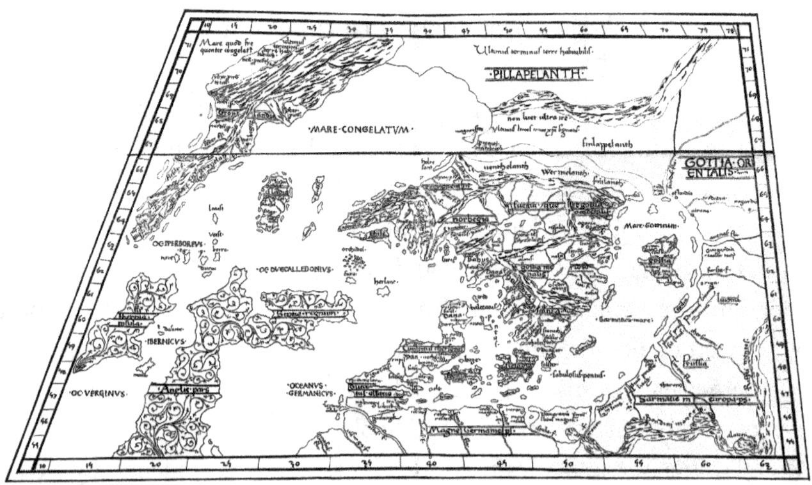

The *Zamoiski Map*, 1468.

"Zamoiski Map." A. E. Nordenskiöld, *Facsimile-atlas to the early history of cartography with reproductions of the most important maps printed in the XV and XVI centuries* (Stockholm: P.A. Norstedt & söner, 1889), plate XXX. Toronto Reference Library, Baldwin Collection.

survey the region. As maps were copied, more and more information was tested, some added, some removed. Mistakes were made. On the *Olaus Magnus Map* frozen ice sheets were correctly shown off the northeast coast of Iceland. However, these ice sheets would show up twenty years later on the *Zeno Map*,[7] incorrectly rendered as solid land masses, as actual islands and not as ice, by someone who knew nothing of what he was copying.

With the discoveries of the *Clavus*, the *Zamoiski*, and the *Olaus Magnus Maps* over the years, it became obvious that the material drawn by Nicolo the Younger had been copied from a number of older sources — not from his ancestors as he suggested. As one historian of cartography wrote, "Zeno's map and book are an uncritical compilation of heterogeneous material from older sources belonging to various dates and places, presumably put together for the purpose of giving Venice, the author's native city, the credit for the discovery of America more than a century before Columbus."[8] With this as one of his possible motives, Nicolo Zeno took this compilation of older sources and made it into something which became famous.

Given Zahrtmann's position with the Royal Danish Navy, his should have been the final judgment on the *Zeno Stories* and its map. It wasn't however. Arguments supportive of Forster, Zurla, Major, and the Zeno family continued in spite of more logical and more clearheaded voices. This had become a discussion between logic on one side and the faithful on the other. According to the faithful, you either believed or you were blind to the truth. Sadly, like any theological discourse, talk of the *Zeno Stories* had become an argument about the unknowable.

In 1898, Frederick Lucas, a London lawyer, wrote what is considered the most comprehensive work on the *Zeno Stories* and its history. The title of Lucas's book, *The Annals of the Voyages of the Brothers Nicolo and Antonio Zeno in the North Atlantic about the end of the Fourteenth Century and the Claim founded thereon to a Venetian Discovery of America: A Criticism and an Indictment*, makes clear his intent. He blasted apart the histories of men like Forster and Major, not only claiming they were apologists for the *Zeno Stories*, but that they were concocting excuses for the ridiculous. The "criticism and indictment" that Lucas directed at these historians was for their abuse of history, for the fraudulent repainting of the past.

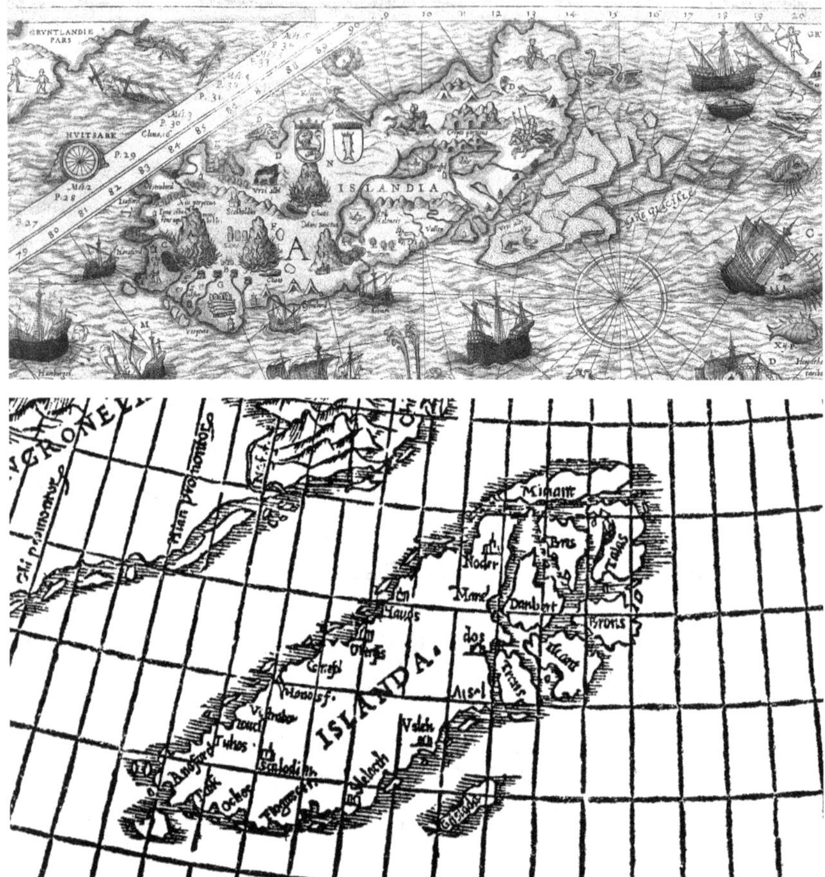

(upper) The *Olaus Magnus Map of Iceland*, 1572 print from a 1539 original. Masses of ice are shown along the northeast coast. (lower) The Zeno Map of Iceland, 1558. The ice is incorrectly shown as a group of islands.

(upper) "Olaus Magnus Map." Carta marina, opus Olai Magni Gotti Lincopensis, ex typis Antonii Lafreri Sequani, Rom, 1572 coloured engraving, National Library of Sweden, Map collection, KoB, Kartor, 1 ab.

(lower) "Zeno Map." Niccolò Zeno, *The voyages of the Venetian brothers, Nicolò & Antonio Zeno to the northern seas, in the XIVth century, comprising the latest known accounts of the lost colony of Greenland; and of the Northmen in America before Columbus* (London: The Hakluyt Society, 1873). Toronto Reference Library, Baldwin Collection.

Lucas asserted that these pro-Zeno, pro-Sinclair historians "have seemed to find a strange delight in exercising their ingenuity upon endeavors to account for untruths, to explain away difficulties, to excuse mistakes, and to prove that, if certain things had not been such as they undoubtedly were."[9] Lucas reviewed every major map, article, and book that discussed the *Zeno Stories* — over three centuries of references. He methodically dissected the claim that Henry Sinclair was Zichmni, or that Zichmni ever existed, reminding the reader that "notwithstanding the powerful position and great fame attributed by Zeno to Zichmni, his name was unknown to historians."[10] Lucas described the Zichmni-Sinclair connection asserted by Forster and Major and by the Sinclair family as "altogether destitute of foundation."[11]

Lucas also attempted to clear up the confusion over the growing belief among some historians, and particularly among the Sinclair family, that Zichmni, a.k.a. Henry Sinclair, had discovered America. Lucas wisely noted that, "the Zeno narrative nowhere suggests that Zichmni reached either Estotilanda or Drogio, [the New World] but distinctly states that he failed to find them." However, the clarity of Lucas's thought did not shake the beliefs of the Sinclairs or stop them from advocating the supremacy of their ancestor. By the end of the nineteenth century, in some circles at least, it was persistently believed that Earl Henry Sinclair had preceded Columbus by a hundred years, even in the face of Lucas's research.

As this battle between the two Zeno camps, the believers and the non-believers, continued into the twentieth century, a new body of critically important information on the Zeno claims was discovered among the ancient documents stored in the Venetian archives. In 1933, Andrea Da Mosto, the Venetian State Archivist, went looking for the truth behind the *Zeno Stories*. Da Mosto's position allowed him unlimited access to the archives in his search for the footprints that the Zeno family and the brothers Nicolo the Knight and Antonio may have left behind. As the State Archivist, Da Mosto was able to delve deeper into the archives than Cardinal Zurla had in the early nineteenth century, and so was able to discover a remarkable and previously unknown chapter in the history of this noble Venetian family.

Da Mosto's research, which was published in a larger book on Venetian genealogy, is a revelation. According to Da Mosto, we know that our Nicolo, Carlo's brother and the man who would come to be called Nicolo the Knight, was still fighting against the Genoese until 1381. In 1383 he was appointed ambassador to Hungary but never served. In 1388 he was elected to the legislative body of Treviso, just north of Venice. In 1389 he led a squad of naval galleys in the Gulf of Venice, moved to southern Greece as Military Governor in 1390, and returned to Venice in 1392. It is clear from these records that our Nicolo the Knight spent most of the 1380s, indeed most of his life, in or around Venice.[12]

The next decade brought Nicolo's downfall. In 1394 he was accused of having committed embezzlement during his time as Military Governor in Greece.[13] In 1396, after the case was argued in the Venetian criminal courts, Nicolo the Knight was sentenced harshly. He was forced to pay both a sizeable fine as well as compensation to the victims. More critically, he was excluded from public office for five years. For a man who had spent his life in public service, that must have been a great sadness. He withdrew from public life, but was still in Venice in 1400 when his last will and testament was dated.[14] He died soon after. The Venetian archives held no mention of his supposed northern adventures or the discoveries of new lands, no Prince Zichmni, no knighthood. The archival material uncovered by Da Mosto painted a portrait of Nicolo and Antonio that was comprehensive and unexciting. For me, that was the end of the *Zeno Stories*. Nicolo the Younger's elaborate story of letters home describing strange islands, a partnership with a warring prince named Zichmni, and a knighthood bestowed for heroic deeds appears to be a fantastic fabrication made a century and a half after the fact, possibly to erase the stain of crime on a noble family.

In 1558 Venice was enormously rich, one of the greatest cities in Europe. It was an empire with trading partners throughout the known world. It was a city of art experiencing a great renewal, the home of Titian, Veronese, and Palladio. It was a city of grand old families who were probably very cruel to those stained with even the faintest memory of past crimes by their forbears. Carlo the Lion was jailed briefly late in his career, but his heroism and fame erased his misdeeds. Antonio, the youngest son, was a family man without distinction. However, the dreadful deeds of their brother Nicolo must have followed the family for generations. Embezzlement is not only a crime, it is a breach of trust and a violation of official duty, two sins especially serious among a community as tightly woven as the Venetian nobility. A century and a half later, for the forty-three year old Nicolo the Younger, namesake of the fifteenth-century Zeno and a member of one of the leading families in Venice, maybe if this dark mark on his ancestry could not be changed it could at least be papered over.

Nicolo the Younger appears to have reconfigured his ancestral black sheep into a valiant knight and a daring discoverer. He fabricated a Nicolo the Knight who was both prudent and brave, a skillful military leader generous with his power, a noble gentleman, and a caring son of Venice. He gave his ancestor a knighthood, bestowed on him by the Great Zichmni, a prince, warlike and brave, the victor of mighty battles, master of the sea and "as worthy of immortal remembrance as any other who has ever lived in this world." Who would dare question the nobility, the wisdom, the power of one as "worthy of immortal remembrance" as the Great Zichmni of Frislanda? Nicolo the criminal and the embezzler, was reborn as Sir Nicolo Zeno, the Knight. Who can blame Nicolo the Younger for his attempt to whitewash the past? As he made clear in the introduction to his book, the Zenos had a long noble ancestry, and pride is an important family trait.

It is difficult to hold ill feelings towards Nicolo the Knight or the Zeno family. This was the embarrassment of a grand Venetian family. However, his 1394 fraud charge took Nicolo out of the running for a death in Greenland. It also explained the stories written by Nicolo the Younger in 1558. They were simple fabrications, tales of the exotic north he would have heard spoken of in Venice. The map we know is not a *Zeno Map*. Nicolo the Younger copied it. Venice was the centre for those sort of stories and a repository for those sort of maps. For Nicolo, they all served to write a history unlike the one his ancestor had actually lived. The archival research was the death knell for the Zeno saga. Or at least it should have been.

Two very different attitudes towards the Zeno problem have evolved: rational cynicism and blind faith in the truth of Nicolo's story. When Henry Sinclair was added to the mix, Forster's forceful way of arguing made everything seem like a certainty. History was led to believe that the original documents proving the voyages could be found somewhere in the Venetian archives, and that Nicolo's map had undergone the critical analyses of master geographers while hanging in the family home. Both claims were wrong. Nicolo appears to have concocted the entire story to whitewash his ancestor's crimes. Moreover, even if the Zeno stories were true, the belief that Antonio, Nicolo the Knight, or Zichmni had visited the New World is based on an incorrect translation. However, for centuries, simply because Nicolo the Younger belonged to the great Zeno family of Venice, readers of the *Zeno Stories* bowed to his nobility and accepted the tales as being truthful. In turn, the Sinclairs had a marvelous new ancestor, Henry the Holy. The next critical question was how Henry Sinclair had gotten to Guysborough.

15
MYTH BECOMES HISTORY

It seems that some of the Mi'kmaq leadership and a few members of the government of Nova Scotia who helped authorize the construction of the Guysborough monuments have accepted the *Zeno Stories* as being mostly truth, or at least have never bothered to delve too deeply into the theories that these two monuments represent. I think they cannot be blamed, perhaps. The Zeno legends have simmered for centuries in a historical fog. No one knew what was real. Moreover, the Sinclair Clan, with men like Forster and Major in their court, had enough intellectual ammunition to defend their peculiar historical position and understandable family pride. They could show as clearly as the finely written, published page how their ancestor, Henry Sinclair, was believed by some to have sailed with Antonio Zeno to the New World. However, for more than a century, there has been serious doubt about the *Zeno Stories*. The truth has been available, at least since the publication of Zahrtmann, Lucas, and Da Mosto's research. Their convincing refutations have put the advocates of the Zeno adventures in a difficult and untenable situation.

On the older monument in Guysborough, the one located on the shore east of the town, a specific writer had been referenced. The monument stated that it represented, "the claim for Prince Henry's supposed voyage as described in Frederick J. Pohl's authoritative book: *Prince Henry Sinclair His Expedition to the New World 1398*." According to this claim, in addition to the *Zeno Stories*, the monument was based fundamentally on the work of this Frederick Pohl.

In 1961, Frederick J. Pohl, an American editor, author, and playwright, published his first book of speculative history, *Atlantic Crossings Before Columbus*. In it he told the stories of the early Phoenicians, of Brendan of Ireland, and of the Vikings. Before the Viking settlement of L'Anse aux Meadows was discovered in northern Newfoundland, Pohl argued passionately that Vinland could only refer to Cape Cod. He was a dreamer of historical fantasies, and Henry Sinclair was among them. In *Atlantic Crossings Before Columbus*, Henry Sinclair got his own chapter, the last and longest in the book. It was clear that Pohl, like Forster and Major before him, was taken by the story. Pohl did more for Sinclair's image than had ever been done before. He gave him actions, power, a life. Pohl was writing fiction, but he brought Henry Sinclair out of the fog of legend and gave him a history, albeit a make-believe one.

Pohl, it seemed, did not have access to Da Mosto's archival research. This is understandable. The archival research was from a little-known Italian document published in 1933 by the Venetian State Archivist, so not easily accessible. Besides, Pohl had an interest in speculative history, but he was not a historian. He wrote about history that might have been.

A review of Pohl's book in *The Catholic Historical Review*[1] stated that, though Pohl's theories were interesting, he lacked "objective arguments" and relied mostly on "unproven assumptions." The review specifically pointed to his treatment of the *Zeno Stories* in order to underline one of Pohl's fundamental weaknesses: a belief in the fabulous. The critic wrote, "The wholesale acceptance of the Zeno tale without a word of justification is surely amazing in the light of solid evidence of its spuriousness in whole or in part."[2] By the time Pohl was writing, the *Zeno Stories* were simply no longer accepted by serious historians. Too much of their foundation had been eroded: the dates had been proven wrong, the map was a sixteenth-century copy, the fantastic Zeno geography had not survived the test of time, and then there were those fraud charges.

Pohl should have listened to the critic's rebuke and left the *Zeno Stories* to the world of once upon a time. He did not. Henry Sinclair's New World settlement became Pohl's most important theory, that for which he is remembered. As the monument in Guysborough claims, it was Pohl's second book, his 1974 *Prince Henry Sinclair: His Expedition to the New World in 1398*, that formed the intellectual basis — the proof — for the belief currently being advanced by the Sinclair Society, at least a few of the Mi'kmaq leaders, and some members of the government of Nova Scotia. Pohl tried to claim with some authority that, "the authenticity of the narrative has been established."[3] He was wrong. The authenticity of the *Zeno Stories* has never been established, but unfortunately that did not stop people from believing.

Pohl was very clear that everything in the *Zeno Stories* should to be considered authentic and true. The names, dates, and places just needed to be changed to fit with reality. He believed that the Zichmni character was Henry Sinclair, and that Sinclair, along with Antonio Zeno and a navy of several hundred men, sailed to the New World in 1398, specifically to Guysborough Harbour. Pohl believed that Henry Sinclair settled there over the winter and returned to Scotland in the spring. However, Pohl does more than just provide a framework of dates, travels, and discoveries. Pohl is writing historical fiction; he gives Henry Sinclair a personality. He claims Sinclair's initial meeting with Nicolo the Knight at Frislanda was nothing less than "a dramatic meeting of two notable men." It is as if Pohl was writing a script. He has Nicolo the Knight teaching Henry Sinclair the new skill of compass navigation and the latest casting methods for naval artillery. Pohl gave his legendary figures skin and bones and daily lives. Nicolo and Henry became friends. In Pohl's hands they became human. None of it was real, but this technique of storytelling worked. Believers believed him.

We actually know very little about Henry Sinclair, but what is known is mostly insignificant. Just as no reference has ever been found in the Venetian archives of the Zeno adventures in the North, no mention has ever been found in the Scottish archives of Henry Sinclair's supposed cross-Atlantic discovery, no city building, and no surveying of new lands. Nonetheless, through Pohl's lens, Sinclair has been painted as a hero. According to Pohl, Earl Henry Sinclair, "conceived it to be the duty of a lord to labor night and day to cause disorder to cease, and to redress wrongs, and defend all honest men against robbers."[4] In Pohl's hands he became a grand nobleman: honest, true, and good.

Not only did Pohl give Henry Sinclair a personality, he commissioned him with duties and outfitted him with a navy, all simply on the strength of the few threads of information in the *Zeno Stories* that refer to Zichmni of Frislanda. Most important, however, Pohl has Henry Sinclair sailing to the New World. Referencing the Zeno story of the fishermen's visit to the regions of Estotilanda and Drogio, Pohl claimed that although "the discovery of those lands was the fisherman's; the conception of the trans-oceanic expedition was Earl Henry's."[5] Even though the fishermen made the journey on their own, Henry was cast as an adventurer and a hero with visions of the New World in his head. This is fiction. With nothing to base it on, Pohl built an elaborate history out of mythic fog and helped make Henry Sinclair a bit of a saint in the process.

Even though Nicolo the Younger claimed that the wind had blown the Zeno crew back to Greenland, there was no doubt in Pohl's mind that Henry Sinclair and Antonio Zeno did indeed reach the New World with a significant number of ships and men. As they made their supposed landfall, according to Pohl, "there can be no doubt of the identification of Trin Harbour. It was Guysborough."[6] On the *Zeno Map,* the Trin Harbour written about in the *Zeno Stories* is clearly located on the tip of Greenland, but Pohl appears to have ignored the *Zeno Map*. Instead, he based his decision on the mention of "a spring of pitch" and a "smoking hole" that were said to have been seen in the distance of Trin Harbour by Antonio Zeno when he first landed. We know nothing else about the pitch or the smoke and nothing about the location other than Nicolo the Younger claimed it was the southern tip of Greenland. However, a mid-twentieth-century American geologist named Henry Hobbs, who was a fervent supporter of the *Zeno Stories*, had claimed the fourteenth-century mention of pitch and smoke could only point to eastern Nova Scotia.[7] It was a case of quasi-science appearing to support the make-believe.

Pohl elaborated his theory to include the smallest details. Not only did he claim the exact location for Sinclair's landing, he gave the landing an exact date. According to Pohl, Henry Sinclair must have sailed into Guysborough Harbour on Sunday, June 2, 1398. The date was calculated as the probable date of Trinity Sunday. Pohl's rationale for Zichmni naming his discovery Trin Harbour was that Henry Sinclair, being such a holy man, must have named his discovery in honour of Trinity Sunday. Therefore, Sinclair must have discovered Trin Harbour on Trinity Sunday 1398 — June 2. Make sense? That year, 1398, had evolved after the Zeno supporters discovered that Nicolo the Knight had been in Venice during the 1380s, so could not have been sailing in the North Atlantic. They shifted the voyage to the 1390's and rearranged the dates so that 1398 would gave Nicolo and Antonio enough time to get to Frislanda, for Nicolo to die in Greenland, and for Henry Sinclair to have discovered the New World before his death in Scotland in 1400. This is the sort of reasoning that Pohl and his followers have used, all knitted together from "tissues of fiction," as Admiral Zahrtmann called the *Zeno Stories*, all for the purpose of making the story more believable.

All this specificity of detail was built on the vague geographical suggestions of what is now considered by most to be a sixteenth-century Italian forgery. Perhaps it seemed of little harm. However, the whole thing — the Forster and Major books, Pohl's theories, and claims of the believers — begins to become serious when the story enters the realm of the Mi'kmaq legends. This is not a place to try and spin "tissues of fiction."

One of the most important legends in Mi'kmaq traditions is the story of Glooscap, the visiting teacher and great leader who lived among them and who the Mi'kmaq believe helped shape and refine their society. The legend is not only central to Mi'kmaq oral tradition but also plays a significant role in Western history. Glooscap is part of an almost forgotten history, kept alive for centuries by the integrity, clarity, and tenacity of Mi'kmaq storytellers and the truth of their legends. As the representation of a foreign community that visited and lived in the Americas before the European Age of Discovery, Glooscap is key to the story of New World exploration. This early history of the Mi'kmaq is so critically important to Western history because the early history of eastern Canada is the earliest history of the New World, and the history of those first centuries of discovery and settlement is fragile. Who came when, what they did while here, and what they may have left behind are key to future understanding of New World history. The fabricated stories of early visitors may seem insignificant at first, but changing history, complete with erecting stone monuments to little-known Scotsmen and revising revered Aboriginal legends, suggests nothing less than a fundamental shift in the way we understand our past.

Pohl declared, in the same authoritative tone he used with so many other elements in the story, "There can be no doubt that Henry Sinclair was Glooscap." His reasoning? He claimed "Jarl Sinclair" sounded like "Glooscap." In the late eighteenth century, Reverend Forster had claimed that "Zichmni" sounded like "Sinclair." Now Pohl was carrying on the same faulty tradition. "Jarl Sinclair" doesn't sound like "Glooscap." "Zichmni" doesn't sound like "Sinclair." The reasoning is without foundation.

At the core of Pohl's argument for the Glooscap-Sinclair connection was a list he devised of seventeen different elements of the Glooscap legend that appeared to match the life of Henry Sinclair, the Henry Sinclair that Pohl had fabricated. For example, Pohl claims Sinclair arrived by ship. So had Glooscap. Pohl claims Sinclair used a sword. So had Glooscap. Sinclair explored Nova Scotia. So had Glooscap. According to Pohl, both men had similar, "unusual" characters. He painted both men with so broad a brush as to make all these vague parallels inevitable. They both carried swords? Explored Nova Scotia? Unusual characters? Pohl appears to have been making it up as he went along, concocting a Henry Sinclair persona to match the Mi'kmaq legends while keeping the parallels general enough so they would not appear suspiciously inaccurate.

Pohl's historical fiction was finely crafted. He constructed a neatly arranged story around a very faulty premise, supplying details as he needed them, relying on outrageous explanations of implausible feats. According to Pohl, Sinclair settled in Guysborough for the winter with only a few men and the rowboats. His navy had left him. Though stranded, he explored Nova Scotia, laid the foundations for a number of settlements, and then built his own ship — hull, mast, rigging, sails, and all — and sailed back to Scotland in the spring. The claim that a handful of men built an ocean-going sailing ship in the eastern Canadian wilderness during a few months in the winter is so unrealistic to make it the stuff of fantasy, not serious history. Yet Pohl's book had a willing audience.

It is at this point that Pohl, the Sinclair Society, the Mi'kmaq, and the province of Nova Scotia go from appearing to be the purveyors of a romantic fiction to being active players, wittingly or unwittingly, in what might be viewed as a bizarre manipulation of history. Pohl's book was published in 1974. The monument at Halfway Cove was built in 1985. In 1998 at the Boylston Park monument, some of the Mi'kmaq Elders were celebrating the six-hundredth anniversary of Henry Sinclair's supposed visit to Guysborough shoulder to shoulder with members of the Sinclair family. That was less than twenty-five years after Pohl's book.

Even odder than these two monuments is a strange flag that I first saw flying outside the local Mi'kmaq government offices in Guysborough. I found it so odd because it seemed almost Mediaeval looking. It had a pure white background with a large red cross, a five pointed star in one corner and a crescent moon in the other. The cross on the flag was very similar to the red cross on the sail of Henry Sinclair's ship shown on the monument in Boylston Park. The cross made the ship look like it might have been used during the Crusades. That did not surprise me. However, the crescent moon and the five pointed star seemed to be Islamic images, appearing often on the flags of Islamic countries. The Turkish and the Pakistani flags are good examples. The juxtaposition of these images — the Christian cross and the Islamic star and crescent moon — looked so unusual in Nova Scotia and flying in front of the Mi'kmaq offices that it was very difficult to really understanding what I had seen.

Throughout my research on Henry Sinclair I kept coming across references to the Sinclair Clan being involved in the lore of the Crusades through their supposed association with the Knights Templar. The more I read, the more I realized that the Knights Templar were part of the Sinclair story, and I began to see the Mi'kmaq flag differently. There was something haunting about the flag, and I began to think that the Henry Sinclair connection to the Knights Templar may have had something to do with it.

The Mi'kmaq flag was a powerful statement about something, but it was difficult to imagine about what. I began looking at traditional Mi'kmaq visuals, but nothing about the flag seemed traditional. The first description of what appears to be this flag I found in a scholarly article from 1992 describing the Mi'kmaq St. Anne's Festival, an annual religious celebration in

The Mi'kmaq Grand Council Flag.

honour of the Mi'kmaq patron saint. Before that day in 1992 there seemed to be no earlier mention of this Mi'kmaq flag with the red cross, at least none that I could find. The writer of the 1992 article attended the festival and described the flag as "seen flying everywhere."[8] That it had been hung in such profusion was unusual. It seemed to have appeared quite suddenly. I also found an image of the flag in a Dalhousie University graduate thesis from 1996, but the student gave no reference for its source.[9]

A book called *The Sinclair Saga,* published in Halifax in 1999 by a writer named Mark Finnan, seems to hold some clues. Like Pohl, Finnan appears to have been a firm believer in the *Zeno Stories* and in the fundamental truth of the Henry Sinclair legend. Most important, he showed an illustration of the Mi'kmaq Grand Council flag and explained where he had seen it.[10] Finnan described attending a Sinclair conference in August 1997, organized and hosted by members of the Scottish Sinclair family in the small town of Kirkland, on the Orkney Islands off the far northern coast of Scotland. According to Finnan, one of the conference leaders was Niven Sinclair, a name I recognized from the Guysborough monuments. Some Mi'kmaq leaders were also at the conference: the Mi'kmaq historian Peter Christmas; Don Julien, the executive director of the Confederacy of Mainland Mi'kmaq; and Kerry Prosper, the chief of the Afton Mi'kmaq band, the region in which Guysborough is located. Chief Prosper's name appears on one of the Guysborough monuments alongside Niven Sinclair's.

Finnan described how, at a reception held during this Sinclair Conference, the Mi'kmaq representatives presented their Grand Council Flag to the host town of Kirkland. This was the flag with the red cross, the five-pointed star, and crescent moon. When the flag was displayed, Finnan claims, "On seeing the flag, a Templar historian attending the reception immediately commented on the fact that this flag was practically a mirror image of a flag sometimes used by the Templar fleets during the crusades."[11] According to Finnan's account, this similarity between the Templar flag and the Mi'kmaq flag was further highlighted by Niven Sinclair in a presentation he gave at the conference. As Finnan wrote of the two flags, "to most of the attendees this was taken as further circumstantial evidence that Prince Henry Sinclair, whose family had known connections to the Templars, had made it to Nova Scotia."[12]

This was the first concrete reference to a source I had seen. Finnan's book displayed the two flags side by side, and there is no doubt that they were almost identical. Each flag has a large distinctive red cross running through the centre of a white rectangular field, and both flags also have a star and a crescent moon shown in each of the two corners on the left side of the flag. Was it possible that a Templar flag had been adopted by the Mi'kmaq? Could Henry Sinclair and the Templars actually have visited Guysborough during the winter of 1398? Six hundred years later and, remarkably, the two flags were still almost identical. Was that possible?

The two flags shown at the Sinclair Conference, August 1997. (left) The flag said to be the Fleet Battle Flag of the Knights Templar and (right) the Mi'kmaq Grand Council Flag.

I realized the Knights Templar might provide some answers. At least it was a place to start. The Templars were real. They have a history: authentic, documented, and well-studied. However, there are also multiple layers of mythical stories attached to them, many of them growing out of eighteenth- and nineteenth-century fantasies.

The real history of the Order started with nine knights in 1118. Twenty years before, the First Crusade had ended in the capture of Jerusalem by the Christian armies. Travel to the Middle East soon became a dangerous journey for the growing number of Christian pilgrims coming to the Holy Land. These nine knights presented themselves to the King of Jerusalem, Baudouin I, the brother of the man who had helped capture the city during the First Crusade, Godfroi de Bouillon. The knights pledged to safeguard the Holy Land. Taking an oath of poverty, they then moved into a wing of the ruined royal palace.

The idea of this new Order was both logical and ingenious. Their goal was to act as warrior knights to protect European Christian pilgrims, but they were also monks and lived the strict life of a monastic community. They could be trusted. They belonged to Rome. In their pure white tunics with red crosses, they provided a powerful image for their role as protectors of Christianity's most holy relics. The Templar image became an icon of stability, safety, and faith.

Within twenty years, the Templar Order had grown beyond all expectations. It became wealthy, acquiring significant properties throughout Britain, Europe, and the Middle East. It was powerful. Through the twelfth and thirteenth centuries the Templar Knights became some of the principal money handlers in Europe. They helped establish the institution of banking. When the last of the Holy Land was returned to the Muslims in 1291, the Templars retired to Europe but continued to use their religious houses to control the European money system. They were known as honest bankers and well-connected statesmen. Kings used them, popes used them. The Order, especially without the drain of its vast expenditures in the Holy Land, remained a wealthy and powerful force. They became the stuff of legend.

Their mystique in history was assured by the arrest of the entire order by the French king, Philip IV, on Friday, October 13, 1307. Philip needed money. In order to get it, he arrested every Templar living in France in one superbly organized move. The knights were charged with heresy, sexual license, and worshipping idols. Other European countries followed suit and arrested the Templars under the same charges, all with the blessing of Pope Clement V, a close ally of the French king. The goods and territories of the Templars were seized. Five years after the initial French arrests, the pope dissolved the Order, and in 1314 the last Grand Master of the Templars, Jacques de Molay, was burnt at the stake in Paris. The Knights Templar were destroyed.

Some believe that a group of Templars escaped during their persecution in France and sailed to northern Scotland, to the Sinclair lands.[13] The legend of this Sinclair-Templar connection, however, began to appear only in the eighteenth and nineteenth centuries, relatively recently. It is a story that has no original documentation to corroborate it, but it is also impossible to disprove.[14] For those few Templars who might have escaped capture, almost anything would have been possible, and so those who might have slipped into the fog of history have only added to the fantasy. It is what has made legends grow around the Order with such great fertility.

In all the research on the Knights Templar, I could find no flag like the ones shown at the Sinclair Conference, the ones that apparently connected Henry Sinclair, the Mi'kmaq, and the Knights Templar. No flag with a red cross, a star, and a crescent moon appeared anywhere in Templar history. The red cross appeared on the white tunics they wore as uniforms. On the battlefield they carried a simple and easily recognizable banner of a black square and a white square, one above the other, sometimes with a black cross on the white.[15] However, nowhere in the literature could I find an image of any other flag flown by the original Templars.

In the several weeks after finding the images of the two flags side by side in Finnan's book, I sent out emails to two of the Mi'kmaq who had been at the 1997 conference and to the Templar historian at the conference who Finnan credits for supplying the image of the Templar flag. I had hoped to get some information from them on the Mi'kmaq flag, on its origins and its history, and also some insight into the flag that the Templar historian at the Sinclair Conference had claimed was a Templar flag. At the same time I sent out similar requests for information on the flag to two of the world's most respected Templar specialists, Malcolm Barber, professor of mediaeval history at the University of Reading, and Helen Nicholson from the History Department at Cardiff University.

The two Mi'kmaq who had attended the Sinclair conference did not respond to my questions, nor did the Templar historian from the Sinclair Conference. In contrast to this silence, the two Templar scholars, both internationally recognized historians, responded immediately and concisely to my questions regarding the two flags. Neither Professors Barber nor Nicholson had ever seen the flag said to be a Templar flag that had been shown at the Sinclair Conference. According to them, it was not in Templar history and not original to the Templars. The Templars had not flown a flag like this. These two scholars, more than anyone, would have recognized any flag that the Order had flown, and they not did recognize this one.

According to Finnan, at the 1997 conference Niven Sinclair claimed that, "the similarity of the two flags was either a remarkable coincidence or evidence of contact between Europe and North America involving the Templars."[16] The similarity may be neither. The flags do not appear to be a coincidence. Their iconography is almost identical except the vertical axis has been flipped so that one flag is a mirror image of the other. Nor do these two flags appear to be evidence of early contact. There has been no history written of the Mi'kmaq using a flag given to them in the fourteenth century by a Scottish Earl or by the Knights Templar. There are no records, no documents. If the Mi'kmaq had been given such a flag, representing evidence of such early contact, it would be all through the history books. Could the flag be a modern attempt at binding Henry Sinclair's history, through his supposed Knights Templar roots, to that of the Mi'kmaq?

There is at least one historical image associated with the Knights Templar that includes a five pointed star and a crescent moon, but the image is only a fantasy drawn from the imagination of a nineteenth-century French magician and occultist named Alphonse Louis Constant.[17] Constant wrote under the name Eliphas Levi. In 1854, Levi published a book titled *Dogme et Rituel de la Haute Magie* in which he included an illustration of a strange beast he had drawn: an androgynous form, part human, part goat, both winged and cloven hoofed. He called the creature Baphomet and cloaked it in Knights Templar mythology.

Levi claimed this Baphomet creature he designed was one of the idols worshipped by the Knights Templar. Levi wrote, "in our profound conviction, the Grand Masters of the Order of the Templars adored Baphomet, and caused it to be adored by their initiatives."[18] During their fourteenth-century torture in France, a number of Templars spoke of a Baphomet in their confessions, but the term Baphomet is believed to have been an early Westernized form of Mohammed, the Prophet of Islam, a reference made during Templar trials to the their life in the Middle East.[19] In the mid-nineteenth century, Levi took this possible Knights Templar reference to Mohammed as having been the name of an actual idol worshipped throughout the Order. He added the star and the crescent moon to his drawing as a reference to their association with the Middle East. No original image of any such icon has ever surfaced from the time of the Templars. The goat-headed, winged beast was only in the imagination of Levi the Magician. His Baphomet image appears to be pure nineteenth-century fiction. To Levi, writing about magic and the occult, it was supposed to represent the great dualities of the cosmos: light/dark, good/evil, male/female. However, with the name of the Knights Templar welded on, it gave Levi some gloss of historical validity.

Levi's nineteenth-century image of the idol Baphomet became well known. Moreover, it gave those interested in the Knights Templar a mysterious, new image to grasp onto. By some, Levi's Baphomet image was believed to be something actually used by the Knights Templar, an idol worshipped by them. It was not, but some may still believe it was. With the red cross copied from the Templar tunics and with the star and the crescent moon copied from a much more recent illustration such as Levi's Baphomet, someone could have designed a flag that appeared to have originated from the Templars. That may have been the source to the Templar-like flag that was shown at the Sinclair Conference in 1997. Might it also be the basis for the Mi'kmaq flag? As the Chair of the Sinclair Conference noted, the similarity of the two flags is undeniable.

This flag with the red Templar cross and the star and the moon appears to have no early history among the Mi'kmaq. When I tried to find the meaning of the flag, the explanations that had been recently published appeared confused. The most official explanation is included in

"Prominent Flags of the Mi'Kmaq Nation," a section of the website First Nation History[20] written by Daniel Paul, a well-known Mi'kmaq elder. Daniel Paul shows two Mi'kmaq flags. The first, the Mi'kmaq National Flag, is a white flag with a graphic of two simple flags with their staffs crossed and what appears to be a sunrise drawn between them. Paul writes that this Mi'kmaq National Flag was first raised in Listuguj, Quebec, in 1900 and then in Halifax, Nova Scotia, in 1901. The symbolism appears to be completely Christian. Paul explains it as representing "the Father, Son and The Holy Spirit" and "Christ who was crucified on the Cross."[21]

Daniel Paul's website also gives an explanation of the second flag, the Mi'kmaq Nation Flag or the Grand Council Flag. This is the flag that the Mi'kmaq presented at the Sinclair conference and which now flies in front of some of the buildings that house their offices. Unlike the Mi'kmaq National Flag, Paul gives neither a location nor a date when this Grand Council Flag was first raised.[22] Only the iconography is explained. The white background is said to represent "the purity of creation,"[23] yet at the annual Mi'kmaq St. Anne's Festival, held in 1991, where the flag was said to be "seen flying everywhere,"[24] the Mi'kmaq explained that the white background represented "the extensiveness of the Mi'kmaq territory within the Atlantic Provinces."[25] Paul's website explains that the red cross represents "mankind and infinity"[26] while at the 1991 festival it was explained to simply represent the church.[27] The crescent moon represents either "the forces of night"[28] or "the land of the Mi'kmaq."[29] The star is the sun.[30] The meaning of these images seems uncertain. The iconography appears not to have developed with time, certainly not six hundred years of it, but seems to be much more recent and is still evolving and unsure.

The seeming confusion of what this flag represents strikes at the heart of Mi'kmaq legends, and the Mi'kmaq legends are key to the writing of New World history. Those ancient legends tell of early visitors. That is why the *Zeno Stories*, and in turn the Henry Sinclair legends, sound almost plausible. Yet they are not. This confused sense of history has harmed the clarity of the ancient stories long remembered by the Mi'kmaq. The legend of Glooscap is now shrouded in the murky fog of what most historians now consider a sixteenth-century Italian forgery.

Woven into these stories has been the suggestion that the Knights Templar somehow controlled, or were responsible for, or had hidden away the Holy Grail. At various times in the past, the Grail has been believed — by those who believe such stories — to have been a wide range of different holy objects. Since the publication of the 1982 book *The Holy Blood and the Holy Grail* by Michael Baigent, Richard Leigh and Henry Lincoln and the subsequent *The Da Vinci Code* by Dan Brown in 2003, the Holy Grail is now thought by some people to be the two thousand year old bloodline of Jesus.

No longer is it seen as an object: a cup used at the Last Supper, or the bowl that held the blood shed on the cross, or a platter, or a tray, or a box, or mystical tablets. Now it is the specific genetics of a single bloodline supposedly started two thousand years ago. The modern-day Grail believers think that Jesus and one of his followers, Mary Magdalene, had children. They claim that the Marriage Feast of Cana, the well-known water into wine miracle, stands as proof. In their eyes, only a groom would have been responsible for providing wine at his own wedding. After the marriage and a brief life together, Mary supposedly sailed across the Mediterranean with the children, apparently to Marseilles in the south of France. So began a two-thousand-year-old lineage. There are no records. However, it seems that the Sinclairs have become part of this holy DNA mythology. Remarkably, some of the modern Sinclairs have begun to believe that a tiny but extremely important bit of this holy DNA might be running in their veins.[31] Their story also has Henry Sinclair taking his holy blood to Guysborough along with the Grail protectors, the Knights Templar, in his command.[32]

The Sinclair story has been included in much that has been written about the Knights Templar and the Holy Grail. Not surprisingly, perhaps one of the most complete works in this category of history has been written by a member of the Sinclair family, a writer named Andrew Sinclair, cousin of Niven Sinclair. It is Andrew Sinclair's 1992 book *The Sword and the Grail: The Story of the Grail, the Templars and the True Discovery of America* that most thoroughly and clearly explains the story of Henry Sinclair and his visit to the North America. In his title, the "True Discovery of America" of which Andrew Sinclair speaks is Henry Sinclair's supposed landfall in Guysborough. Sinclair is forceful in what he believes. He claims that, "With the help of the sea skills and wealth of the Templars, a St. Clair prince tried to found a new Jerusalem in the New World, landing with three hundred colonists, first in what is now Nova Scotia, and then in New England, a hundred years before Columbus."[33] These are the sort of claims, a New Jerusalem and all, that have been embraced by some as serious history. That is why the monuments have been built in Nova Scotia. Fundamentally, it is this remarkable claim made by some members of the Sinclair family that the new Mi'kmaq flag appears to represent.

Andrew Sinclair expanded on Pohl's theory that Henry Sinclair came to Guysborough in 1398, spent the winter, and left in the spring. According to Andrew Sinclair, Earl Henry was busy. The writer has his ancestor establishing an empire in the New World, an empire "run by the Military and Monastic orders." He claims that Henry settled in Guysborough and built his ships, then headed south along the coast to discover New England. Henry had supposedly organized a group of monks he left behind on Cape Breton Island to plant crops over the winter. By the time Henry returned from his winter voyage, sailing in his ocean-going fleet built from what nature could supply him, Andrew Sinclair claims the monks in Nova Scotia "would have already gathered their first crops." All of this appears to be based solely on the *Zeno Stories*.

Moreover, although the *Zeno Stories* are clear on very few things, Zeno the Younger definitely claims that a mythical prince named Zichmni landed and settled for a brief period on the southern tip of Greenland, not anywhere in North America. That is really all Nicolo the Younger wrote in terms of discovery: no Henry Sinclair, no Guysborough, no Knights Templar, no Holy Grail, and no flag. These other claims are based on a mistranslation of an already fictional story, and are served up as true history, published as if it were reality. The modern Sinclair Society has been attempting to carve a niche in history, and they have been convincing enough to bring some of the Mi'kmaq and some of the provincial government leaders along with them.

To the Sinclairs, the Holy Grail is a key element in their historical association with the Knights Templar. When the Grail was thought to have been an object — a cup or bowl — Rosslyn Chapel, the Sinclair family chapel, was said to have housed it secretly, hidden inside a column. Now that the Grail is seen as holy DNA, the focus has shifted. In the recent past, writers have attempted to weave together a number of theories to support this new historical construction: Sinclairs fighting in the Crusades, Knights Templar escaping to Scotland carrying treasure, and Earl Henry Sinclair's supposed stay among the Mi'kmaq with Grail Knights keeping guard.

Some members of the modern Sinclair family are involved in a project to map their DNA. At first glance, this Sinclair DNA-mapping project might seem like a simple family venture. However, I discovered that this investigation began with the remarkable hypothesis, advocated by the founder of the project, Steve Sinclair, that "when enough myths persist, there may be a grain of truth in them. There may be some basis in reality to the legends of our association with the Templars, a Holy Bloodline, the Prince Henry St. Clair stories about early voyaging to the New World, and more."[34] This hypothesis is stated quite clearly. Many of the Sinclairs appear to take it very seriously.

DNA from the Son of God makes for a great story. Is this mythology, the idea of being an ancestor of God, what helped captivate the Mi'kmaq about the Sinclair claims of Henry the Holy's visit with the Knights Templar? The Mi'kmaq were and continue to be a strongly Christian community. The explanation given for the iconography of the Mi'kmaq National Flag makes that clear. One of their great historical figures, Chief Membertou, was baptized by the French in 1610, the first Aboriginal leader to be baptized by the Jesuits in the New World. The Mi'kmaq Christian faith has been one of the foundations of their community. If Henry Sinclair and the Templar Knights had actually visited Nova Scotia, settled among them, and even sired offspring, or at least if the Sinclairs had convinced the Mi'kmaq that they may have, as far-fetched as it sounds, this would bring the legendary bloodline of Jesus to the shores of Guysborough and into the homes of the modern day Mi'kmaq. To the Mi'kmaq, that might have been important. It could have been enough of a reason for embracing the Sinclair story as one of their own legends.

Clearly there was also support for the Sinclair legend from the provincial authorities. Both the Nova Scotia Department of Natural Resources and the Nova Scotia Department of Economic Development and Tourism were thanked on the Sinclair monument erected in Boylston. In June 1998 the Nova Scotia Legislative Assembly, the chief governing body of the province, adopted a formal resolution recognizing the Henry Sinclair legend, his trip to the New World with "12 ships and 300 crew,"[35] and his 1398 landing in Guysborough. The resolution congratulated the Sinclair Society and wished them "every success in their quest to authenticate the arrival of Prince Henry in North America."[36]

Presenting the two flags side by side at the 1997 conference was just what was needed in order to suggest that there had been a relationship between Henry Sinclair and the Mi'kmaq. Given that the Sinclair family was believed by some to have had Templar roots, the connections must have fallen neatly into place. The underlying premise had been laid by centuries of mythmaking: from Zeno to Zichmni; from Zichmni to Henry Sinclair; from Greenland to Guysborough. With the matching iconography of the two flags, in the eyes of both the Sinclair Society and some of the Mi'kmaq leaders, over a few months in 1398, Henry Sinclair, the Knights Templar and the Holy Grail had visited Eastern Canada. For those attending the 1997 conference, it seems that the two flags were perhaps the final proof.

The Prince Henry saga, the two monuments that have been erected in Guysborough, and the matching flags that appear to look like they originated from the Templars, all starkly illuminate our centuries-old search for something that continues to call out from the distant past. It is the "lost chapter" that Reverend Patterson referred to at the end of the nineteenth century. These forgotten ancient visitors have been called pirates, rovers of the sea, and white men who came before the French. Now there are those who claim they were knights and farming monks led by a fourteenth-century Scottish earl who had the blood of the Holy Grail flowing in his veins.

Is it not obvious that this region of the world holds the key to a confused but mysterious history that seems to have faded into the deepest corners of long ago, a remarkable past that we sense was almost erased from memory just as the European Age of Discovery was beginning? But we have not been able to forget that lost past. The nineteenth-century historians of Saint Peters wrote about it, the Mi'kmaq recall it in their legends, and it still has the power to make us search for answers. The frustration of not knowing is clear. The flag that the Mi'kmaq now fly, said by some to have been born of one the Knights Templar once flew, is a powerful reminder that we continue to struggle in this search.

The ruins at Saint Peters, in the form of deeply buried memories possibly once built by the hands of ancient settlers, remind us of that forgotten history much more powerfully than banners of Templar-like iconography or modern monuments based on the sixteenth-century Zeno letters. A story is written in these ruins. The voice of an ancient canal, shown on the earliest maps, cannot be silenced. What was here? Who left such marks on our land?

We are searching for clues amid the darkness of a time long ago, a time lost not just to the small island of Cape Breton but lost to all human history. The island, as it did when shipping ruled the world, may again represent a critical point of transition in the world. Someday it may be home to the discovery and understanding of a remarkable lost chapter in our past. Who were these rovers of the sea, these maritime adventurers who were able to build on such a massive scale? Their memory refuses to be forgotten.

Epilogue:

ATTEND TO THE ORIGINAL FACTS

> To say anything about the nature of things you must attend to the facts, facts in their original form. The trouble with knowledge is that it keeps chiseling things away.[1]
>
> —Mencius

One of the most visually memorable stories told by the Mi'kmaq is their legend that before the time of European settlement they were visited by a floating island that had come to rest just off their shore. The island had tall trees on it, and on the trees the Mi'kmaq thought they could see bears, which seemed to be crawling among the branches.[2] The floating island turned out to be a massive ship, the trees its tall masts, and the bears crawling through the branches were the crew in the rigging. Some of the visitors came to shore in a smaller boat they had lowered from their ship, and one of them, clothed in white, addressed the Mi'kmaq with signs of friendship. Historians believed this legend was the Mi'kmaq account of one of their first visits by Europeans, so the visit was thought to have occurred during the late fifteenth or early sixteenth century, the era of some of the earliest European maritime adventures. However, like so much of the region's early history, this may be an attempt by those scholars who first recorded the Mi'kmaq legends to fit this floating island story into a European framework, the only framework these early historians would have imagined. Moreover, this European attribution assumes that the Mi'kmaq, born on the coast and considered master navigators and sailors, would have been so astounded by the colossal presence of these small European ships that they would have considered them floating islands.

Another important memory that the Mi'kmaq record in their legends gives an even more specific description of who these visitors may have been. The Mi'kmaq claim that these earliest visitors used marks for writing, "a mark standing for a word."[3] What culture was writing with graphic characters or marks, each character representing a word? What culture was sailing ships so large they could easily have been mistaken for floating islands, with masts so dense in number that they that would have been mistaken for trees? What country's maritime crews were clothed in white robes as their standard uniform? Although the early maritime history of China was not available to nineteenth- and twentieth-century historians, we now know that these early Mi'kmaq legends appear to point very specifically to the Chinese fleets that were sailing for hundreds of years before the first European visits to the New World.

When the focus is shifted away from an exclusively European influence behind the mysterious history of the Island of Seven Cities, an early Chinese presence becomes logical in every element of the discussion. For example, the cannon found in the ruins at Saint Peters was seen as unimportant, yet, archaic and simple in its construction, it was a curiosity when found because the iron of which it was made was of such an unusually high quality, the best iron the local blacksmith had ever seen. It is a small element in the research and is hardly enough evidence on which to base a rewriting of New World history. However, these many individual memories, records, observations, and legends, when seen and woven tentatively together for the first time, begin to build a strong and unshakable foundation for the theory of pre-Columbian Chinese settlement in the region.

Similarly, the ruins on Mount Grenville cannot be explained away simply as a badly managed building project started and finished in a single winter in 1793 by a small group of English soldiers. Why would they have built on the top of a hill, cutting down trees and levelling wilderness in the frozen weather, when the much more convenient site of the earlier French ruins lay abandoned on the shore? The raised platform on the mountainside, an area already cleared of wilderness, with a sweeping view of the bay and ocean beyond, must have been seen as even more convenient. The French cartographers had shown the outline of this platform along with the roads connecting it to the shore almost a century earlier. Who built the ruins that the French drew?

Then there is the mystery of the small fort on the shore of Saint Peters. It raises too many difficult questions to be catalogued with such certainty as a simple structure left behind by a seventeenth-century New World entrepreneur. Earlier settlers, the *Compagnie de Cap-Breton*, appear to have mentioned the fort in their correspondence as already built; Denys, not liking where the entrance was placed, wanted it moved; the fort's walls were constructed not of roughly mounded earth but of seemingly carefully constructed and compacted earth layers, just as the Chinese built; archaeologists found no remains of pickets or post holes in the layered earth walls suggesting that the walls had never been used to hold the wooden palisade typical of a fort built by early European settlers. This list of clues suggests another, different, and earlier story behind these ruins. Added to this was the discovery by the team of archaeologists of an older layer of remains found under the ruins of Nicolas Denys's fire. This deeper level of history has never been investigated. There is more to the story.

And then there is the enigma of the canal. All we know is that there was a canal across this isthmus that appears to have been built before Europeans began settling the area. It is shown on the earliest maps of the region, dating back to the 1490 Columbus map of the Island of Seven Cities and repeated by Lescarbot, Champlain, Sanson, and Coronelli. In 1597 the captain of the *Hopewell* called it a "road" on which one of his ships had become stuck. In 1606, to underline its presence across the isthmus, Champlain, who lived in the region, claimed there was an entrance through to the centre of the island from the south, from the Saint Peters side across the isthmus. Nicolas Denys appears to have built the Haulover Road to drag boats across the isthmus through this canal, and

Ensign Prenties, thinking that this "communication" had been dug by the French military in the early part of the eighteenth century, described the cut — as seen through the knowledgeable eyes of a sailor — as once having been able to accommodate large French warships. The ancient canal at Saint Peters cannot be ignored. The maps are clear. But perhaps it can be explained. Were the Chinese mining gold here in Nova Scotia, using this short canal to ferry their barges of ore from the goldfields of the mainland across into the Bras d'Or Lakes, the Arm of Gold, and out to the deep water port on the east coast of Cape Breton?

David Ingram's narrative confirms the Chinese presence. The Mi'kmaq storytellers were so sure in the "the shape and figure of ships, and of their sails and flags" that Ingram was convinced, again through the knowledgeable eyes of a sailor, that these were Chinese ships the Mi'kmaq were describing. To Ingram, the fact that the Chinese had been visiting the coast seemed secondary to the suggestion that the Northwest Passage had been clear and free of ice, and once used to sail across the top of the world. Did the British already know that the Chinese had been to the Americas?

Ingram's casual mention of horses and elephants no longer serves to discredit his narrative, as it did in the late sixteenth century, but appears now as solid proof. Who else but the Chinese were able to carry such a collection of large animals on their ships? Even if this strange cargo were a fantasy from Ingram's mind, would he have thought of elephants? Yet we now know this was possible for the early Chinese fleets. The records are clear. The Chinese ships were known to carry both domestic and wild animals, for food, trade, and as labour, and even generations after the Chinese had stopped sailing it is possible that distant relatives of this Chinese cargo could still be found in the Americas.

We no longer have reason to dismiss Ingram's reports — or the Mi'kmaq claims — because of their seeming outrageous "incredibilities." In the same way, we no longer can so easily ignore the early Mi'kmaq legends that the ruins in Saint Peters were built by settlers "before the French." For centuries these Aboriginal claims of early visitors to their land have been overlooked. No wonder the Mi'kmaq have embraced the Sinclair story and all it means. Someone finally listened to them. Sadly, however, there were other motives behind the sixteenth-century Zeno letters that have come to form the basis for this new rendition of history. As Pohl's reviewers claimed, the *Zeno Stories* is "now considered spurious in whole or in part." The remarkable adventure of Henry Sinclair and the Templar Knights and their pre-Columbian visit to North America depends on this collection of letters that, since Da Mosto's exhaustive mid-twentieth-century research in the Venetian archives, have been shown to be sixteenth-century forgeries written to help erase the fraud charges of a fourteenth-century Zeno ancestor. It is not the stuff on which to build the history of a region and the history of its people, and is a sadly unstable base on which to build monuments hoping to celebrate a great proud past.

Nonetheless, the unfortunate introduction of the *Zeno Stories* in an attempt to reframe New World history has helped highlight one very important element of the past: the remarkable map of the Far North and the ancient cartographers who drew it. Before Europeans had the technical ability, there was a well-surveyed map of Greenland. Where had this map come from? As with so much of this story, we are forced to ponder the question of who had the ships, the technology, and the manpower to make such a survey before the fifteenth century. Consistently, the answers to the nagging questions of who possibly could have done these things — ships like floating islands, cannon formed of remarkable iron, canals cut in the wilderness, raised platforms on hillsides, surveys made and maps drawn of little known northern coastlines — all seem to intersect in one place, Ancient China. In each and every case, China had the ability to build, to sail, to transport, to survey, and to organize all of this. Gradually and patiently over the coming generations, China may provide the answers to many of the historical mysteries which continue to linger in our past.

There is more work to be done. Explaining the theory of early Chinese settlement and the possible reasons behind these settlements is just a first tentative step in writing a new history of the region. The theory needs to be tested. An archaeological dig of the ruins in Saint Peters and of Cape Dauphin is the next step. And there are other sites on Cape Breton Island that may add to the full understanding of this remarkable history. We may be at a turning point, a beginning and an ending, and as was said of an earlier theory, changing our long-held convictions is one of the most difficult of human journeys.

Acknowledgements

This book could not have been written without the unconditional love of my family. To each of them individually, thank you for helping to build a solid, lasting, and trustworthy foundation on which to stand.

To Marian Hebb, who never stopped believing that this story needed to be told. I hope this book stands as a small recognition of your unfailing support.

To the staff of the Toronto Reference Library, especially the librarians of the Baldwin Collection, thank you.

Thank you to Dundurn Press and to all those who helped make this book possible: Sheila Douglas, Carrie Gleason, Margaret Bryant, Courtney Horner, and Jim Hatch. To my editor, Michael Melgaard, who helped make sense out of the early draft of this manuscript and who guided it through to the final publication, thank you. And especially to Kirk Howard, the publisher of Dundurn Press, thank you for believing that this story is an important chapter in Canadian history.

Finally, to my good friends Rob and Beth. They continue to be the very best companions anyone could hope for on this journey. To them, my love.

Notes

Prologue: A Shipwreck's Tale

1. Samuel Walter Prenties, *Castaway on Cape Breton: Ensign Prenties' Narrative of Shipwreck at Margaree Harbour, 1780,* ed. G.G. Campbell (Wreck Cove, NS: Breton Books, 2001), 10.
2. Ibid., 68.

Introduction: The Path to the Second City

1. For a concise history of the project, see the following three short videos: "The Island of Seven Cities, Part One: History and Geography," https://www.youtube.com/watch?v=KkxIP-gLLxU; "The Island of Seven Cities, Part Two: The Site," https://www.youtube.com/watch?v=PWKeATzqXPQ; "The Island of Seven Cities, Part Three: The Indigenous People" https://www.youtube.com/watch?v=O4NDdiQZNvk.
2. Daniel Boorstin, *The Discoverers: A History of Man's Search to Know His World and Himself* (New York: Vintage Books, 1985), 476.
3. "The Island of Seven Cities, Part Two: The Site."
4. Ibid.
5. Ibid.

1: The Ruins on the Shore

1. David Lee, "The French Forts on St. Peters Bay," in *Agenda Paper* (Ottawa: The Historic Sites and Monuments Board of Canada, 1981), 345.
2. Robert Le Blant, "Les Compagnies du Cap-Breton 1629–1647," in *Revue d'histoire de l'Amérique française* 16, no. 1 (1962), 87.
3. Lee, "French Forts," 345.
4. Clarence-Joseph d'Entremont, *Nicolas Denys, Sa Vie et Son Oeuvre* (Yarmouth, NS: L'imprimerie Lescarbot Ltée, 1982), 464.
5. Nicolas Denys, *The Description and Natural History of the Coasts of North America (Acadia)*, trans. and ed. William R. Ganong (Toronto: Champlain Society, 1908), 176.
6. Sieur de La Roque, *The 1752 Census of Isle Royale (Known as Cape Breton Island) as a Result of the Inspection Made by Sieur de La Roque* (Pawtucket, RI: Quinton Publication, 1997), 14.
7. Thomas Pichon, *Genuine Letters and Memoirs Relating to the Natural, Civil, and Commercial History of the Island of Cape Breton and Saint John from the First Settlement there to the Taking of Louisbourg by the English in 1758* (London: J. Nourse, 1760), 38.
8. Lee, "French Forts," 347.
9. Eric Krause, *The Built History of Port Toulouse, Isle Royale, Actual and Proposed, 1713–1758,* 1, 1 (Cape Breton, NS: Krause House Info-Research Solutions, 1998, revised, 1998, 2004), 5.
10. Thomas C. Haliburton, *History of Nova Scotia* (Belleville, ON: Mika Publishing, 1973).
11. R.G. Haliburton, "Lost Colonies of Northmen and Portuguese," *Popular Science Monthly*, 27 (May 1885), 48.
12. Richard Brown, *A History of the Island of Cape Breton* (Belleville, ON: Mika Publishing Company, 1979), 89.
13. Robert R. McLeod, *Markland or Nova Scotia: Its History, Natural Resources and Native Beauties* (Toronto: J.L. Nichols Company, 1902), 495.
14. George Patterson, "The Portuguese on the North-East Coast of America and the First European Attempt at Colonization There: A Lost Chapter in American History," *Proceedings and Transactions of the Royal Society of Canada for the Year 1890* 8, section 2 (1891), 169.
15. Ibid.

2: Rovers of the Sea

1. Denys, *The Description and Natural History*, 178.
2. Ibid.
3. Ibid.
4. Ibid.
5. Birgitta Wallace, *Nicolas Denys Fort Saint Pierre Archaeological Report*, unpublished report for the Historic Sites and Monuments Board of Canada, 1986, 55.
6. Ibid., 21.
7. Ibid.
8. Ibid., 29.

3: The Ruins on Mount Grenville

1. Lee, "French Forts," 351.
2. Ibid., 352.
3. Canada Historic Sites and Monuments Board of Canada, "Fort Dorchester, or 'Fort Grenville', St. Peter's, Cape Breton," *Agenda Paper* 39 (Ottawa, 1966), 19.
4. Ibid., 20.
5. Ibid., note 21, 20.
6. Ibid., note 18, 20.
7. Brown, *A History of the Island of Cape Breton*, 407.
8. Denys, *The Description and Natural History*, note, 178.
9. Canada Historic Sites and Monuments Board of Canada, *Agenda Paper* 39: 20.
10. Tony E. Walker, *St. Peter's Canal: A Narrative and Structural History* (Ottawa: National Historic Parks and Sites Branch, Parks Canada, Department of Indian Affairs and Northern Affairs, 1973), 102.

4: The Mark of an Ancient Canal

1. Richard Hakluyt, T*he Principal Navigations, Voyages, Traffiques, and Discoveries of the English Nation, XIII,* 2 (Edinburgh: Edmund Goldsmith, 1889), 62–76.
2. Ibid., 68.
3. Ibid.

4. Ibid.
5. Ibid., 69.
6. Samuel de Champlain, *Voyages of Samuel de Champlain, 1604–1618*, ed. W.L. Grant (New York: Charles Scribner and Sons, 1907), 117.
7. Denys, *The Description and Natural History*, 179.
8. Lee, "French Forts," 349.
9. Ibid.
10. Ibid.
11. Prenties, *Castaway on Cape Breton*, 68.
12. Brown, *A History of the Island of Cape Breton*, 418.
13. Walker, *St. Peter's Canal.*
14. Ibid., 27.
15. Ibid., 36.
16. Ibid., 35.

5: A Cannon from the Past

1. Patterson, "The Portuguese," 164.
2. Ibid.
3. J.G. Bourinot, "Cape Breton and Its Memorials of the French Regime," *Proceedings and Transactions of the Royal Society of Canada for the Year 1891* 9, section 2 (1892), 173–339.
4. Ibid., 284.
5. Ibid., 285.
6. Patterson, "The Portuguese," 164.
7. Ibid., 169.
8. R.G. Haliburton, "Lost Colonies," 48.
9. Joseph Needham, *Science and Civilisation in China*, vol. 5, VII (Cambridge: Cambridge University Press, 1986), 284.
10. Ibid., 341.
11. Ibid., note g, 296.

6: The Adventures of David Ingram

1. James A. Williamson, *The Cabot Voyages and Bristol Discovery under Henry VII* (Cambridge: Hakluyt Society at the University Press, 1962), 211.
2. Jean Alfonce, *Les Voyages Avantureux du Capitaine Ian Alfonce, Sainctongeois* (Poitiers: Pelican par Ian de Marnef, 1559), 28–29.

3. Antoine Simon Maillard, *An Account of the Customs and Manners of the Micmakis and Maricheets Savage Nations* (London: Hooper and Morley, 1758), 33.
4. Silas Tertius Rand, *A Short Account of the Lord's Work among the Micmac Indians* (Halifax, NS: William MacNab, 1873), 5.
5. David Ingram, "The Relation of David Ingram, from the Principal Navigations by Richard Hakluyt," *March of America Facsimile Series* 14 (Ann Arbor, MI: University Microfilms, 1966), 557.
6. Ibid., 562.
7. Ibid.
8. Ibid., 557.
9. Ibid., 562.
10. Ibid.
11. Edward L. Dreyer, *Zheng He: China and the Oceans in the Early Ming Dynasty, 1405–1433*, Library of World Biography Series (New York: Pearson Longman, 2007), 59, 89.
12. Rayner Unwin, *The Defeat of John Hawkins: A Biography of His Third Slaving Voyage* (London: George Allen and Unwin Limited, 1960), 311.

7: The Treasure Fleets

1. Louise Levathes, *When China Ruled the Seas: The Treasure Fleet of the Dragon Throne, 1405–1433* (New York: Simon and Schuster, 1994), 42.
2. Joseph Needham, *Science and Civilisation in China*, vol. 4, III (Cambridge: Cambridge University Press, 1971), 464.
3. Levathes, *When China Ruled the Seas*, 43.
4. Ibid., 41.
5. Ibid., 53.
6. Dreyer, *Zheng He*, 112.
7. Teobaldo Filesi, *China and Africa in the Middle Ages*, trans. David L. Morison (London: Frank Cass with the Central Asian Research Centre, 1972), 13.
8. Levathes, *When China Ruled the Seas*, 72.
9. "The 'foot,' or chi, referred to here was probably between 10.5 and 12 inches in length." Ibid., 19.
10. Levathes, *When China Ruled the Seas*, 175.
11. J. Ding, Ch. Shi, and A. Weintrit, "An Important Waypoint on Passage of Navigation History: Zheng He's Sailing to West Ocean," *International*

Journal on Marine Navigation and Safety of Sea Transportation 2, no. 1 (September 2007), 291.

12. Dreyer, *Zheng He*, 51.
13. The Kangnido chart presented to Zhu Di by the Korean ambassador in 1403.
14. Levathes, *When China Ruled the Seas*, 175.
15. Ibid., 179.
16. Needham, *Science and Civilisation in China*, vol. 4, III, 527.

8: A Culture Forgotten

1. Martin Booth, *Opium, A History* (New York: St. Martin's Press, 1996), 128.
2. Travis W. Hanes and Frank Sanello, *The Opium Wars: The Addiction of One Empire and the Corruption of Another* (Naperville, Illinois: Sourcebooks, Inc., 2002), 296.
3. Booth, *Opium: A History*, 110.
4. Hanes and Sanello, *The Opium Wars,* 21.
5. Booth, *Opium: A History*, 110.
6. Ibid., 115.
7. Hanes and Sanello, *The Opium Wars,* 292.
8. Booth, *Opium: A History*, 148.
9. Ibid., 128.
10. Hanes and Sanello, *The Opium Wars,* 39.
11. Ibid.
12. Keith McMahon, *The Fall of the God of Money: Opium Smoking in Nineteenth Century China* (Lanham, MD: Rowan and Littlefield Publishers, 2002), 208.
13. Hanes and Sanello, *The Opium Wars,* 159.
14. McMahon, *The Fall of the God of Money*, 75.
15. Ibid.
16. Ibid., 74.
17. Booth, *Opium: A History*, 162.
18. McMahon, *The Fall of the God of Money*, 206.

9: History Through a New Lens

1. Jacques Gernet, *A History of Chinese Civilization* (Cambridge: Cambridge University Press, 1996), 408.
2. Hanes and Sanello, *The Opium Wars,* 214.
3. Dreyer, *Zheng He*, 65.

4. Ibid., 32.
5. Ibid., 34.
6. Hart, 171.
7. Ibid., 172.
8. Ibid., 142.
9. Needham, *Science and Civilisation in China*, vol. 4, III , 488.

10: History Takes a Turn

1. Needham, *Science and Civilisation in China*, vol. 5, VI, 400–01.
2. Denys, *The Description and Natural History*, 167.
3. Ibid., 103.
4. Reuban Gold Thwaites, ed, "Lower Canada and Iroquois: 1642-1643." *The Jesuit Relations and Allied Documents: Travels and Explorations of the Jesuit Missionaries in New France*, vol. 24 (Cleveland: The Burrows Brothers Company, 1898), note 9, 310.
5. John N. Grant, *Historic Guysborough: A Portrait of Home* (Halifax: Nimbus Publishing, 2004), xi.
6. A.C. Jost, *Guysborough Sketches and Essays* (Guysborough, NS: Kentville Publishing Company, 1950), 38.
7. Grant, *Historic Guysborough*, ix.
8. Ibid., x.
9. Harriet Cunningham Hart, *History of the County of Guysborough, Nova Scotia* (Belleville: Ontario: Mika Publishing Company, 1975), 61.
10. Harriet Cunningham Hart, *History of Canso, Guysborough County, N.S*, vol. 21 (Halifax, NS: Historical Society Collections, 1927), 50.
11. Denys, *The Description and Natural History*, note 1, 168–69.
12. F.G. Speck, "Beothuk and Micmac," *Indian Notes and Monographs* no. 22 (New York: Museum of the American Indian, Heye Foundation, 1922), 149.
13. F.G. Speck, "Some Micmac Tales from Cape Breton Island," *Journal of American Folklore* 27, 107 (1915), 60.

12: Evolution of a Myth

1. Frederick Lucas, *The Annals of the Voyages of the Brothers Nicolo and Antonio Zeno in the North Atlantic about the End of the Fourteenth Century and the Claim Founded Thereon to a Venetian Discovery of America: A Criticism and an Indictment* (London: Henry Stevens and Son, 1898), 3–4.

2. Brian Smith, "Henry Sinclair's Fictitious Trip to America," New Orkney Antiquarian Journal, vol.2 (2002), 5. http://www.alastairhamilton.com/sinclair.htm.
3. William Herbert Hobbs, "Zeno and the Cartography of Greenland," Imago Mundi, vol. 6 (1949), 15–19.
4. Lucas, *The Annals of the Voyages of the Brothers Nicolo and Antonio Zeno*, 22.
5. Ibid., 28.
6. Abraham Ortelius, "The Peaceable or the Fourth Sea, Called by the Spaniards Mar Del Sur," *Theatrum Orbis Terrarum, 1570, Series of Atlases in Facsimile*, 1st series, vol. 3 (Amsterdam: N. Israel, 1964).
7. Richard Hakluyt, *The Third and Last Volume of the Voyages, Navigations Traffiques, and Discoveries of the English Nation* (London: George Bishop, Ralfe Newberie, and Robert Barker, 1600), 127.
8. Andrea di Robilant, *Irresistible North: From Venice to Greenland on the Trail of the Zen Brothers* (New York: Alfred A. Knopf, 2011), 133.
9. Ibid., second note, 133.
10. Vincenzo Coronelli, Libro dei Globi, *1693, Theatrum Orbis Terrarum: Series of Atlases in Facsimile,* 4th series, vol. 5 (Amsterdam: Theatrum Orbis Terrarum, 1969), first edition globe, Venice, 1688.
11. Ibid., second edition globe, Venice, 1692–93.
12. Pierre-François-Xavier de Charlevoix, *History and General Description of New France* (Chicago: Loyola University Press, 1962), 105.
13. Ibid., 20.

13: The *Zeno* Stories Come of Age

1. Johann Reinhold Forster, *History of the Voyages and Discoveries made in the North* (Dublin: Printed for Luke White and Pat Byme, 1786), 178.
2. Ibid., 199.
3. Placido Zurla, *Di Marco Polo e degli altri viaggiatori Veneziani più illustri dissertazioni: con appendice sopra le antiche mappe lavorate in Venezia e con quattro carte geografiche*, vol. 2 (Venice: Picottiani, 1819), 18.
4. Ibid., 20.
5. R.H. Major, *The Voyages of the Venetian Brothers, Nicolò and Antonio Zeno to the Northern Seas, in the Fourteenth Century, Comprising the Latest Known Accounts of the Lost Colony of Greenland; and of the Northmen in*

America before Columbus (London: Hakluyt Society, 1873), xxxv.
6. Ibid., xxv.
7. Ibid., xlvii.
8. Ibid., xxxii.
9. Thomas Sinclair, *Caithness Events: A Discussion of Captain Kennedy's Historic Narrative, and an Account of the Broynach Earls, to which is Added a Supplement of Emendations of 1899* (Wick: W. Rae, 1899), 139.
10. Roland William Saint-Clair, *The Saint-Clairs of the Isles Being a History of the Sea-Kings of Orkney and Their Scottish Successors of the Sirname of Sinclair* (Buckland, New Zealand: H. Brett, 1898), 445.

14: The Battle for History

1. C.C. Zahrtmann, "Remarks on the Voyages to the Northern Hemisphere, Ascribed to the Zeni of Venice," *Journal of the Royal Geographical Society of London*, vol. 5 (1835), 108.
2. Ibid.
3. Ibid., 109.
4. Edward Heawood, "Claudius Clavus and the early Geography of the North," *The Geographical Journal*, vol. 36, no. 6 (December 1910), 686–89.
5. Ibid., 389.
6. A.E. Nordenskiöld, *Facsimile-Atlas to the Early History of Cartography with Reproduction of the Most Important Maps Printed in the XV ad XVI Centuries* (New York: Dover Publications, 1973), 52–61.
7. Haraldur Sigurdsson, "Some Landmarks in Icelandic Cartography Down to the End of the Sixteenth Century," *Artic* 37, no.4, "Unveiling the Artic" (December 1984), 400.
8. Ibid.
9. Lucas, *The Annals of the Voyages of the Brothers Nicolo and Antonio Zeno*, 56.
10. Ibid., 96.
11. Ibid., 97.
12. Andrea Da Mosto, *I Navigatori Nicolè e Antonio Zeno* (Firenze: Felice Le Monnier, 1937–1940), 298–300.
13. Ibid., 299.
14. Ibid., 300.

15: Myth Becomes History

1. Michael Wolfe, "Review of Frederick J. Pohl's, Atlantic Crossings Before Columbus," *The Catholic Historical Review*, vol. 48, no. 3 (October 1962), 415–16.
2. Ibid., 416.
3. Frederick J. Pohl, *Atlantic Crossings Before Columbus* (New York: W.W. Norton and Company, 1961), 228.
4. Ibid., 235.
5. Frederick J. Pohl, *Prince Henry Sinclair: His Expedition to the New World in 1398* (New York: Clarkson N. Potter, 1974), 107.
6. Pohl, *Atlantic Crossings*, 254.
7. Ibid., 248.
8. Janet Elisabeth Chute, "Ceremony, Social Revitalization and Change: Micmac Leadership and the Annual Festival of St. Anne," *Papers of the Twenty-Third Algonquian Conference*, ed. William Cowan (Ottawa: Carleton University, 1992), 49.
9. Leslie Jane McMillan, *Mi'kmawey Mawio'mi: Changing Roles of the Mi'kmaq Grand Council from the Early Seventeenth Century to the Present*, M.A. Thesis, Dalhousie University, 1996, 200. http://www.nlc-bnc.ca/obj/s4/f2/dsk2/ftp04/mq24981.pdf.
10. Mark Finnan, *The Sinclair Saga* (Halifax: Formac Publishing Company, 1999), 82–85.
11. Ibid., 82.
12. Ibid., 83.
13. Andrew Sinclair, *The Sword and the Grail: The Story of the Grail, the Templars and the True Discovery of America* (Edinburgh: Birlinn Limited, 2005), 31.
14. Robert L.D. Cooper, *The Rosslyn Hoax? Viewing Rosslyn Chapel from a New Perspective* (Surrey: Lewis, 2007), 32.
15. Personal correspondence from Helen Nicholson, History Department, Cardiff University.
16. Finnan, *The Sinclair Saga*, 82–83.
17. Éliphas Lévi, *Secrets de la Magie* (Paris: Robert Laffont, 2000), 158.
18. Éliphas Lévi, *The Mysteries of Magic: A Digest of the Writings of Éliphas Lévi with Biographical and Critical Essay by Arthur Edward Waite*, 2nd edition (Secaucus, New Jersey: University Books, 1974), 209.
19. Malcolm Barber, *The New Knighthood: A History of the Order of the Temple* (Cambridge: Canto, 1995), 320.

20. Daniel Paul, "Prominent Flags of the Mi'kmaq Nation," *We Were Not Savages*. http://www.danielpaul.com/Mi'kmaqFlags.html.
21. Paul, "Mi'kmaq National Flag."
22. Paul, "Mi'kmaq Nation Flag/Grand Council Flag."
23. Ibid.
24. Chute, "Ceremony, Social Revitalization and Change," 49.
25. Ibid.
26. Paul, "Mi'kmaq National Flag."
27. Chute, "Ceremony, Social Revitalization and Change," 49.
28. Paul, "Mi'kmaq National Flag."
29. McMillan, *Mi'kmawey Mawio'mi*, 200.
30. Paul, "Mi'kmaq National Flag."
31. Steve Sinclair, "Methodology — A Second Hypothesis," St. Clair Research: The Sinclair/St.Clair DNA Study. http://www.stclairresearch.com.
32. Andrew Sinclair, *The Sword and the Grail*, 127.
33. Andrew Sinclair, *The Sword and the Grail*, back cover.
34. Steve Sinclair, "Methodology — A Second Hypothesis."
35. Raymond White, Guysborough — Port Hawkesbury, "Resolution 353," Parliamentary Debates (Hansard) Province of Nova Scotia, Legislative Assembly, 02 June 1998, 613. http://nslegislature.ca/index.php/proceedings/hansard/c56/57_1_h98jun02/#[Page 613].
36. Ibid.

Epilogue: Attend to the Original Facts

1. Mencius, *Mencius*, trans. David Hinton (Washington, D.C.: Counterpoint, 1999), 149.
2. Silius Tertius Rand, *Legends of the Micmacs* (New York: Longmans, Green, and Company, 1894), 225.
3. Ibid., 226.

Selected Bibliography

Alfonce, Jean. *Les Voyages Avantureux du Capitaine Ian Alfonce, Sainctongeois.* Poitiers: Pelican per Ian de Marnef, 1559.

Barber, Malcolm. *The New Knighthood: A History of the Order of the Temple.* Cambridge: Canto, 1995.

———. *The Trial of the Templars.* 2nd ed. Cambridge: Cambridge University Press, 2006.

Boorstin, Daniel J. *The Discoverers: A History of Man's Search to Know His World and Himself.* New York: Vintage Books, 1985.

Booth, Martin. *Opium: A History.* New York: St. Martin's Press, 1996.

Bourinot, J.G. "Cape Breton and Its Memorials of the French Regime." *Proceedings and Transactions of the Royal Society of Canada for the Year 1891* 9, section 2 (1892): 173–339.

Bradley, Michael. *Holy Grail Across the Atlantic: The Secret History of Canadian Discovery and Exploration.* Toronto: Hounslow Press, 1988.

Brown, Richard. *A History of the Island of Cape Breton.* Belleville, ON: Mika Publishing Company, 1979.

Canada, Historic Sites and Monuments Board of Canada. "Fort Dorchester, or 'Fort Grenville', St. Peter's, Cape Breton." *Agenda Paper* 39. Ottawa, 1966. 18–21.

Champlain, Samuel de. *Voyages of Samuel de Champlain, 1604–1618*. Edited by W.L. Grant. New York: Charles Scribner's Sons, 1907.

Charlevoix, Pierre-François-Xavier de. *History and General Description of New France*. Chicago: Loyola University Press, 1962.

Chute, Janet Elisabeth. "Ceremony, Social Revitalization and Change: Micmac Leadership and the Annual Festival of St. Anne." *Papers of the Twenty-Third Algonquian Conference*. Edited by William Cowan. Ottawa: Carleton University, 1992.

Cooper, Robert L.D. *The Rosslyn Hoax? Viewing Rosslyn Chapel from a New Perspective*. Surrey: Lewis, 2007.

Coronelli, Vincenzo. *Libro dei Globi, 1693. Theatrum Orbis Terrarum: Series of Atlases in Facsimile*, 4th series, vol. 5. Amsterdam: Theatrum Orbis Terrarum, 1969.

Da Mosto, Andrea. *I Navigatori Nicolo e Antonio Zeno*. Firenze: Felice Le Monnier, 1937–1940.

d'Entremont, Clarence-Joseph. *Nicolas Denys, Sa Vie et Son Oeuvre*. Yarmouth, NS: L'imprimerie Lescarbot Ltée, 1982.

Denys, Nicolas. *The Description and Natural History of the Coasts of North America (Acadia)*. Translated and edited by William R. Ganong. Toronto: Champlain Society, 1908.

Ding, J., Ch. Shi, and A. Weintrit. "An Important Waypoint on Passage of Navigation History: Zheng He's Sailing to West Ocean." *International Journal on Marine Navigation and Safety of Sea Transportation* 3, *no.* 1 (September 2007): 285–93. http://www.transnav.eu/Article_An_Important_Waypoint_on_Ding,3,40.html.

Dreyer, Edward L. *Zheng He: China and the Oceans in the Early Ming Dynasty*. Library of World Biography. New York: Pearson Longman, 2007.

Filesi, Teobaldo. *China and Africa in the Middle Ages*. Translated by David L. Morison. London: Frank Cass with the Central Asian Research Centre, 1972.

Finnan, Mark. *The Sinclair Saga*. Halifax: Formac Publishing Company, 1999.

Forster, Johann Reinhold. *History of the Voyages and Discoveries made in the North*. Dublin: Printed for Luke White and Pat Byrne, 1786.

Gernet, Jacques. *A History of Chinese Civilization*. Cambridge: Cambridge University Press, 1996.

Grant, John N. *Historic Guysborough: A Portrait of Home*. Halifax: Nimbus Publishing, 2004.

Hakluyt, Richard. *The Principal Navigations, Voyages, Traffiques, and Discoveries of the English Nation*. XIII, vol. 2 Edinburgh: Edmund Goldsmith, 1889.

———. *The Third and Last Volume of the Voyages, Navigations, Traffiques, and Discoveries of the English Nation*. London: George Bishop, Ralfe Newberie, and Robert Barker, 1600.

Haliburton, R.G. "Lost Colonies of Northmen and Portuguese." *Popular Science Monthly* 27 (May–October 1885): 40–51.

Haliburton, Thomas C. *History of Nova Scotia*. Belleville, ON: Mika Publishing, 1973.

Hanes, Travis W., and Frank Sanello. *The Opium Wars: The Addiction of One Empire and the Corruption of Another*. Naperville, IL: Sourcebooks, Inc., 2002.

Harrisse, Henry. *The Discovery of North America: A Critical, Documentary, and Historic Investigation*. Paris: H. Welter, 1892.

Hart, Harriet Cunningham. *History of Canso, Guysborough County, N.S.*, vol. 21. Halifax: Nova Scotia Historical Society Collections, 1927: 1–34.

———. *History of the County of Guysborough, Nova Scotia*. Belleville, ON: Mika Publishing Company, 1975.

Heawood, Edward. "Caludius Clavus and the Early Geography of the North." *The Geographical Journal* 36, no. 6 (December 1910): 686–89.

Hobbs, William Herbert. "The Fourteenth-Century Discovery of America by Antonio Zeno." *The Scientific Monthly* 72, no. 1 (January 1951): 24–31.

———. "Zeno and the Cartography of Greenland." *Imago Mundi* 6 (1949): 15–19.

Ingram, David. "The Relation of David Ingram, from the Principal Navigations by Richard Hakluyt." *March of America Facsimile Series*, no. 14. Ann Arbor, MI: University Microfilms, 1966: 557–62.

Jost, A.C. *Guysborough Sketches and Essays*. Guysborough, NS: Kentville Publishing Company, 1950.

Krause, Eric. *The Built History of Port Toulouse, Isle Royale, Actual and Proposed, 1713–1758*. Cape Breton: Krause House Info-Research Solutions, 1998, revised, 1998, 2004. http://fortress.cbu.ca/search/9813.htm.

Le Blant, Robert. "Les Compagnies du Cap-Breton 1629–1647." *Revue d'histoire de l'Amérique française* 16, no. 1 (1962): 81–94.

Lee, David. "The French Forts on St. Peters Bay." *Agenda Paper*. Ottawa: The Historic Sites and Monuments Board of Canada, 1981: 344–60.

Levathes, Louise E. *When China Ruled the Seas: The Treasure Fleet of the Dragon Throne 1405–1433*. New York: Simon and Schuster, 1994.

Lévi, Éliphas. *Secrets de la Magie*. Paris: Robert Laffont, 2000.

———. *The Mysteries of Magic: A Digest of the Writings of Éliphas Levi with Biographical and Critical Essay by Arthur Edward Waite*. 2nd edition. Secaucus, NJ: University Books, 1974.

Lucas, Frederick. *The Annals of the Voyages of the Brothers Nicolo and Antonio Zeno in the North Atlantic about the End of the Fourteenth Century and the Claim Founded Thereon to a Venetian Discovery of America: A Criticism and an Indictment*. London: Henry Stevens and Son, 1898.

Maillard, Antione Simon. *An Account of the Customs and Manners of the Micmakis and Maricheets Savage Nations*. London: Hooper and Morley, 1758.

Major, Richard Henry. *The Voyages of the Venetian Brothers, Nicolò and Antonio Zeno to the Northern Seas, in the Fourteenth Century, Comprising the Latest Known Accounts of the Lost Colony of Greenland; and of the Northmen in America before Columbus*. London: Hakluyt Society, 1873.

McLeod, Robert R. *Markland or Nova Scotia: Its History, Natural Resources and Native Beauties*. Toronto: J.L. Nichols Company, 1902.

McMahon, Keith. *The Fall of the God of Money: Opium Smoking in Nineteenth Century China*. Lanham, MD: Rowan and Littlefield Publishers, 2002.

McMillan, Leslie Jane. *Mi'kmawey Mawio'mi: Changing Roles of the Mi'kmaq Grand Council from the Early Seventeenth Century to the Present*. M.A. thesis, Dalhousie University, 1996. http://www.nlc-bnc.ca/obj/s4/f2/dsk2/ftp04/mq24981.pdf.

Mencius. *Mencius*. Translated by David Hinton. Washington, DC: Counterpoint, 1999.

Mote, Frederick W. and Denis Twitchet, editors. *The Cambridge History of China, vol. 7: The Ming Dynasty, 1368–1644*. Cambridge: Cambridge University Press, 1988.

Needham, Joseph. *Science and Civilisation in China*. 6 vols. Cambridge: Cambridge University Press, 1954.

Nicholson, Helen. *The Knights Templar: A New History*. Stroud, England: Sutton Publishing, 2001.

Nordenskiöld, A. E. *Facsimile-Atlas to the Early History of Cartography with Reproduction of the Most Important Maps Printed in the XV and XVI Centuries*. New York: Dover Publications, 1973.

Ortelius, Abraham. *Theatrum Orbis Terrarum, 1570*. Series of Atlases in Facsimile, 1st series, vol. 3. Amsterdam: N. Israel, 1964.

Patterson, George. *A History of the Country of Pictou, Nova Scotia*. Belleville, ON: Mika Studio, 1972.

———. "The Portuguese on the North-East Coast of America and the First European Attempt at Colonization There. A Lost Chapter in American History." *Proceedings and Transactions of the Royal Society of Canada for the Year 1890* 8, section 2 (1891): 127–73.

Paul, Daniel. "Prominent Flags of the Mi'kmaq Nation — Mikmaq Nation Flag." *We Were Not The Savages*. http://www.danielnpaul.com/Mi'kmaqFlags.html.

Pichon, Thomas. *Genuine Letters and Memoirs Relating to the Natural, Civil, and Commercial History of the Island of Cape Breton and Saint John from the First Settlement there to the Taking of Louisbourg by the English in 1758*. London: J. Nourse, 1760.

Pohl, Frederick J. *Atlantic Crossings Before Columbus*. New York: W.W. Norton and Company, 1961.

———. *Prince Henry Sinclair: His Expedition to the New World in 1398*. New York: Clarkson N. Potter, 1974.

Prenties, Samuel Walter. *Castaway on Cape Breton: Ensign Prenties' Narrative of Shipwreck at Margaree Harbour, 1780*. Edited by G.G. Campbell. Wreck Cove, NS: Breton Books, 2001.

Rand, Silas Tertius. *A Short Account of the Lord's Work among the Micmac Indians*. Halifax: William MacNab, 1873.

———. *Legends of the Micmacs*. New York: Longmans, Green, and Company, 1894.

Reid, John G. *Acadia, Maine, and New Scotland: Marginal Colonies in the Seventeenth Century*. Toronto: University of Toronto Press, 1981.

Robilant, Andrea di. *Irresistible North: From Venice to Greenland on the Trail of the Zen Brothers*. New York: Knopf, 2011.

Roque, Sieur de La. *The 1752 Census of Isle Royale (Known as Cape Breton Island) as a Result of the Inspection Made by Sieur de La Roque*. Pawtucket, RI: Quinton Publication, 1997.

Saint-Clair, Roland William. *The Saint-Clairs of the Isles Being a History of the Sea-Kings of Orkney and Their Scottish Successors of the Sirname of Sinclair*. Buckland, New Zealand: H. Brett, 1898.

Sigurdsson, Haraldur. "Some Landmarks in Icelandic Cartography Down to the End of the Sixteenth Century." *Arctic* 37, no. 4, "Unveiling the Arctic" (December 1984): 389–401.

Sinclair, Andrew. *The Discovery of the Grail*. New York: Carroll & Graf, 1998.

______. *The Sword and the Grail: The Story of the Grail, the Templars and the True Discovery of America*. Edinburgh: Birlinn Limited, 2005.

Sinclair, Steve. St. Clair Research: The Sinclair/St. Clair DNA Study. http://www.stclairresearch.com.

Sinclair, Thomas. *Caithness Events: A Discussion of Captain Kennedy's Historic Narrative, and an Account of the Broynach Earls, to which is Added a Supplement of Emendations of 1899*. Wick, Scotland: W. Rae, 1899.

Smith, Brian. "Henry Sinclair's Fictitious Trip to America." *New Orkney Antiquarian Journal* 2 (2002). http://www.alastairhamilton.com/sinclair.htm.

Speck, F.G. "Beothuk, and Micmac." *Indian Notes and Monographs*, no. 22. New York: Museum of the American Indian, Heye Foundation, 1922.

______. "Some Micmac Tales from Cape Breton Island." *Journal of American Folklore* 27, no. 107 (1915): 59–69.

Thwaites, Reuben Gold, ed. "Lower Canada and Iroquois: 1642–1643." *The Jesuit Relations and Allied Documents: Travels and Explorations of the Jesuit Missionaries in New France*, vol. 24. Cleveland, OH: The Burrows Brothers Company, 1898.

Unwin, Rayner. *The Defeat of John Hawkins: A Biography of His Third Slaving Voyage*. London: George Allen and Unwin Limited, 1960.

Walker, Tony E. *St. Peter's Canal: A Narrative and Structural History*. Ottawa: National Historic Parks and Sites Branch, Parks Canada, Department of Indian Affairs and Northern Affairs, 1973.

Wallace, Birgitta. "Nicolas Denys Fort Saint Pierre Archaeological Report." Unpublished report for the Historic Sites and Monuments Board of Canada, 1985.

Wallace, W. Stewart. *A Sketch of the History of the Champlain Society*. Toronto: The Champlain Society, 1981.

White, Raymond. Guysborough — Port Hawkesbury. "Resolution 353." *Parliamentary Debates (Hansard)*. Province of Nova Scotia, Legislative Assembly. June 2, 1998: 613. http://nslegislature.ca/index.php/proceedings/hansard/c56/57_1_h98jun02/#[Page 613].

Williamson, James A. *The Cabot Voyages and Bristol Discovery under Henry VII*. Cambridge: Hakluyt Society at the University Press, 1962.

Wolfe, Michael. "Review of Frederick J. Pohl's, Atlantic Crossings Before Columbus." *The Catholic Historical Review* 48, no. 3 (October 1962): 415–16.

Zahrtmann, C.C. "Remarks on the Voyages to the Northern Hemisphere, Ascribed to the Zeni of Venice." *Journal of the Royal Geographical Society of London* 5 (1835): 102–28.

Zeno, Nicolo. *De I commentarii del Viaggio in Persia di M. Caterino Zeno il K. & delle guerre fatte nell'imperio persiano, dal tempo di Vssuncassano in quà, libri dve; et Dell scoprimento dell'isole Frislanda, Eslanda, Engrouelanda, Estotilanda, & Icaria, fatto sotto il polo artico, da due fratelli Zeni, M. Nicolò il K. e M. Antonio, libro vno: con un disegno particolare di tutte le dette parte di Tramontana da lor scoperte*. Venice: Francesco Marcolini, 1558.

Zurla, Placido. *Di Marco Polo e degli altri viaggiatori Veneziani più illustri dissertazioni: Con appendice sopro le antiche mappe lavorate in Venezia e con Quattro carte geografiche*. vol. 2. Venice: Picottiani, 1819.

Index

Acadians
- Beaubassin, 21–22, 120
- Cheticamp, 24, 27–28
- Etang des Berges, 120
- Guysborough, 120–21
- Mi'kmaq and, 121

Africa and the Chinese fleets, 14, 92, 97–98
African Americans in Guysborough, 121
Alfonce, Jean, 87–88, 114

Baigent, Michael, 183
Baphomet, 180–81
Barbaro, Daniel, 138–40
Barbaro, Marco, 139–40, 147
Barber, Malcolm, 180
Beaubassin, 21–22, 120
Bergier, Clerbaud, 120–21
Bolyston Park, 123, 129–31, 175, 186
Boston, 120
Bourinot, John George, 36, 40, 77–81, 83, 101
Boxer Rebellion, 106–07
Bras d'Or Lakes, 11–12, 28, 34, 36, 57, 60, 61, 63–72, 75, 112–13, 191
British East India Company, 103
British Secretary of State, 90
Brown, Dan, 183
Brown, Richard, 36, 57
Burrows, Samuel, 27–28

Cabot, John, 13, 65, 87, 95
Cannon
- Chinese, 80–83
- European, Petriera, 79
- Louisbourg, 76–80, 83
- Saint Peters, 13, 40, 76, 79–81, 83, 84, 102, 189, 192

Canso, 11
Canso Strait, 11, 112, 117–18
Cape Cod, 170
Cape Dauphin, 14–24, 60, 76, 110, 112–13, 124, 192
Cape of Good Hope, 98
Cartier, Jacques, 87
Casey, Bill, 19–22
Catholic Historical Review, The, 170
Champlain, Samuel de, 64–65, 68–69, 72, 109, 190
Champlain Society, The, 41–42, 45

Chancewell, 62–63, 68, 90, 111
Charlevoix, P.F.X. de, 150, 159
Chedabucto Bay, 118, 122
Cheticamp, 24, 27–28
Chicago Exhibition of 1873, 156
China
canals, 110
cannon, 80–83
Confucius, 98, 107
elephants, 92, 191
gold, 112–13, 118, 191
horses, 92, 96, 191
Lao Tzu, 107
Mencius, 107, 188
opium, 102–08
response to Seven Cities Publication, 18–24
settlement in the New World, 83–84, 87–88, 90–93, 110–14, 189, 191, 192
ships and ocean travel, 94–100, 189
Chinese ambassador, Ottawa, 19–23
Chinese Cultural Centre, Toronto, 19
Chow, Cheong Pak, 20
Christianson, David, 16
Christmas, Peter, 176
Clavus, Cladius, 161–63
Clavus Map, 161–63
Clement V, Pope, 179
Collins, Rev. W.H., 107
Columbus, Christopher, 16, 65–66, 68, 72, 109, 123, 148, 156, 157, 163, 165, 184, 190
Compagnie de Cap-Breton, 28–30, 37, 46, 48, 55, 190
Confucius, 98, 107
Constant, Alphonse (Eliphas Levi), 180–81
Cook, James, 151, 153, 158
Coronado, Vasques de, 90
Coronelli, Vincenzo, 66–69, 73, 109, 149, 159, 190
Crusades, 175, 177–78, 185

Da Mosto, Andrea, 165–66, 169, 170, 192
Da Vinci Code, The, 183
Darwin, Charles, 15–16, 18
De la Roque, Sieur, 30
De Lyonne, Martin, 119
De Molay, Jacques, 179
Denmark, 103, 149, 160, 161, 163
Denys, Nicolas
Fort Saint Pierre, 29–31, 37, 38–46, 109, 190
Guysborough, 117–22
Haulover Road, 69–70, 72, 190
Saint Peters, 29–31, 37, 38–46, 48, 51, 55, 59, 60, 69, 109, 190
Department of Indian and Northern Affairs, Canada, 59, 73
DesBarres Manor, Guysborough, 122–23
Desportes, Pierre, 28–29
Drogio, 136, 157, 165, 172

elephants, 92, 191
Elgin, Lord, 111
Ellis Entertainment, 23–24
Estotilanda, 132–33, 136, 140, 146–50, 157, 159, 165, 172
Etang des Berges, 120
eunuchs, 96–99

Finnan, Mark, 176–77, 179–80
Forster, Johann Reinhold, 151–57, 159–60, 163, 165, 167, 169, 170, 173, 174
Fort Dorchester (Fort Grenville), 47–60
Fort Saint Pierre, 27–37, 38–46
Fortified Manors, 117
Frislanda, 132–36, 140, 146, 147, 149, 150, 153–54, 156, 159, 167, 171, 172, 173

Ganong, William, 39–46, 47, 57–59, 101–02, 108, 111, 121
Gaozong, Emperor, 95
Genghis Khan, 95
giraffes, 98
Giunti, Tommaso, 145
Glooscap, 128, 130, 131, 133, 173–74, 182
gold, 112–13, 118, 191
Graves, Rev. R.H., 107
Greenland, 135–42, 148–50, 154, 157, 161–62, 167, 172–73, 184, 186, 192
Gulf Stream, 98
Guysborough, 118–31, 137, 158, 168, 169, 171–77, 183, 184–86

Hakluyt, Richard, 91–92, 147–48, 159

Halfway Cove, 123, 125–29, 130, 131, 158, 169, 175
Haliburton, Robert Grant, 35, 39, 44, 80–81, 83
Haliburton, Thomas Chandler, 34–37, 43–45, 56–60, 75, 80, 91, 101–02, 105, 108, 111
Halifax, 11, 73, 124, 176, 182
Hawkins, John, 88
Historic Sites and Monuments Board of Canada, 45–46, 58
History Television, 23
Hobbs, Henry, 172
Holy Blood and the Holy Grail, The, 183
Holy Grail, 126, 183–86
Hong Kong, 106
Hopewell, 62–64, 68, 90, 95, 190
horses, 92, 96, 191
Huxley, Thomas Henry, 16

Iceland, 161–64
Ingonish, 24
Ingram, David, 88–93, 95, 102, 114, 147, 191
Island of Seven Cities, The, 12, 13, 24, 65, 66, 76, 87, 189, 190
Island of Seven Cities, The,
    documentary, 23–24, 124
    McGill Course, 20–21
    publication, 15–24
    SDX Joint Publishing Company, 23
    videos, 15, 194
Isle Madame, 58

Jerome Point, 30–31, 36, 39–40, 51, 53, 109
Jesuits, 108
    Mi'kmaq, 185
    De Lyonne, Father Martin, 119
Julien, Don, 176

Kellys Mountain, 14
Kenny, Edward, 73
Kublai Khan, 95
Kirkland, Scotland, 176–77
Knights Templar
    flags, 175, 177, 179–81, 187
    Sinclair family, 126, 175, 177, 179–80, 183–87

La Giraudiere, 119
L'Anse aux Meadows, 170
Lao Tzu, 107
Leigh, Charles, 62–63
Leigh, Richard, 183
Lescarbot, Marc, 64–65, 68, 72, 109, 190
Levi, Eliphas (Alponse Constant), 180–81
Lincoln, Henry, 183
Louisbourg, 31, 53, 76–83
Lucas, Frederick, 163–65, 169

Macarmick, William, 56, 58
MacDonald, Rodney, 17–18
Madagascar, Strait of, 97
Maillard, Pierre, 88
Major, Richard Henry, 155–60, 163, 165, 169, 170, 173
Manchurians, 102
Marcolini, Francesco, 132, 138–39, 141, 146, 152
Matthew, 95
McGill University, Montreal, 20–21
McGregor, Rev. James, 72–73
Mencius, 107, 188
Mercator, Gerardus, 145–47
Mi'kmaq
    Acadians and, 120–21
    Grand Council flag, 175–77, 179–82, 184, 186, 187
    Guysborough, 118, 122
    history, 13–14, 18–19, 22, 23, 88, 90–91, 114, 118
    legends, Glooscap, 128, 130, 131, 133, 173–74, 182
    legends, pre-Columbian visitors, 188–89
    legends, Saint Peters, 13, 35–36, 40, 44, 47, 59–60, 91, 101, 110
    Membertou, 185
    National Flag, 182, 185
    Prenties, Samuel, 11, 28
    Sinclair Monument, 127–31, 169, 171
Ming Dynasty, 14, 95, 99, 102
Minion, 88
missionaries
    De Lyonne, Martin, 119
    Jesuits, 108, 119, 185
    Maillard, Pierre, 14, 88

Moletius, Josephus, 145
Moore, George, 56–59
Mount Grenville (Mount Granville), 34, 39, 47–60, 61, 69, 74–75, 83–84, 109, 189–90

Needham, Joseph, 81, 113
Nicholson, Helen, 180
Northwest Passage, 90–91, 191
Norway, 129, 130, 154, 160, 161
Nova Scotia Government
  Cape Dauphin Ruins, 16–18
  Department of Natural Resources, 131, 185
  Nova Scotia Museum, 16
  Office of Economic Development, 131, 185
  Sinclair Monument, 131, 169, 171, 185, 186

Ogilvie, James, 56
Olaus Magnus Map, 162–64
opium
  Boxer Rebellion, 106–07
  British East India Company, 103
  opium use in China, 102–08
  Opium Wars, 105–07
Ortelius, Abraham, 146–48

Patterson, George, 37, 40, 76–81, 83, 101, 186
Paul, Daniel, 182
People's Daily, China, 21
Petriera, 79
Philips, William, 120
Pichon, Thomas, 31
Pilgrim Fathers, 62, 95
Pohl, Frederick J., 127, 169–76, 184, 192
Popular Science Monthly, 39
Port Toulouse, 40, 50–52
Portuguese, 40, 70, 77, 79, 83, 101, 128
Prenties, Samuel
  canal, 11–12, 28, 72, 73, 75, 111, 191
  Mi'kmaq, 11
  Saint Peters, 11–12, 28, 72, 73, 75, 111, 191
  shipwreck, 9–12
Prosper, Chief Kerry, 127, 176–77

Ptolemy
  Geographia, 143, 145, 162
  Library of Alexandria, 143
  maps, 160, 161
Purchas, Samuel, 92

Ramusio, Giovanni, 144–45, 147
Rand, Silas Tertius, 88
Rosslyn Chapel, 126, 184
Ruscelli, Girolamo, 143–45

Saint-Clair, Roland, 157–58
Saint Peters
  canal, 11–12, 13, 34, 59, 61–75, 83, 110, 112–13, 187, 190–91
  cannon, 13, 40, 76, 79–81, 83, 84, 102, 189
  Denys, Nicolas, 29–31, 37, 38–46, 48, 51, 55, 59, 60, 69, 109–10, 118, 190
  Fort Dorchester (Fort Grenville), 47–60
  Fort Saint Pierre, 27–37, 101–02, 187
  Island of Seven Cities, 9, 13, 24
  Jerome Point, 30–31, 36, 39–40, 51, 53, 109
  Mount Grenville, 34, 39, 47–60, 61, 69, 74–75, 83–84, 101–02, 109, 187, 189–90
  Prenties, Samuel, 11–12, 28, 72, 73, 75, 111, 191
  stones from canal excavation, 74
Sanson, Nicolas, 66, 67, 68, 73, 109, 190
Scandinavia, 144, 157, 160, 161, 162
SDX Joint Publishing Company, 23
Sinclair, Andrew, 183–84
Sinclair, Henry
  Forster, Johann Reinhold, 153–54, 169, 174
  Glooscap, 128, 130, 131, 133, 174
  Guysborough Monuments, 123–31, 132–33, 137, 158
  Knights Templar, 175, 177, 179–81, 183–87
  Lucas, Frederick, 163–65, 169
  Major, Richard Henry, 156–58, 165, 169, 170
  Pohl, Frederick J., 127, 169–76, 184
  Saint-Clair, Roland, 157–58

Sinclair, Andrew, 183–84
Sinclair, Thomas, 156–57
Zichmni, 137, 148, 153, 154, 156, 157, 165, 171–74, 184, 186
Zurla, Placido, 154
Sinclair, Niven, 176–77, 180, 181, 183
Sinclair, Steve, 185
Sinclair, Thomas, 156–57
Sinclair Conference 1997, Kirkland, 176–77
Sinclair Monuments, Guysborough, 123–31, 132–33, 137, 158, 169–71, 175–77, 184, 186
Sinclair Society of North America, 127, 130, 131, 156, 157, 171, 175, 184, 186
Song Dynasty, 95
Spanish, 88–89, 92, 103, 128

Tartars, 88
Times, London, 105, 107
Toronto, 18, 19, 131
Transactions in the Royal Society of Canada, 40, 76–77, 79, 83
Treasure Fleets, 12, 14, 19, 38, 81, 92–93, 94–100, 109–13
Treaty of Nanking, 106
Treaty of Tordesillas, 128
Trin, Greenland, 136, 148, 157, 172–73

United Empire Loyalists, 121

Victoria, Queen, 105
vikings, 170
Vinland, 170

Walker, Edmund, 41
Wyatt, James, 121

Yongle Empire, 95–100
Yuan Dynasty, 95

Zahrtmann, Admiral C.C., 159–60, 163, 169, 173
Zamoisky Map, 162–63
Zeno Family
Antonio, 132–36, 139, 140–42, 146–50, 152, 154, 157, 165–66, 168, 169, 171–73
Carlo the Lion, 134–36, 152, 165, 166
Nicolo the Knight, 132–37, 139–50, 152, 154, 165–68, 171, 173
Nicolo the Younger, 132–37, 138–50, 151–57, 160–63, 166–68, 172, 184
Zeno Map, 140–49, 154, 155, 157, 159–64, 167–68
Coronellli, Vincenzo, 149, 159
Mercator, Gerardus, 145–47
Moletius, Josephus, 145
Ortelius, Abraham, 146–48
Ruscelli, Girolamo, 143–45
Zahrtmann, Admiral C.C., 159–60, 163
Zeno Narrative, Zeno Stories, 132–37, 138–50, 191–92
Barbaro, Daniel, 138–40
Barbaro, Marco, 139–40, 147
Charlevoix, P.F.X. de, 150, 159
Da Mosto, Andrea, 165–66, 169, 170, 192
Forster, Johann Reinhold, 151–57, 159–60, 163, 165, 167, 169, 170, 173
Giunti, Tommaso, 145
Hakluyt, Richard, 147–48, 159
Lucas, Frederick, 163–65, 169
Major, Richard Henry, 155–58, 159–60, 163, 165, 169, 173
Marcolini, Francesco, 132, 138–39, 141, 146, 152
Pohl, Frederick J., 127, 170–76, 184, 192
Ramusio, Giovanni, 144–45, 147
Saint-Clair, Roland, 157–58
Sinclair, Thomas, 156–57
Sinclair Monuments, Guysborough, 126–31
Zurla, Placido, 154–55, 159–60, 163, 165
Zheng He, 19, 96–99
Zhu Di, Emperor, 95, 98
Zichmni, 135–37, 140–42, 146–50, 153–54, 156–57, 162, 165–68, 171–74, 184, 186
Zurla, Placido, 154–55, 159–60, 163, 165

www.ingramcontent.com/pod-product-compliance
Lightning Source LLC
Chambersburg PA
CBHW070910270326
41927CB00011B/2516

9781459733121